Victory Through Valor

A Collection of World War II Memoirs

by Dr. George J. Despotis, Donald E. Korte,
and Matthew Lary

REEDY PRESS

THROUGHOUT HISTORY, MANKIND HAS STRUGGLED TO PRO-
CURE AND MAINTAIN THE CONCEPT OF FREEDOM. THERE-
FORE, WE DEDICATE THIS BOOK TO ALL WORLD WAR II VET-
ERANS AND THEIR FAMILIES. THROUGH THEIR SACRIFICES
AND VALOR, THEY HAVE BESTOWED THE GIFT OF FREEDOM
TO FUTURE GENERATIONS.

Reedy Press, PO Box 5131, St. Louis, MO 63139, USA

Library of Congress Control Number: 2008934296

ISBN: 978-1-933370-38-5

cover art by Kevin Belford

back cover art by James Whitney

For information on all Reedy Press publications visit our website at www.reedypress.com.

Printed in the United States of America
20 21 22 23 34 5 4 3 2

Contents

Foreword

The Second World War was the largest armed conflict in human history and is one of the greatest events to impact the lives, cultures, and civilizations of the human race. To attempt to understand the shear tragedy experienced during this war overwhelms the human spirit. It is estimated that 50 to 60 million people lost their lives as a direct result of the conflict, with substantially more who sustained either irreversible physical or emotional trauma. The countless, innocent children who had to experience the horrors of war during their childhood perhaps represents one of the greatest tragedies. In reality, few people's lives on earth went unaffected.

The United States of America was not the first to engage in the struggle against the fascist tyrannies, but in the end the contribution and determination of U.S. forces ensured victory. In all, 13 million Americans served in the conflict with more than 400,000 deaths and more than 670,000 being wounded. The European Theater of Operations clearly contended with the Pacific Theater with respect to size and human tragedy. The largest battle fought by American soldiers in that theater (and in the history of the United States) was the Ardennes Campaign, commonly known as the Battle of the Bulge.

By December 1944, German armies were in retreat, and many Allies felt that the war was almost won. The German army had been mauled and expelled from France, losing much equipment and many men in the process. And yet somehow, with almost complete secrecy, Hitler had been able to assemble thirty divisions totaling nearly a half million men in the Ardennes region for a last-ditch offensive against four vastly outnumbered U.S. divisions. On December 16, the Bulge offensive started with an armored thrust involving thirty German divisions against the four surprised and under-equipped American divisions. Bad weather eliminated the advantage that the Allies enjoyed in the air, and as the elite Panzer divisions advanced, Hitler remained confident of achieving his goal: To divide the American and British forces and capture the port of Antwerp, thereby setting the stage for a stronger German position in a negotiated peace. Hitler's plan would then have the German military force regroup and head east to confront and defeat the Soviet Union, assuming there would be a negotiated peace on their western borders.

The tenacity and determination of the American soldiers dogged the

Axis advance from the first day. As the weeks passed, the Allied High Command—and 600,000 American soldiers—turned and faced the threat, and it became clear that the German army would not achieve its goals. Delaying actions fought in defense of key crossroads and villages allowed the Allies to consolidate and relocate their forces to coordinate an effective defense. By the end of January 1945, Hitler's army had been forced back roughly to its starting point. The Allied victory at the Battle of the Bulge, which ultimately involved over one million soldiers, destroyed the last, best units of the German army and marked the decisive end for the Third Reich. With Germany unable to wage war, it was the beginning of the end of World War II.

✻   ✻   ✻

The stories and specific battles of the Second World War have been charted by thousands of historians and are generally well researched and documented. The decisions of great leaders and the movements of vast armies are cornerstones of our understanding of this crucial period of world history. However, the American success in World War II was the product of a *national* effort, and while it might be said that the arsenal of democracy and the armed forces of the Unites States exceeded the sum of its parts, they carried the strength *of* those parts. Whether serving as a rifleman or a truck driver, a medic or a radio operator, a clerk or a factory worker, it was this great and unsurpassed generation of American people who provided that strength through their tireless service and sacrifice. The tenacity and valor of this generation continues to amaze subsequent generations.

From the start, the specific goal of this book was to capture and memorialize the voices and personal accounts of these soldiers and patriots. This work began several years ago with the cooperation and encouragement of the Gateway Chapter of The Veterans of the Battle of the Bulge in St. Louis, Missouri. Initially, the focus revolved around accounts from the Battle of the Bulge, as this is the common thread of the veterans within this organization, and also because it is the largest U.S. military battle that involved severe wartime and weather-related conditions. However, our project was expanded to include interviews from any World War II veteran or World War II–era citizen, since many of the instances of great courage and perseverance fell outside that timeframe and theatre of operation. Many examples of the greatest dedication could not be summed up in the events of a month or two. They could only be seen through the tireless efforts of those behind the front line, whether working in a motor pool, maintaining the ability of the army to function, or even working in a factory in the United States to build the equipment that would allow our soldiers to survive and succeed.

These are their stories, in their own words. Or rather, these are highlights of their stories—with the attendant limitations, since the interviews were typically so fascinating and rich in material that they grew to some length—a length that was far too great to fit into the few pages that the size of this book would allow. Consequently, a great deal of material had to be omitted. Years of experience cannot be efficiently condensed into a few pages, and the events related in the following pages capture only a glimpse of that story. This is not mentioned to daunt those of you who are seeking to learn about these soldier's experiences "at the ground level," but rather to encourage you to seek out the veterans in their neighborhoods and ask them directly about their war experiences.

For those of you who want to explore the specific accounts of our interviewed veterans in greater depth and to perhaps actually view the videotaped interviews, we encourage you to search for the Victory through Valor website, which will be established within the next few years. The proceeds from this book, as well as any charitable contributions to a specific foundation yet to be established under the Victory Through Valor name, will be used to fund this project. Another one of the goals of our website and foundation will be to identify all those U.S. soldiers who paid the ultimate sacrifice during the Ardennes Campaign and engrave their names on a dedicated memorial to commemorate these heroic individuals. Our World War II veterans continue to vanish, and along with them goes the opportunity for us all to understand their personal commitment, sacrifices, and experiences. The courage and valor that emanated from this generation as a bright beacon led us through one of the most devastating crises in the history of mankind and one of the greatest triumphs in American history. It is to all of our World War II veterans and their families that we dedicate this book.

—Dr. George J. Despotis, Donald Korte, and Matthew Lary

Acknowledgments

The authors would like to thank the following people for their significant contributions to the Despotis Book Project: The Eden United Church of Christ in Affton, Missouri, under the guidance of Pastor Jacoba Koppert has graciously allowed us the use of their meeting rooms for a number of the veterans' interviews. We also express our appreciation to the following individuals: Matt Lary (primarily), Jeryldine Tully, Sean Keough, and Don Hensley, who served as interviewers or camera crew for the vast majority of the interviews; Roger K. Imhof for his recruitment of WWII veterans for the project; Tina Riemer for her editorial assitance; and Marilyn Korte (primarily), Joyce Kleine, Donna Shaheen, and Carter Transcription Services who worked tirelessly to convert the audio from the interviews to many of the transcripts that formed the basis of this book. The memoirs of James Lewis, Frank Camm, and Phillip McKnight were drawn upon heavily, in lieu of interview transcripts, for the preparation of their sections. The following members of the St. Louis Gateway Chapter, Veterans of the Battle of the Bulge were instrumental in championing the Despotis Book Project to their membership: Harold Mueller, Kent Stephens, and Jim Johnson. Our appreciation is also submitted to the Battle of the Bulge National Organization for their support of this project. Finally, we express our appreciation to the St. Louis Gateway Chapter of the Battle of the Bulge for their enthusiastic support of this project from its conception and for financing the publication costs of this book.

James Parker

Date of Birth:
August, 1921

Place of Birth:
St. Louis, MO

Military Assignment:
U.S. Regular Navy

Military Duties:
Sonarman

Highest Rank Achieved:
Chief Petty Officer

Postwar Occupation:
Journeyman Heavy Equipment Operator

Jim enlisted in the Navy in October of 1940 and took his basic training at the Great Lakes Naval Center in North Chicago, Illinois. He was sent to Pearl Harbor in December of 1940 and was present as a Seaman First Class on the USS *Oglala* on December 7, 1941. Jim subsequently served on a number of vessels, including the *Elvida*, the *L. E. Thomas*, and the USS *George K. MacKenzie* (Korean War). Jim left the Navy in 1957, having received the U.S. Presidential Citation, Pearl Harbor Medallion, five Good Conduct Medals, Asiatic–Pacific and the European–African–Middle Eastern Service Ribbons, World War II Victory Medal, Navy Occupation (Japan), Philippine Presidential Unit Citation, American Defense, and American Campaign medals.

What time did you wake up on the morning of the Pearl Harbor attack?

About 3:30, because I was on messenger watch on the main deck of the *Oglala*, which was a minelayer, in my white uniform, regulation white uniform. I was on duty until 7:30, and then I had breakfast and read the Sunday funnies down in the compartment. I was going up the ladder to put the flag up at 8:00, and it said five minutes to eight when a torpedo went off in two compartments. The ladder I was on acted like a diving board—it flipped me over backwards and I did a back flip and landed on both feet in the compartment I just left on the steel deck. So I got up the ladder. I went to my locker; I looked in my locker for my wallet but I thought I'll be back. I get topside and they said abandon ship, so I went over to the gangway, and the cruiser we were tied up to (the *Helena*). As I was going across the bow, a Japanese plane strafed on by, at deck level and I looked at him, eyeball to eyeball. He looked at me as he went by; we never lost contact with our eyes. He was surprised to see me, and I was surprised to see him. Nobody was afraid; we were just surprised. And I never did put the flag up. About thirty years later I saw a picture of the ship capsizing, and the flag still wasn't up.

So you got off of the ship as fast as you could.

No. I went over to the cruiser *Helena*, which we were tied up to. So I went to board the ship there, a man came up to me from the dock, and he had a bullet right through his jaw, right through his teeth. And every time he opened his mouth, blood came out all over his white uniform. And when he closed his mouth, blood would pulse out of his jaws. I got another sailor off the cruiser, and I told him, "Take this man to the sick bay. It's an emergency." I found out later that he made it.

So you went from your ship that was capsizing, you went over to the other ship and starting helping?

Yeah. Momentarily, they said, "If you don' have a rifle, get off the ship." I didn't have a gun, so I got off the cruiser and went out on the dock. I thought I better get in that warehouse over there. I had no money; my wallet was on the ship that went down. So I walked to the receiving station, since I knew a friend of mine who was going to radio school, and right away they said go down the steps there and get those oily clothes and shoes off and put on some new clothes. So that's what I did.

So getting back to the attack on your initial ship—you said the torpedoes hit and within five minutes, it capsized?

No, it took about a half hour, forty-five minutes. I wasn't on her when she tipped over. Part of the bridge ripped off on the dock when she rolled over. She was outside the cruiser *Helena* to act as a blister. Well, right away they towed her away from the blister, the stern of the cruiser so they wouldn't pin her in against the dock when she sank. My ship turned over against the dock and then sank on her port side.

How far was your ship from the *Arizona*?

About one thousand yards, about a half mile. I was standing on the dock when the *Arizona* got the bomb. That was during the second wave. That bomb went down through the stainless steel deck right into the magazine. When the magazine blew, it blew her bottom out. She rose up; her water line went up about six feet, then she went right back down again. Never did come up again. Then the *Nevada* tried to get underway, and the Japanese probably thought, "They're going out to the channel; we'll sink her right in the channel. That'll close up Pearl Harbor for half a year." But the quartermaster on the *Nevada* saw what was going to happen, so he backed her into the trees, stern first, propeller, rudders. Backed her right in the trees. They call that Nevada Point now. They made an officer out of him, too, for saving the battleship.

When the second wave came in, we started to repel them. Then we shot the locks off all the magazines, and got the ammunition out so we could fire. A lot of the people at Hickham Field, they couldn't even fire a rifle. All the ammunition was locked up in the storerooms. And the same way on the ships. They had to shoot all the locks off to get the stuff since it was peacetime. Like the *California*. When she sank, she had her bottoms open on Friday for inspection, her double bottoms, and she still had them open during the attack. That's why she sank so quickly. She was wide open. She didn't have a double hull. She flooded real fast. I don't know how many torpedoes she got; it's all in the history books.

When did you go to sleep that night?

It was after dark. When they turned the lights out I went to bed with everybody else, at the receiving station. And then about eleven o'clock that night they started waking us up. They come around, you, you, you, you, and you just volunteered you know. Woke up a hundred men out of their bunks, and we went down the street. Fifty-foot motor launches, sixty-foot motor launches. They took us out to the battleship *California*. It was still sinking. We tried to get some papers off so they wouldn't get ruined by the salt water. She went down six feet while I was on her, and then they said abandon ship. So I left the battleship *California* down at cargo, and then I got over to the air station. And we shot four of our own planes down. Everybody was trigger-happy. They killed one pilot, too.

After the attack, I was on the scullery machine, running through 10,000 men a day, six battleships sunk. You ate two meals: breakfast and you got in line for supper; there was no lunch. Just one continuous line. Machine was built for 600, and I was running through 10,000 men a day. The chief boson mate, he saw me and said, "You're the only man who knows how to run that machine the way you run it." "Well, they're finding where my ship is." We found it across the street and set up a temporary office in a bowling alley. Then they forgot where I was. The chief boson mate said, "Can't Parker come over and run the scullery machine? He's the only man I can find who can run it. Go ahead Parker and run it."

In the days following the attack, what was your role?

I went back to the receiving station, and they sent me out to the gate vessel, and I used to open and close the gate to let the friendly ships in and out—and keep the enemy submarines out. Usually, when a carrier started coming in, they would get about halfway over my gate. I laid the cable on the floor of the ocean, the channel. And about the time she'd get halfway through, I'd figure about where her propellers were, I started pulling that cable up off the floor, hoping I wouldn't catch the propellers. I never did. I took it all the way in, so nobody could follow the carrier in.

I usually kept the gate closed, and we also had an indicator net too, so if somebody did get through, this indicator net would set off flares, and you could follow the flares through the channel. They wouldn't know that they hit the indicator net. But the big net, they couldn't get through that big wire. They would tell me when a ship was coming in or when it was leaving and I'd be standing there. I'd throw the brakes off, and that would sink the cable and open the gate you know. The buoys would go all the way across and then when they'd get across there I'd get about where the propellers were, I'd start pulling that in fast, as fast as I could. Two big Westinghouse winches powered the system.

When did you leave Pearl Harbor?

I operated out of Pearl Harbor for two and a half years after the attack.

So the main duty for your ship was antisubmarine. How would you deliver the depth charges?

Echo range. You had to know the bow of your ship and the location of your underwater sound gear. That's dead time. Your depth charger was way back on the stern three hundred feet away. Well, the depth charger passes over that submarine. It's all figured mathematically. So you figure I'll fire three seconds early or fire three seconds late. Sometimes we'd fire a thirteen-charge pattern, with each one's a three hundred-pound depth charge. Sometimes I'd fire a twenty-six-charge pattern. A double pattern. I'd say, "Stand by for a double pattern." I'd fire K-guns and lay thirteen charges, and by that time they got them all related, and I'd lay another thirteen charges, twenty-six charges all together.

Were the depth charges just pushed or rolled off the back of the ship?

Gravity rolled them off. The K-guns, they fired them. You get three K-guns on both sides of the ship; you got two racks on the stern. Of course, they don't have those anymore. Everything's done with rockets now.

Charles Branson

Date of Birth:
Russel, KY

Place of Birth:
July 1925

Military Assignment:
87th Division

Military Duties:
Radioman

Highest Rank Achieved:
Sergeant

Postwar Occupations:
Commercial/Residential Architect

Charles enlisted in the Army and was inducted on January 31, 1944. He took his basic training at Tyler, Texas, and obtained additional training with the Signal Corps at CP Frannin TexLine Communications and for ordinance training at Aberdeen Proving Grounds. After departing from New York, he crossed the Atlantic on the *Queen Mary* and arrived in England. He was later transferred to Scotland for further ordinance training before being deployed in the ETO. He fought in France, Belgium, and Germany predominately with the 87th Division (7th Army). Charles was awarded the two Bronze Stars, Purple Heart, Combat Infantry Badge, Rifle Sharp-Shooter Badge, Army of Occupation Medal, European–African–Middle Eastern Ribbon, World War II Victory Medal, Good Conduct Medal, two Overseas Bars, Missouri World War II Award for Patriotic Service, and the French Jubilee of Liberty Medal. He returned to the United States in May 1946 and obtained a bachelors degree in architecture from Washington University and subsequently began his career as a registered commercial/residential architect.

What was basic training like?

I graduated from high school early and went down to Jefferson Barracks and was interviewed for enlistment. The interviewer happened to be the conductor for the high school band, and he said, "I have a good place for you in communications, because Morse code has a sound like chords on a piano." Or something of that sort. So I started with communications down in Texas. And from Texas I went to Aberdeen Proving Grounds for training in booby traps, the use of explosives, primer cords, and this sort of thing. Since I was too young to go over, I also helped teach the trainees about booby traps. So whenever I had a little bit of explosive left over, I buried it in the creek because I had booby traps set, and they would step on those boards and the charge would go off, and I'd say, "See, you've already started to learn about booby traps."

I'll always remember the last day of training. I took this little package of explosives, and I had buried it in the creek in the sand so I would have a final explosive sendoff for the troops. And so who comes down but the general for Aberdeen, and he sat right down in the front row on the end seat just in front of us. And I said, "Oh my goodness," and I had already set it off. And it went "Boom," and all the sand and mud and everything was all over him. The sergeant says to me, "Well, we're shipping right now." But I went down and said, "Sir, I want to apologize to you for what I put you through." And he says, "I got one thing to tell you, soldier." And I thought, "Well, here it comes." "I would suggest to you that you use a little less powder next time." So I remember that from when I started, and I learned to listen to my training people. I wouldn't be sitting here today if I hadn't followed what the men that went before me taught me from their experiences.

Where did you go after your time at Aberdeen?

I went over on the *Queen Elizabeth*, and I listened to my sergeant again. He says, "Charlie, get a top bunk." And so when we went down to the bottom of the ship, I climbed into the top bunk, and I couldn't quite figure out why, so he says, "They throw up above you, and you don't want to be down below." So I saw a notice that the chaplain would like to have an assistant, and I volunteered for that, which was a big step for me. Changed my attitude a lot towards people. So that was well worthwhile, and what was to come as far as our activities go. They took us off the ship, and we ended up to Scotland because they didn't want to relay anything that was going to happen before the invasion. And so we had a lot of target practice there, and I shot competitively in high school, so I was already pretty good from the competitions that we had. And I had a range in my folks' basement, so I got to where I could light a kitchen match without knocking the match over. One time we went up into the hills for target practice, and they had everybody from the different companies. We all pitched in a pot who'd get the best scores. After a few rounds, they moved the target down five hundred yards. So I knew all about windage, to allow for that, and also the height, the drop of the bullet, and I was the only one out of the whole group that got a bulls-eye. And so they brought up the target to see that it was true, and it was. I can remember the company officer saying, "Branson, where did you learn to shoot like that?" So I said, "Oh, I've been around."

Describe your entry into the European Theatre of Operations?

We were loaded onto trains to get to ships for the invasion. I was to land on Omaha Beach, but we were loaded on another ship, and so we went up the coast from where the heavy fighting was. We landed at Le Havre, and that was where the Germans were expecting us to land. So we went ashore there. I remember going over the side on the ropes and I had my radio on me, I had my burp gun, a carbine, and my pack. Well, I can't swim, so when he dropped the ramp a little early and when I went down that ramp, the water was about up to here, and I had to bounce so I wouldn't drown in the water. So I got ashore that way, and we were lucky when it started at the main beaches, that evidently they pulled all their troops out of Le Havre, although there were still troops there and some of the Italian troops as well. After that we went ahead and got up there beyond the beach and started up the road. I remember going in the first street up there, and this guy stepped out, and he's walking towards us and he gives us an obnoxious arm gesture.

Do you remember your first combat engagement?

After landing at Le Havre, we fought from there up, taking towns ,and we were clearing out the villages, towns. Most of them had apartments right on the street, where you went in through a common entry and then there's a door on one side and another door on the other side. So you worked as a team on those, because what they were doing, we found out, was one of us would go in one door and German would come out and fire from the other door. So what we did, one guy would go in one side, and the other guy would guard the other door. Well, we broke in and no sooner we did and I saw this leg, and I started firing when he came out and these are some of the stories I would like to forget. As a young kid that had been brainwashed and that sort of thing, I killed him. I don't like remembering that story, but as you know I said some stories you forgot about, but I've never forgotten that one. That was one of my first that hardened me for what I had to do in the coming weeks and months.

Oscar Covarrubias

Date of Birth:
March 1919

Place of Birth:
East St. Louis, IL

Military Assignment:
Third Army, 949th Field Artillery Battalion

Military Duties:
Driver in a Field Artillery Battery

Highest Rank Achieved:
Technician Fifth Grade

Postwar Occupation:
Mechanic

Oscar was drafted in June of 1941. He took his basic training at Ft. Leonard Wood, Missouri, and received additional training at Camp Iron Mountain, the Mojave Desert, and at Ft. Bragg, North Carolina, before being shipped overseas. He arrived in Glasgow, Scotland, in late June of 1944 and was sent over to France shortly thereafter. Oscar served as a driver and artilleryman and was a member of the 949th Field Artillery, which was sent with the 3rd Army to relieve Bastogne. He was awarded the Good Conduct Medal, two Overseas Bars, World War II Victory Medal, American Defense Medal, and the Europe–Africa–Middle Eastern Ribbon with four Battle Stars (Northern France, Ardennes, Rhineland, and Central Europe). Oscar left the service in November of 1945 and pursued a career as a mechanic.

How did you get to Europe?

I went overseas on the *Queen Elizabeth I,* the biggest ship ever built. The *Queen Elizabeth* was being built in England when the war started, and to keep it safe from bombs (because that was a short distance for German planes to cross), they brought it to New York, where it was finished as a troop carrier.

We went to the New York harbor. We walked up ten stories, and there was this big ship with a catwalk and a little door opened halfway up the side. There were 22,000 troops on the *Queen Elizabeth*, but it was made to carry only 2,500 passengers. There were so many people, some took turns sleeping on the decks. We were billeted in one of the ship's theaters. We slept in hammocks, three to a frame, and they were so close together we struggled to get our duffle bags between them so we could climb into them. And since we were in artillery, we had guard duty on a five-inch gun on the fantail to watch for German subs, but we didn't have any problems. The ship was divided into three sections, and you had to stay in your section to keep the ship level. One of the ship's pools was a secondary kitchen and dining room. We got two meals a day and had to walk up and down these steps; I still don't know if it was worth climbing them for that stinking food.

How did the weather affect your experiences in Europe?

France was rainy and muddy. We stalled at the Saar River, where we ran out of food, gasoline, ammunition, everything. Meanwhile, the Germans built a big force and attacked through the Ardennes Forest. We were already down there in the mud. Every night the Germans would fire a self-propelled 150 mm howitzer and shell through our gun positions. So when the call came from the Bulge, we were glad to move out.

The night we pulled in we dug our holes, which we lined with our raincoats and our blankets. We had a couple of little candles that we lit and placed pine boughs over them and snow over that. But after that first night, we were out in the elements. You didn't dare go in a building because buildings were good targets for the enemy.

What was your most intense battle or firefight?

I remember one piece of woods that was full of Germans. We cut and they called the artillery to clean it up, but we couldn't get through so we barraged them. The next day we couldn't believe the damage. Big trees that looked like somebody had just broken them; our artillery cut them down. There were pillboxes where the Germans had hidden, and they dug a big ditch and covered it with logs, leaves, and snow. There were body parts everywhere. We had six-inch artillery, 155s, howitzers, and I drove the Number 4 gun. A lot of times we ran over bodies; there was no other way to go through. So we plowed through, knocked down trees, and ran over everything in the way.

Alex Deeken

Date of Birth:
July 1924

Place of Birth:
St. Louis, MO

Military Assignment:
XVIIIth Corps Airborne, 54th Signal Battalion

Military Duties:
Jeep Messenger

Highest Rank Achieved:
Private First Class

Postwar Occupation:
Display Artist

Alex enlisted in December of 1942, took his basic training at Camp Kohler, California, and left from Boston to go overseas in August of 1943 for additional training in Iceland. After about a year there, his group was sent to Swindon, England, before crossing the Channel in December of 1944, landing at Reims, France. Alex's military duties included transferring messages from Corps to Division Headquarters via jeep. He served with the XVIIIth Corps in Reims, Paris, andBastogne, ending up on the outskirts of Berlin at the close of the war. He earned the Good Conduct Medal and the European Theatre Service Medal. Alex returned to the United States in December of 1945 and pursued a career as a display artist.

Describe your trip overseas.

From Boston we left the harbor on one single boat, not a convoy, and went to Iceland; it was scary. Half the time we slept on deck, but we all got sick. You had to go a long way down to get your chow, but many times it wasn't edible so we bought candy bars from the PX.

One morning, about three days out, we were on deck around five o'clock and they decided to test the machine guns. It sounded like somebody hammering on sheet metal with a sledgehammer. We thought we were being attacked! This went on for seven days. Then we landed in Iceland and went to Reykjavik. Our camp—three Nissen huts—was close by. They said we had one of the best-looking camps from the air. Reykjavik had a lot of lava rock, so they made the roads with that rock.

We joined the 54th Signal Battalion. There was A Company, B Company, and Headquarters. I was assigned to Headquarters, and I drove a jeep as a messenger, 'cause I guess I was too young for radio. We were in Iceland almost a year. They used to send us on detail. P-38s were popular; they'd come down and practice strafing you.

We shipped out in July after D-Day. We went to Scotland on an English boat with hammocks you had to string, so we slept on the floor. Then we went by train down to England, where we stayed until the Battle of the Bulge. There, the colonel who commanded 18th Corps took over the 17th, 13th, 101st, and the 82nd Airborne divisions. He volunteered us for airborne, but we were to go in on gliders. So we had to take glider training, which meant a pay boost. A C-47 would pull two gliders and then cut them off. The pilots of these gliders were forced-out airline pilots or army pilots. And they'd always say, "I'm on top." They tried to scare you; we had no parachutes. There was twenty-four of us on each glider.

And I was scared because one day I saw one of the English cigar-shaped gliders being towed behind one of their planes. The glider broke in two, and all these guys tumbled out; half went underneath the plane. Guys were hanging on and falling out, but the pilot had to cut them loose or the whole plane would go down. That was the most tragic thing I ever saw.

November, we learned we were to be in an airborne operation over the Elbe and Rhine Rivers. The Battle of the Bulge had started, so they loaded up in C-47s. We landed over Reims, and a jeep was waiting for us there. I knew we were going to Belgium, where the breakthrough was. There were four of us in the Jeep, and only I knew how to drive, so I had to drive for five hours in blackout. That was where you had little lights on top of the fenders, and there were two little taillights on the car in front of you. As long as you could see those two lights, your distance was good, but if not you were too far back. Longest trip ever.

Glen Jarvis

Date of Birth:
March 1922

Place of Birth:
Frank Clay, MO

Military Assignment:
First Army, 467th AAA AW/SP Battalion

Military Duties:
Machine Gunner on a Half-Track

Highest Rank Achieved:
Technician Fifth Grade

Postwar Occupation:
Machine Operator—Loy-Lange Box Company

Glen was drafted in December of 1942 and took his basic training at Camp Stewart, Georgia, with further training at Ft. Dix, New Jersey, Camp Picket, Virginia, and in California at Camps Ibis, Coxcomb, and Young. He was given additional training in England before landing on Omaha Beach on D-Day. He served with the 467th AAA AW/SP Battalion through France, Belgium, Holland, Luxembourg, Germany, and Czechoslovakia. Glen was awarded the American Theatre Campaign Ribbon, Europe-African-Middle Eastern Theatre with Bronze Service Arrow, D-Day arrowhead, Victory Ribbon, five Battle Stars (Normandy, Northern France, Ardennes, Central Europe, Rhineland), and three Overseas Service bars. Glen returned to the United States in December of 1945 and pursued a career as a machine operator at the Loy-Lange Box Company.

Describe your first battlefield engagement.

I landed at Omaha Beach on D-Day. I was a machine gunner on a half-track. When we got on the beach, our first half-track hit a bomb hole, and the skipper on this landing craft backed off and circled around, and he came back to a different spot and we got off. But I guess the Seabees had a route cleared from land mines across the beach, and we got as far as we could, but we couldn't get off the beach. There was a big gun position up on this bluff, and we couldn't get by it until finally one of the big battleships came in close to the beach and blasted that gun position out. We went up a country road, and we felt like the war was over, just getting off that beach, 'cause the Germans had been raining mortar shells and artillery on us all day. The shells had started hitting close, and we had several casualties, mostly guys with shrapnel wounds. One of our medics took a direct hit, and I don't think they ever even found his dog tags. Before we went into St. Lo, the big 155s had been sitting behind us firing over us, and every time they'd fire the ground and trees would shake, and sometimes when we'd hear those guns go off, we'd stand up on our toes to keep from getting the shock. But usually we were in the half-tracks, outposting for the artillery. We'd pull in a field, off to one corner, and set up for any enemy planes that come in. But we were constantly getting shelled by artillery and one thing we learned fast, when we pulled in we'd dig a hole. And then if we were going to be there for a while, we'd dig the half-track in, which sometimes took several hours. We'd dig it deep enough so the ground would be level with the half-track, and we'd drive it down in the hole.

That must have been hard to do for a whole half-track, especially with the cold.

Yeah, it was. I think we dug enough holes over there to bury half of St. Louis, but that's what saved us a lot of times. We'd be on these half-tracks, and when we'd hear these shells coming in, we'd jump in a hole. One time we were up in Germany, and we pulled in this little orchard. We had two half-tracks and another guy with a tank sitting in there, and the Germans had zeroed in on us with these railroad guns, and we heard these shells coming. We jumped into a hole, and they hit the half-track on the gun turret and knocked the turret off. There was a basement set up there where we had our kitchen, and every time we started to run to get into the basement, another shell would come in. Sometimes we'd be moving up at night, and a German plane would come in and drop flares and light up like daytime, and sometimes a tank would be sitting in the middle of the road burning, and we'd just go around it and keep on going.

So where did you serve during the Bulge?

We were in Bastogne, and the Germans were bombing all of the houses, and we weren't allowed to get in a house, so we had stay out in an open field. The ground was so hard we couldn't dig foxholes, and we'd sleep on the ground in our sleeping bags. The next morning they would be frozen to the ground, and we'd have to dig them out with a pick and shovel. But we went into Bastogne with Patton's 3rd Army, and we had been way down south. We drove a couple days getting up there, and the Germans had us surrounded. They had knocked out all the antiaircraft, and when we got close to Bastogne, all the bridges were knocked out across some of these little streams, so we had to go cross-country. Our American tanks were parked along the road, pointing out to keep the road open to get us in there, and there were dead soldiers all along the road. When we got into Bastogne, our 101st Airborne had the Germans stacked up like cord wood out in the fields there. And the first night we got in there, the German planes came in around sundown, their low-level bombers, and we cut loose. It looked like Fourth of July. We knocked down some of them, but so many guys fired on them we didn't know who was firing on whom. But they never came back, and the next day or so the weather broke, and our planes—looked like thousands of them—got into the air. After that we started to advance, and the next big thing was the Rhine River. When we got to the Remagen bridgehead, we set up our antiaircraft guns, and the 90 mm was way back behind us. They started firing at these planes over us, and shrapnel was falling down, and some of our guys got hit in the back. And that was the first time the Germans used their jet planes in combat. They stayed up high enough that we were firing on them, but we couldn't reach them with the .50 caliber machine gun and the other half-tracks had 37 mms, but they couldn't hit them either. Some of our fighter planes came up there, so we'd have to stop firing. I saw a couple of our planes run together up there, I think a P-38 and a P-47.

Clarence Goldsmith

Clarence volunteered for service in September of 1943 and took his basic training, parachute school, and OCS at Ft. Benning, Georgia. He went overseas on the *Queen Elizabeth* and landed in Glasgow, Scotland, in February of 1944. Clarence crossed the Channel on D-Day, parachuting behind enemy lines in support of the Normandy landings. He fought with the 82nd Airborne Division in the European Theatre of Operations. Clarence earned the Combat Infantry Badge and was awarded two Purple Hearts, the Silver Star, two Bronze Stars, and the European Theatre Service Medal with four Battle Stars for the Normandy, Holland, Ardennes, and Rhineland campaigns. He returned to the United States in June of 1946 and pursued a career in education.

Date of Birth:
March 1924

Place of Birth:
East St. Louis, IL

Military Assignment:
82nd Airborne, 504th Parachute Infantry Regiment

Military Duties:
Paratrooper and Platoon Leader

Highest Rank Achieved:
Captain

Postwar Occupation:
Superintendent of School District 189

What was your first battlefield engagement like?

At Leicester, England, I was reassigned on temporary duty to the 505th Regiment when the 504th could not be refitted and reinforced in time for the impending D-Day invasion. On June 6, 1944, I jumped with the 505th Parachute Infantry Regiment of the 82nd Airborne Division parachuting a few kilometers from St. Mere Eglise near the small village of Neuville-

au-Plain on the road to Monteburg. I landed with two others from my stick into an area where a small company of German defenders just happened to be assembled to go on defense. Before we could get out of our harness, we were immediately surrounded and disarmed. As paratroopers were dropping near us, the German defenders, not wanting to fire their weapons thus giving away their position, spread eagled us on the ground and smashed our hands with their rifle butts. So on my very first day of combat I had two broken hands. The Germans locked us in a barn knowing they had to quickly leave to avoid other paratroopers in the vicinity. After a short period of time, we broke out of the barn to join other troopers and moved toward our objective. A medic put splints and tight bandages on our hands, and that's how I spent the next thirty-five days. As a platoon officer, I took the two from my platoon, and with an assembled group of scattered troopers, headed toward Neuville-au-Plain to locate my company. The ground was covered with weapons bundles so I was able to arm myself. Firing the weapon was difficult but could be accomplished. The time was 3:00 a.m., but our little group of paratroopers found our platoon assembled near our objective at Neuville-au-Plain, where I then assumed command of my platoon. I stayed with my platoon for all thirty-five days before returning to Leicester, England, where proper medical care was rendered. Bones were reset, and after five weeks I was returned to the 504th Parachute Infantry to prepare for out next combat jump, this time Operation Market-Garden at Nijmegen, Holland on September 17, 1944.

Describe the role the weather played during the Battle of the Bulge.

When we left Sissone, France, early in the morning on the 18th to confront the Germans at Werbomont, there were about three inches of snow on the ground. So the snow came early on. We didn't think too much about it because we didn't know what lay ahead. We left in stake-bed trucks, not the old Army deuce-and-a-half most people see in films, but tractor-trailer trucks with room for about fifty people in each truck. Since there was not enough room really to sit down or lay down, most of us stood up all the way to Werbomont, Belgium. Every couple of days, it seemed like there was new snow. There was fresh snow at Lierneux, as we seized and took the high ground. Herresbach, required a twelve-mile march, and there were snow drifts sometimes two or two and a half feet deep. Our platoon was the point platoon, and it was so difficult breaking trail that every twenty minutes we'd have to change the trail-breaker. Breaking trail in that amount of snow was absolutely exhausting. Of course, when we broke trail, it meant that everybody behind attempted to walk in the same tracks to minimize the effort. Our company was spread out in about fifteen-yard intervals in two columns, and we were strung out for a quarter of a mile.

Are there any individuals fallen or otherwise that you would like to pay a tribute to?

That would be very hard to answer because there were really so many outstanding men known for their bravery. If you really wanted to nail one person down, I could mention our commanding general. His name was Jim Gavin, Major General Gavin. He was everywhere. He wanted to lead but also wanted to perform reconnaissance and monitor front-line conditions. There were times on the front line when he would show up next to you with an M1 rifle. He always carried an M1 rifle and thought my Thompson submachine gun was a poor choice of weapon. He wanted a rifle with firepower and punch. This man was a great morale builder. Everybody in the division seemed to have great regard for him, and that's not the way you find too many commanding generals, but that's the way his soldiers found him.

What was the most intense battle or firefight that you were engaged in during the war?

That is very difficult to answer. Normandy was very tough, and Market-Garden was even tougher. We were nearly wiped out crossing the Waal River in canvas boats, losing 40 men with 130 wounded for the two companies in the first wave. The Battle of the Bulge was also tough. The Germans were on the attack, having just crossed the Ambleve River, and had taken the little town of Cheneaux in the northern sector. We had detrucked at Werbomont two days before and had gone through Rahier, a small village that we took without too many problems because there were few Germans there. In fact, I only remember a probing patrol that advanced that far. But in the village of Cheneaux, the Germans had moved in in force with a great deal of armor. The 1st Battalion bore the brunt of the battle for Cheneaux attacking from the south and the 3rd Battalion, of which I was a member, attacked from the north. In two days of fighting, we were able to regain that town and run the tanks out. That was probably one of the toughest fights, maybe because it was our first real fight in the Ardennes. Our regiment was awarded the Presidential Unit Citation for that one battle, marking the first Unit Citation awarded in the Ardennes Campaign. Cheneaux was the first village to be retaken from the Germans, around December 19 or 20.

You've mentioned your hands already, the injuries you sustained there. Were you wounded at any other time?

Yes, I was hit with shrapnel and small arms on March, 24, 1945, which happens to be my birthday, when I was with the 17th Airborne Division. We were in Lyon, France, at a camp set up for us in preparation for the next combat jump. We knew there was probably going to be just one more parachute jump before the war was over, and as young paratroopers, many of us wanted to make that last jump. Division Headquarters asked for volunteer veteran platoon leaders to temporarily go to the 17th Airborne because, although the division had been tested in combat, they had not made a combat jump. Our objective was to prepare the way for ground forces to cross the Rhine in the area near Wessel, Germany, and clear out the landing zone areas for our gliders. Against the advice of everyone in the Officer's Club, I went TDY to the 17th and was hit with shrapnel before I left the plane, hit again on the way down, and hit with small arms fire again after I landed. It was not my day. On that particular jump, it seems as if the Germans really knew we were coming, and we encountered more antiaircraft fire there than any place I'd ever been. This time, the 513th jumped from a C46, a plane not before used to transport paratroopers into combat. It was a larger aircraft than the C47 with two doors permitting exiting from both sides. Without the two doors, many of us possibly could not have jumped, but we all got out after the plane was riddled and disabled. The plane was burning and may have had more than a hundred holes in it and with most of the troopers on the plane already hit. As jumpmaster and with the plane losing power, I ordered three seriously injured troopers, not able to jump on there own, to be put out of the plane, thus giving them a chance to make it down safely. The rest of us exited at the last minute, although nowhere near our drop zone, at about 250 feet. The plane was lost and both the pilot and copilot killed.

When you landed, were you in a relatively safe area, or were there Germans right on top of you?

We landed almost in the middle of a German gun emplacement, probably about 150 yards away, in sort of a wooded area. It was not our drop zone. It was a British landing zone, and the British 6th Airborne were going to make a glider landing onto that particular area. We dropped on the road to the gun emplacement, and the Germans opened up with all the small arms they had, the most damaging an MG-42. Everyone was hit, and I was shot through the knee to go with previously sustained shrapnel wounds in the back and shoulder. I managed to roll into a drainage ditch along the side of the road, still in my parachute harness, and to pull three paratroopers into the ditch with me. The Germans kept firing, but they would not come out to attack. Two of us laid down enough fire to keep them in their gun emplacement. That was kind of a rough day. The British paratroopers came in after what seemed like hours, but it was really only about twenty minutes later. They wiped out the gun emplacement and got us back to a British aid station. I later ended up at the 76th General Hospital in Liege, Belgium. That was the end of the war me. From my stick in this jump, I was the only survivor. and I was awarded another purple heart and a silver star for my actions.

Marvin East

Marvin enlisted in the spring of 1943 and took his basic training at Camp Edwards, Massachusetts. He went overseas from Camp Kilmer on the *Queen Mary,* leaving on December 23 and landing January 1 in Glasgow, Scotland. He crossed the Channel on D-Day, landing at Omaha Beach, and fought with the 110th AAA Mobile Gun Battalion through France, Belgium, Luxembourg, and Germany. He was awarded the Good Conduct Medal, Bronze Arrowhead (D-Day), and European Theatre Service Medal with four Battle Stars (Northern France, Ardennes, Rhineland, and Central Europe). He returned to the United States in December of 1945 and became a distributor of hydraulic and pneumatic tools.

Date of Birth:
March 1924

Place of Birth:
Denver, CO

Military Assignment:
First Army, 110th AAA 90 mm Mobile Gun Battalion

Military Duties:
Quad 50 Machine Gunner

Highest Rank Achieved:
Technician Fifth Grade

Postwar Occupation:
Distributor of Hydraulic and Pneumatic Tools

So when did you cross the Channel, and what was that like?

Well, we got on the LST, and I don't really remember all the facts. While we were in the marching area, we changed all the tracks to rubber. They had a big sand table there on the shore, which was a mockup of where we were going to land, with models of troops and equipment. I remember going in and looking at that bugger, and we had a captain by the name of Borne, who was probably forty, forty-five. He looked at that thing, and the sweat just began to pour out of him, because he knew we were in it; we were going to get it. They didn't let us out of the marching area at all until they put us on the LST. Now, I don't remember being on the LST that long, and the trip over wasn't too bad. It was pretty steady. And we were sitting on the deck just playing cards and stuff, and every now and then there would be a ping or something from some odd shell that didn't go in the right direction. But that night we had the ramp down because we had tried to land, but had to wait. And there were lights on the deck, so our ship sort of stood out. Then we started taking in wounded from the DUKWs, because they would see our light, and they would come up to our ship and want to unload the wounded. And we had that damn deck full of stuff, and we had to take the wounded and haul them all the way over all that stuff, back to the aft end of the ship where the medics were. That lasted so long; we all got so tired. One guy came off and he is going, "Oh my leg. Oh, my leg. Be careful, my leg." And I said you know we are doing the best we can, buddy. I mean he was really shot up, and I had no sympathy whatsoever. Young and stupid, that's what I was.

How long after the initial landings was it before you were unloaded?

We didn't get off until the next day. In the marching area they swapped our single-barreled, water-cooled, 50-caliber for a Quad 50, air-cooled, in a turret on a trailer. So we got off on the beach the next morning with a 6 by 6, pulling this trailer with the Quad 50 on it. In the beginning, everything was screwed up on the beach, but by the time we got there the beach itself was pretty well cleaned up. I remember splashing in the water, driving up on the beach, making a left turn, and then we made a right turn and went up like a gully. And I remember that is where I saw my first dead German; he was lying there in that gully. I have been back in the gully since, and it has changed a lot, but it is still there. We went to the east at Pointe du Hoc, and the beach goes up like this, but there are several places where the waters run down over some gullies. So you did not have to go straight up over a dune or anything, we could drive up those gullies.

Terry Bye

Terry was drafted in March of 1943 and took his basic training at Camp Edwards, Massachusetts, where he got the nickname "Tex" since he had worked for Texaco before entering the service. He went over on the *Queen Mary* in December of 1943, crossed the Channel on D-Day, and landed at Omaha Beach. Tex served with the 110th Mobile Gun Battery in the Normandy, Northern France, Ardennes, Rhineland, and Central European campaigns and received the European Theatre Service Medal with five Battle Stars and an arrowhead. He returned to the United States in December of 1945 and pursued a career with Texaco.

Date of Birth:
April 1924

Place of Birth:
Yankton, SD

Military Assignment:
First Army, 110th AAA 90mm Mobile Gun Battalion

Military Duties:
Artilleryman

Highest Rank Achieved:
Technician Fifth Grade

Postwar Occupation:
Texaco Petroleum

How long were you in the States, and when did you go overseas?

I think it was April 1943 when we went out to Cape Cod for training on the 90 mm guns, and then we went to Camp Kilmer, New Jersey, before going over to Europe in December of 1943 on the *Queen Mary*. There was something like 16,000 or 17,000 of us on there, and we took shifts sleeping. The *Queen Mary* went all by itself, and it was quite an experience to be out in the middle of the ocean where you can't see anything but water. We changed course about every four and a half minutes or so, because it takes that long for a submarine to set up. Sometimes you'd be lying in that hammock down there on the lowest deck, and you'd hear that thing rotating, picking up messages with the radar, and all of a sudden practically in unison, we were all setting up because we'd hear it making a noise, and we swore to God that we were going to get blown up right there. But we never did. We spent Christmas Day on the *Queen Mary*, and those of us in the lower decks still say to this day that we had kidney stew for Christmas dinner, and the people up above us took all the turkeys for themselves.

You said you arrived in Scotland?

Gourock, Scotland. Then we took a train from there down to Nettlebed, England, and one of the things I remember was that they put us in Quonset huts. There was mud up to your knees, and it was raining a lot. At that point, we became part of England's defense. They put our 90 mm guns in different places along the beach, so when the buzz bombs and the planes came over, we were shooting them down too. So we had a lot of experience there before we went into Normandy.

Did you have much of an opportunity to mingle with the English people?

Oh, yes. Very much so.

How were you received, and what did you think of them?

Well, they were a different kind of people. I wasn't too excited about Britain and the British people, but one time we were billeted in private homes, and there was five of us guys that went to this house. And there was a grandma, a mother, and a daughter, and the daughter was probably twenty years old, and you couldn't ask for better treatment. A lot of stuff was so much different than we were used to in the Army. I mean, you had to go over and light a little pot to heat some water to take a shower—that kind of stuff. But those ladies—I can't recall their names anymore—were just wonderful people.

When did you cross over into France?

We went down to the Plymouth, England, area, and that's where we shipped out. June 6 is when we went into the Normandy area, and most of the people didn't go in until the next day. We were supposed to go in on the fifth, but it didn't work out that way because of the rough weather, and then Eisenhower decided we were ready to go, and we went the next day. We were on an LST and had our equipment on there, and we were up on the top deck when this all took place. There were ships like you could never believe out there, and we were just a bunch of dumb kids. That's why we won the war. It's because we were eighteen and nineteen years old. Hell, we can handle that. That's just a small project. But I think the first thing we saw was a sailor floating in the Channel area about seventeen miles across. Most of us became men overnight, 'cause we started seeing things like this. And when the action started, we really grew up fast. A lot of things happened that I've forgotten, and I leave them forgotten.

Do you remember the process of getting from ship to shore?

At times, some of us were going in by LCIs and some on DUKWs. And they went over the side on the ropes to get into the boats, but on our LSTs, they dropped the front, and that's where we went out from, but it had to be close to the shore for the heavy equipment. But then they opened the front of the LST and started bringing on patients that were injured, since our LST was going to be one of the ones that would take them back to hospitals in England. One of my best buddies from Connecticut and I were there, and all of a sudden they're bringing these guys on, and this officer tapped us and says, "You and you, come with me." So we went back there, and they happened to have a soldier that must have gotten up on the rocks on the beach area there and when the shelling was coming in from our own ships. They had him on the table there, picking chipped rock out of him, and I looked at my friend and said, "Angie, you better get out of here," because he was turning all kinds of colors. You never seen anything like that before in your life. And the doctor said to me, "You better go right with him." So that was one of my experiences going over there. I tell people, I wouldn't take a million bucks for what I've seen, but I wouldn't want to ever do any of it over again. I am not a hero, I'm a survivor. The heroes are still over there, toes up.

Raymond Saul

Date of Birth:
January 1921

Place of Birth:
Jacob, IL

Military Assignment:
4th Infantry Division, 22nd Infantry Regiment

Military Duties:
Radio and Wire Communications

Highest Rank Achieved:
Technician Fourth Grade

Postwar Occupations:
Construction Surveyor; Inspector, Supervisor

Ray enlisted in June of 1940 and took his basic training at Ft. McClellan, Alabama. He went overseas on the *Capetown Castle* and landed in Liverpool, England, in January of 1944. He crossed the Channel on D-Day and landed at Utah Beach. He fought with the 4th Infantry Division through France and Germany and participated in the Normandy, Northern Europe, Ardennes, Rhineland, and Central Europe campaigns. Ray earned the Combat Infantry Badge and was awarded the Good Conduct Medal, American Defense Service Ribbon, European-African-Middle Eastern Theatre Ribbon with Silver Battle Star, Bronze Service Arrowhead, Presidential Unit Citation, and the European Theatre Service Medal with five Battle Stars. Ray returned to the United States in October of 1945 and pursued a career in construction.

What did you do in Britain?

We were in a place called Camp Danberry, England. Pretty close to Doll-ish, and fortunately I didn't get into Slapton Sands, which nobody knew about at the time. Slapton Sands was a very bad situation. They thought they were going to do some training there. The Army moved a lot of English people out of their homes, and they were going to use this area for practice landings, landing craft and like it's a real beach landing. And they actually used live ammunition, but the Germans were right across the English Channel with some torpedo boats, and they came in there during some of the exercises and sank several of our biggest ships. Did a lot of damage and killed a lot of people. And it never got in the papers at the time. Nobody in this country knew about it. Slapton Sands was a disaster, and parts of my 4th Infantry Division were in that operation. Nowadays people know about Slapton Sands, and it's in one of my books on Utah Beach.

When did you cross over into France, and what was that experience like?

Well, I can't remember the exact day, but the St. Lo breakthrough was where we went through the hedgerows in France. We landed at Utah Beach, and the first place that we took was St. Mère-Église, which was up on a hill. The paratroopers had arrived about six hours before we landed, behind the lines three or four miles, and we ran into them as we were taking St. Mère-Église. They were in the treetops and hanging from buildings; they were all over the place. And that was the hardest combat we had up to that point. We had engaged the enemy right on the beach, but then we got away from the beach. General Roosevelt [Brigadier General Theodore Roosevelt, Jr.] told us we weren't going to dig in there; we were going to move on. So we did and I don't know if it was two or three days later, but they relieved my regimental commander, 'cause he wasn't moving fast enough to suit them. Then we came to the town of St. Mère-Église. From then on it didn't seem like it was too difficult fighting, because the Germans were in disarray. They didn't have all the troops in there they needed, and they kept fighting a delay action, so we would keep moving, until we got to St. Lo, and that was a place where we had to break through out of, getting out and into the plain and going towards Paris. We got stopped and we had to go hard fighting. So we leveled St. Lo and moved on, and we got the Presidential Citation for that. And then it seemed like we started moving real fast through France, just one town after another, until we got to the German border, where we were stopped. They put up everything they had at us then.

Kent Stephens

Date of Birth:
January 1924

Place of Birth:
East St. Louis, IL

Military Assignment:
26th Infantry Division, 101st Field Artillery

Military Duties:
Radio Operator/Repairman and Driver for the Red Ball Express

Highest Rank Achieved:
Technician Fourth Grade

Postwar Occupation:
Owner, Retail Hardware Store

Kent had just turned nineteen when he was drafted in early 1943. He received his basic training at Fort Jackson, South Carolina, before going overseas on the *Saturnia* in the fall of 1944. The 26th Division was part of Patton's 3rd Army and was in Metz, France, for R&R when Kent joined them. During the war, he served in France, Germany, Belgium, Luxembourg, Czechoslovakia, and ended up around Linz, Austria. Kent received the Good Conduct Medal and four Battle Stars (Normandy, Northern France, Rhineland, Central Europe). The division started back to the States on a Liberty Ship in November 1945, landing in Newport News, Virginia, on Christmas Day. Kent subsequently became the owner of the long-time owner of a retail hardware store.

Tell us about your time with the Red Ball Express.

My division landed at Cherbourg, France, on September 7, 1944, and we were the first division to land directly from the United States. Maybe two weeks or so after that, Patton made his breakthrough at St. Lo, and he started heading for Paris. Since they needed to get supplies and gasoline up to the front lines faster than the Quartermaster Corps could handle, the Red

Ball Express was set up. I was driving a gasoline truck along with another fellow, and we drove twenty-four hours a day/seven days a week, from about the middle of September to the middle of October. We had German prisoners loading up the trucks in Cherbourg, and then we would head out for Paris. They had one set of roads, which we took going to Paris, and another set of roads for the return trip to Cherbourg. And they blocked all the intersections, so you didn't have to worry about traffic crossing in front of you. So you just put your truck in the convoy and followed the guy ahead of you, and it was a straight shot all the way through. There were two drivers, and one of us would sleep or doze off while the other guy was driving. They had places where you'd occasionally stop and pull in to refuel or change your oil or fix a flat tire, but most of the time we just ate K-rations while we were driving. When you pulled into the refueling area, you were able to get out of the truck. I remember they had coffee and sometimes doughnuts, something to break up the monotony of driving the truck. Basically, everything was all taken care of for you; all you had to do was get in that truck and drive. I drove that Red Ball Express, I think, for about two weeks' time. And that gave Patton and his men around Paris all the equipment they needed, particularly gasoline, which was what they needed to go and pursue the Germans. As far as equipment, number one would be the ammunition. Number two, food. And they also carried replacement clothing and boots.

What were the dangers involved with being a driver on the Red Ball Express?

Well, number one, accidents. Or falling asleep or having a blowout. Something like that would cause a wreck. The Red Ball name came from over here in the States. The moving companies, whenever they had to move furniture or cargo in a hurry, they always lined up what they called a "Red Ball," with a bunch of trucks.

Were there any advantages to being in the Red Ball Express versus being in some other, maybe rear, area assignment?

No, we didn't get any advantages at all, no access to better food or supplies. It was a case where they said we need you, you're gonna go, and that's it. You didn't have any choice. The reason for the Red Ball Express was that this was an emergency. After Patton got up to the front, the war kind of settled down for just a little bit, and then the Quartermaster Companies were able to take over and do the job. But it was a very interesting experience, something different, because the fellows that stayed behind, in my unit particularly, were probably cleaning up equipment or getting things ready for our going up to the front.

Eugene Harmack

Date of Birth:
February 1920

Place of Birth:
St. Louis, MO

Military Assignment:
83rd Infantry Division, 329th Infantry Regiment

Military Duties:
Communications Lineman

Highest Rank Achieved:
Corporal

Postwar Occupation:
Railroad Conductor

Gene was drafted in 1942 and took his basic training at Camp Robinson, Arkansas, with additional training at Ft. Benning, Georgia. He went overseas on a Liberty Ship and landed in Wrekham, Wales, on May 24, 1944. Gene crossed the Channel on June 16, 1944, and landed at Omaha Beach on June 24. He fought with the 83rd Division through France, Luxembourg, Germany, Belgium, and Holland, and he participated in the Normandy, Northern France, Ardennes, Rhineland, and Central Europe campaigns. Gene earned the Combat Infantry Badge and was awarded the Bronze Star with Oak Leaf Cluster with Valor, American Campaign Medal, European-African-Middle Eastern Medal, Army of Occupation Medal, World War II Victory Medal, Presidential Unit Emblem, Good Conduct Medal, and European Theatre Service Medal with five Battle Stars. Gene returned to the United States in November of 1945 and pursued a career as a railroad conductor.

What happened after you landed in France?

We went in and took over for the 101st Airborne at Carentan, which was about seven miles in. Then we went in the hedgerows, which was the toughest fighting for me because we lost so many men. The hedgerows were farmers' fields, and they had hedge trees around each field with a road in the middle, and we would be on one side of a hedgerow, and the Germans would be on the other side with just a road between. One time we needed to call for artillery, but our communication lines had been cut, so I went out and got our jeep, which was under enemy fire, 'cause it had a radio on it. Then the captain called for artillery, and of course, we got the Germans out of there, and I got a Bronze Star for that. But the hedgerows were tough, and then, too, you'd just get your foxhole dug in, and you'd get orders to move out. When the SS Panzers retreated, they would leave snipers behind, tied in trees, and when we'd come along, they would shoot at us. Well, we were laying these lines alongside the road, and they'd be up in the trees shooting at us. It'd just be like the old Western movies where you seen the bullets hitting and the ground coming up. Of course, everybody would turn and shoot, and the trees would just be bare when they got finished. Well, we finally got through the hedgerows, and then we broke loose. We went so fast with Patton; I was on an outpost, about twenty miles out by myself and a few men. My main job was laying the wire for the communications out in front. Then later on, the Signal Corps came in behind us and put in permanent wiring. When we were doing it, if we had time we would put the lines up in trees or on poles so they wouldn't be cut in half by half-tracks and such. But when you're advancing you just lay them on the ground wherever you can. I had a jeep and three men, and if you couldn't go where a jeep would go, two men carried the reel of wire to where we had to go. One time in the hedgerows we thought they were going to use mustard gas, so we had to wear these special suits. They were real heavy and stiff, and they smelled bad, but we only wore them about two days; and they never did use gas.

Did you learn survival techniques as you went along during the Bulge?

Oh yeah. You had to experience things like that all the time, to keep your head down or where you are or when it was time to raise up and look around and not and keep down. And the artillery fire, I mean, the big guns were bad. When we were in the hedgerows and later in Ardennes, we'd get tree bursts from their 88s. In fact, I got hit twice in the hedgerows and in the Ardennes. It was what they called hot shrapnel. But I was lucky. I just got hit in the arms and hands. Nothing serious, more like cuts, and they told me I could get a Purple Heart. I said no, not for that. So I didn't take it. I just wrapped my hands up with rags or whatever was around and went on.

Glenn Lautenschlaeger

Date of Birth:
August 1921

Place of Birth:
Mascoutah, IL

Military Assignment:
First Army, VIIth Corps, 294th Combat Engineer Battalion

Military Duties:
Combat Engineer

Highest Rank Achieved:
Private First Class

Postwar Occupation:
Civil Service

Glenn was inducted in December of 1942. He went overseas on the USS *Excelsior* and landed at Sherborne, England, in December of 1943. He crossed the Channel on June 6 and landed at Normandy Beach. Glenn fought with the 294th Combat Engineer Battalion through France, Belgium, and Germany. Glenn earned the Combat Infantry Badge and was awarded the Purple Heart with an Oak Leaf Cluster, Bronze Star, World War II Victory, and Good Conduct Medals. He received five Battle Stars (Normandy, Northern France, Ardennes, Central Europe, Rhineland), American Campaign, European–African–Middle Eastern (with Bronze Arrow and Silver Star), and Army of Occupation (Germany) Medals. Glenn returned to the United States in November of 1945 and pursued a career in civil service.

The talk around the camps in England must have centered on when the invasion was going to happen. Did you have any personal beliefs on that?

No personal beliefs. I recall being in a large hall, theater, and each and every one was supposed to keep this a secret. We were going to invade the fifth. So it was changed to the sixth, and it was kept secret though. It was kept secret at least as far as we were concerned. We hoped that everybody kept their mouth shut, and I think they did because we invaded Normandy Beach, and we took them a little by surprise, but they had those pillboxes. You could drop a bomb on them, and it wouldn't do a thing, and they had their little holes where they just could put their guns and aim at anything that's outside. We finally got rid of them by throwing grenades in the holes, and that cleaned them out pretty quick. Of course, the paratroopers helped considerably coming in from the rear.

Did you arrive on D-Day or shortly thereafter?

On D-Day, about 5:30—early in the morning—it was dark, kind of a little foggy, which was to our advantage to a certain extent, but we were early enough that they didn't expect us. And that was the big advantage we had. But it was still a sorrowful sight to see your buddy get killed just right alongside of you, and you knew good and well that you could be next at any time. I was one of the lucky ones.

Now arriving and landing on the beaches of Normandy as a combat engineer, you must have had very specific tasks set out for your unit.

They asked us to get rid of the mines and the barbed wire that was out on the beach. We just couldn't go right there and clean those mines out while the Germans were still in the pillboxes. We got some of the mines cleared away so the men could get through and around. But we lost so many men because we were perfect targets. We couldn't shoot through the openings in the pillboxes to get them. The only way was grenades from the top and hope you hit the hole when you threw them in the darn things. Boy, when they were thrown in, they opened the door—well, some got out, but some didn't; lot of them got shrapnel, and it killed them. And that's the only reason we got hold of that Normandy Beach.

What kind of equipment did you use to clear a minefield, and how did you dismantle or defuse a mine?

You just try to neutralize them so they can't explode. After that's done, you just laid them to the side. Of course, you don't want anything driving over them. Once you got that cleared off, you had a pretty decent way of getting other equipment up into the beach. Then the next task was these fencerows. The French had fencerows around the field that marked their fields, and they had one opening to put in cattle or whatever they had. And if you went into that opening, the Germans had three different places set up with foxholes and machine guns. And they just cleaned you right off like flies. So then the tanks couldn't get over the fencerows because a tank is very light metal on the bottom, and they could just clean that tank off, crew and all. So there was a taxicab driver from Chicago. He said, "Glenn, would you help me get some of these railroad ties, and if they get me a welder here, I can weld that on." With permission. Well, he got that welded on and they pierced through those fencerows: It's a mound of ground and then trees on top. So they punched a few holes in there, and they put phosphorus shells in the guns, and they would clean that corner, that corner, and that corner. That's exactly where the Germans were sitting. And once we started doing that, it didn't take us long. Then I don't know what company put up a regular bucket, where they could just scoop the ground out and drive a tank through. Well, once that was going on, it didn't take them long to clear that out.

I've heard that described as something called a hedgehog.

Hedgehog. That was what was sent over afterwards. Then they got a company over here. What they call a hedgehog was a bucket on them, and that scooped that dirt out, whereas this one just punched holes; he punched a few holes and finally the tank, it was loose enough to take the tank and just stay out so it was kind of level, not just way up like this. It was more that they could use their shells and could aim at the different corners.

I guess if a tank was going over it, then its vulnerable belly would be exposed.

Well, that's what happened at the beginning. At first, they thought they could walk into the hedgerow opening. I'm glad I wasn't the first one was told to do it, but right away the more they got in that gateway, that opening, boy, what a perfect target, and they were just mowed right off. There were three machine gun emplacements. There was one in this corner, that corner, and one in this corner. This was the open corner. Then we thought we could go over the built up dirt. With a tank like ours, there is just thin metal on the bottom so all it took was one good shot, and the tank was destroyed. But when he put that thing on, they just kept poking at the mounds, and then the tank could eventually get through.

And this taxi driver from Chicago that you mentioned came up with the idea that your engineer unit welded these onto the first tanks? It sounds instrumental to breaking out of this hedgerow country.

That's how it started. From then on they must have told them about it back in the United States 'cause they got them durn things over there in a hurry, with that bucket.

Were there still lots of land mines in the hedgerow country?

Not in the hedgerow country; not too many. Maybe like this gate opening or something like that, but they were well equipped; they didn't even want that. They just took and cleaned you off. Several tried to get over the top, but you're just like a target. They see you crawl over the top of the hedgerows, even in a bunch of trees, they could easily spot you. So that's why that tank was the best thing, with those phosphorus shells, and when they went in there, it just cleaned them. Not like a bullet; a bullet will just get one or two guys, but this nailed them right there, whoever was there, 'cause that phosphorus burned them all.

You mentioned having some difficulty with your feet from frostbite, trying to get past that. Are there any other physical reminders from your wartime experience that you still live with today?

You bet. I've got shrapnel in my back. It's about three-eighths of an inch from my rear, from my spine, and nobody will take it out. And the wife, she's pretty well taken care of it all now, she always used to take the shrapnel out of my back. Take a little knife and cut. They say it grows out, but this didn't. It would come out to a point, but it just wouldn't get past the skin. So she'd nip it a little, take them out. She took a bunch of that stuff out.

Where were you injured when you received this shrapnel?

The shrapnel was in the Ardennes Forest. They took out as much of the shrapnel as they could with a quick operation but sent me back out right away because they needed all the men they could at that time.

John Conrad

Date of Birth:
May 1924

Place of Birth:
St. Louis, MO

Military Assignment:
44th Infantry Division, 71st Infantry Regiment

Military Duties:
Radio Operator, Combat Infantryman

Highest Rank Achieved:
Sergeant

Postwar Occupation:
Typesetter

John was drafted in February of 1943 and took his basic training at Ft. Lewis, Washington. He spent some time in the ASTP until that program was ended and joined his old outfit in the 44th Infantry Division for maneuvers in Louisiana and Texas. Afterwards, he spent some time in Camp Phillips, Kansas, before being sent overseas on the USS *Monticello,* which was a converted Italian cruise liner. The 44th Division was the first to land at the port of Cherbourg, which had just recently been cleared from debris from the D-Day invasion. John served in France, Germany, and Austria in the Northern France, Ardennes, Rhineland, and Central Europe campaigns. He earned the Combat Infantry Badge and was awarded the Bronze Star, Good Conduct Medal, American Campaign, World War II Victory Medal, French Freedom Medal, Battle of the Bulge Medal, Army of Occupation Medal, and the European Theatre Service Medal with four Battle Stars. In 2007, John was awarded the French Légion d'Honneur. After his discharge from service in 1945, John pursued a career as a typesetter.

Please tell us about the Battle of the Bulge.

Well, maybe you never heard this one, and most people haven't. When people talk about the Battle of the Bulge, everybody assumes more or less that everybody fought at Bastogne. And that's not true. Bastogne was important because it had three or four highways intersecting, and that's where the main fighting was. But there were approximately half a million men on the American side, and half a million Germans on the other side; and they had their equipment, all their jeeps, trucks, weapons, and artillery. All that could not fit in the space around Bastogne. The Battle of the Bulge was approximately fifty to sixty miles long, from Bastogne south. And the people that fought in the Battle of the Bulge was the 1st Army, to the north; and then the 3rd Army butted them, and they came down so far; then my 7th Army was next to the 3rd Army. And my division, the 44th Infantry Division, was right next to the 3rd Army. When Eisenhower sent the 3rd Army up to Bastogne, they vacated something like twenty or thirty miles of front, and so the Germans could have just walked through there. So, when the 3rd Army went up to Bastogne, we were ordered to go north too. The 7th Army was now stretched out to cover about two-thirds of the 3rd Army's previous position, plus we were still covering our own area. At that point we were spread thin as heck, and the Germans knew that too, because they had some good information. There were some Germans there fighting, but not enough to bust through us at the time. So the way I've studied it now through history, when they were stopped up in the Bastogne area, the Germans retreated east and made a big U-turn. When they came back west, they were about fifty miles south of Bastogne, and they attacked us on Christmas Day. They knew we were thinned out, but they didn't know how thin we were. To this day, I don't know if they had all their forces going in and out or were just probing our defenses.

We had quite a fight, but they stopped and retreated. Our intelligence people told us that they thought it was just more or less a feign, but that the Germans definitely are coming back, and we assume they will hit again on New Year's Eve. And it turned out that's the way it was. They hit us New Year's Eve at the south end of the Bulge, in what the Germans called Operation Nordwind, which means North Wind. Most of their infantrymen were covered with white, and their helmets were painted white. And we didn't know whether they were drunk or drugged, but their infantry attacked in lines, just like in the Civil War, which was stupid in the modern war. So we just mowed them down, and they were hollering, "Happy New Year, Yankee bastards." And so we gave them a response, and they didn't break through our lines, but they did some pretty good damage.

At the time, my company was in a little town in northern France, just near the German border. So when they attacked at midnight, we were fighting like heck, and I was radioman in my company. So, at about two o'clock in the morning, my radio rang that they wanted to talk to the captain. And so he got orders to move out, because we're about three-fourths encircled already. And at that time of night, there was no moon, and it was blacker than the ace of spades. You could hardly see a foot in front of you. We were in a town called Bliesbruck, right alongside the Blies River, and were told to go down the road south until we got to the railroad tracks and then go over the railroad tracks to a bridge and cross the river. Now, most of the railroad tracks in that area were built on the top of a hill, maybe thirty, forty, fifty feet up in the air. So we started climbing the hill up to the railroad tracks. But unbeknownst to us, the 63rd Engineers were up there, and they had orders to blow up the track and the bridge. Well, they didn't know we were coming, and we didn't know they were up here. So we got about two-thirds up the hill, and they got the signal to blow. And they did. Man, the tracks flew up, and I was in a group of about a dozen fellows, and we found ourselves flying up in the air backwards, down to the bottom of the hill. As far as I know, none of us were really injured. Probably had a couple of bumps and bruises, I suppose. But we stumbled in small groups around for about a week or so until we got all our companies reorganized.

Are there any individuals either fallen or otherwise that you want to pay tribute to for the role they played?

Yeah, this last company commander, Captain John Hudgins. He was from North Carolina, and there's a saying that an officer is supposed to be an officer and a gentleman, and this fellow was both. I don't know if he was a gentleman because he was from the South or what, but he was a good officer. At the time, I could speak halting German, and he knew that. So I was more or less the official interpreter for my company. Now, I've heard from guys in other companies in my battalion that their officers were more or less conquerors in their attitude, and they'd just go bust open a door and tell the occupants to either stay there or get out, but that our soldiers were going to be staying there that night. And Captain Hudgins was not like that. He'd say, "Conrad, go up and knock on the door and if somebody answers" (we did not know if people were in them or not), he says, "if somebody answers, ask them" and he emphasized "ask" them if we can come in and just sleep on the floor during the night. So I would do that, and if they answered the door I would ask them in my halting German and pidgin English and handwrote them if we could come in and sleep, and most times they said, "Yes." So I respect him for that because the other guys really pushed their weight around.

What would you say was your most important contribution during your time in service?

Well, probably the fact that I was a radioman, and I relayed messages. And one time we were in the Vosges Mountains, and our radios wouldn't work. We couldn't contact anybody, so I went out from our area and found a spot where I could communicate with all the other companies in my battalion and Battalion Headquarters. So they told me to stay there, and I was there for about two days by myself. And any communication had to come through me although I didn't hear it because I'd tell one of the company commanders or wherever, and they'd communicate between their own radios. So I thought that was pretty good. It could have been bad if they had seen me or heard me talking on the radio.

Were you afraid, or was it kind of peaceful for a change?

It was peaceful because there was no shelling whatsoever; I guess they didn't know I was there. And after eleven o'clock or midnight, most communications ceased, so I used to change the dial on my radio, and I picked up a German radio station broadcasting from Belgrade, Yugoslavia. They used to open the program every night playing Lily Marlene, which was popular among the German troops. So I was in France, and the radio signal came all the way across the Adriatic Sea where I picked it up. I guess the conditions were just right. When I got back to my outfit, one of the officers said, "You know, you ought to be given a Bronze Star for putting yourself out like that." And I said, "Well, that's just part of the job."

Lyle Bouck, Jr.

Date of Birth:
December 1923

Place of Birth:
St. Louis, MO

Military Assignment:
99th Infantry Division, 394th Infantry Regiment

Military Duties:
I&R Platoon

Highest Rank Achieved:
Lieutenant Colonel

Postwar Occupation:
Chiropractor

Lyle enlisted in the National Guard in August of 1938; his unit was activated in December of 1940, and he later attended OCS and its advanced course at Ft. Benning, Georgia, also serving as an instructor there. He went overseas in late September of 1944 and was transferred to the battlefield in Belgium in November. He and his men were one of the first units to encounter the Germans at the onset of the breakthrough on December 16 at Lanzerath. After running out of ammunition, Lyle and his men were taken prisoner and survived ordeals in several POW camps before the 99th Infantry Division liberated all of them. Lyle earned the Combat Infantry Badge and was awarded the Distinguished Service Cross, Silver Star, Bronze Star, and the Purple Heart with two clusters. His Intelligence and Reconnaissance Platoon was the most highly decorated unit of World War II, and their story has been eloquently portrayed in Alex Kershaw's book *The Longest Winter*. Lyle returned to the United States, and after a lengthy recuperation at O'Reilly General Hospital, he subsequently pursued a career in medicine.

Could you walk me through as much as you can about your first battle encounter?

Well, our duty as the I&R [Intelligence and Reconnaissance] Platoon was to collect information for the regimental commander, so we ran regimental observation posts. We'd go out and put a couple of men in a tree on the front lines to observe and report what we could see. And then we patrolled into enemy territory to find out where different units were, how strong they were, and what kind of equipment they had. So we were busy doing that on a daily basis. On the 10th of December, Major Kriz told me he had a special assignment for the platoon. We got in the Jeep and went up to the front lines, out of the Division boundary, and went to a hill where the forests were overlooking the village of Lanzerath, Belgium. He said, "The 2nd Infantry Division was here, and they've been pulled out. The 106th Division came in here, and they have not sent anyone to occupy these foxholes. Our right flank is exposed and open. Temporarily, I want you to bring the platoon out here and get into these foxholes until we can get a permanent replacement for you." We went into those foxholes, and I thought that if something happened, we'd need more protection than we have. So we went back to quartermaster, got some saws and axes, and cut down some pine trees. Then we covered up the foxholes with the logs until they looked like igloos, and that's what we did for the next few days. By the 16th of December, we had this position really fortified. We had set up .30 caliber machine guns in foxholes on both flanks and a .50 caliber machine gun on a Jeep in the middle section of our fortified area. When I look back at it, that was probably the luckiest and wisest thing we could have done, because when the combat with the Germans had ended on the 16th, we realized they couldn't locate us. They couldn't figure out how deep we were or how many of us there were. Covering the foxholes with those pine logs, I know for sure protected us from the two-hour artillery barrage that came in earlier that morning. We had a lot of tree bursts, and a lot of shrapnel fell, but we were well protected and had no casualties from the shelling.

So on that morning, when did you receive the first fire?

The artillery came first, and it was for a long time. I wasn't looking at my watch, but all the reports are that there were several hours of artillery. We were on a hill about two hundred yards west of Lanzerath, and there was a tank destroyer unit in the village that we had been regularly communicating with, until they suddenly packed up and left. When I called regiment, they said, "Get someone into the village and see what's going on." So the four of us went into the village, into a house where we had an observation post set up, and we could see the Germans coming on both sides of the road. We went back up to the platoon position, and by now the Germans were filing out of the village looking like they were going to continue on with their march. At that point, we opened fire on them, and that started what was a long day. They regrouped and realized that the fire was coming from up on the hill, so they came across this snow-covered pasture, and there was a farm fence, and as they'd come to that fence they'd get hit. So we repulsed that attack, and they did that three times during the course of the day. Around five o'clock, it was starting to get dark, and I realized we were out of ammunition and had a lot of men wounded. As we were preparing to pull out, the Germans came around on the right side through the back part of our position and stormed us, and since we had no more ammunition, we were captured. I figured that they were just going to shoot us because we had caused so much trouble, but they didn't. We went on down the hill and into a building on the right side of the road, which I was told was a tavern or something.

Do you have any idea of how many Germans you did away with?

I do not know. I read later on that there were two or three hundred. The only thing I know, if you can just picture yourself in a field of snow, and if you killed a chicken and threw it out there the kind of blood that you would see. And if you can imagine how many human beings were lying there, I can't really describe it. It was horrible. But it was something that was happening, and I don't think we looked upon it with any particular feeling.

How close did you come to being killed that day?

It could have ended for me on three occasions. The first was when my hand-held radio was shot out of my hands as I was trying to use it to communicate during the battle. The second was when I got shot in the leg as I got out of my foxhole after were captured. The third was when we were being escorted to the town. As I approached the fence where we inflicted so much damage on the German soldiers, one of the German soldiers, who was enraged with the sight of this carnage, ran up to me and pointed the barrel of his gun at my belly and fired—fortunately, there was only a "click" since he had run out of ammunition. It's ironic that several years prior an aunt of mine had told me that if I survived past my twenty-first birthday, that I would live to be an old man.

How long then were you in this tavern?

It was probably eight or nine in the morning of December 17, which was my twenty-first birthday, when they told us to get up. They started walking us, and we walked all of that day until we got to a place called Stadtkyll, where they put us down in the basement of a railroad station house. The next day, they walked us a short distance, and loaded us on 40 & 8 boxcars. They put seventy-four of us in a boxcar, which was good to keep warm, but the stench was indescribable. There were men that were wounded and defecation and the whole works. We didn't know at the time that that was going to be the beginning of seven long days with no food or water. Well, we got organized. I was Number 7, and we rotated around by numbers. Five men could lie down at one time, and when you got rotated to the window, you could scrape off the frost from our breath on the windows and put it on your tongue, and that was it for water.

We finally got to a prison camp, but there was no room there, so we got on the train again and went to Nuremberg. They put us in a big room and took our clothes. We learned later that they put them in big pressure cookers to wash them. Then they dried them and put them in a big pile, and we had to get what we could get. So I had something that didn't even fit from that point on. And my legs were bitten up from some kind of black bugs after we were there for about three weeks, so that was another problem. They didn't treat you or anything; they said you have to live with it. They gave us a bowl of turnip soup every morning; very little solids, mostly hot water. But the first couple of mornings that was like eating angel food cake, since we'd had nothing to eat for so long. I don't think we were trying to find a way out because I don't know where we would have gone. I don't know if I had the strength physically and mentally to do anything. We just had to sit there, lie there, and receive it. And they put us in a place in this prison camp where they had bunk beds and each one of us got a mattress cover of some kind, which had straw in it, and we had that to lie on. Then we got the turnip soup in the morning, and at night we would get a piece of what they called bread. I never did know what it was. It looked like brown or black bread, with a piece of margarine or some jelly. That was it.

How did you finally get out of the prison camp?

On March 27, 1945, we heard small-arms fire and a lot of shooting, and then we saw some American tanks. So we thought that somebody had broken through the front line, but that wasn't the case. It was a Task Force that General Patton sent to liberate his son-in-law, John Knight

Waters, from the camp. Patton got a spearhead combat team from the 4th Armored Division and told them to break through the lines and go to Hammelburg and liberate the American officers. They had been told that there were around two hundred of us there, but there was really more like fifteen hundred. They had the tanks all lined up to leave, and we got on the second tank. They gave each one of us M3 machine guns, and we took off. Somewhere during the course of the night, the first tank was hit. We figured it was a tank destroyer roadblock that blew the tank up. My buddy Reed from the prison camp and I jumped off the tank and went into some small trees, and from the light of the burning tank, we could see the emplacement that fired on the tank. There were seven or eight German soldiers up there, and we had these grease guns, so we went up through the trees and wiped them out. We got back and gave the message to the tank that we were on, to tell the commander that we had wiped the Germans out and that we could go now. In the meantime, they had turned the column around, and we were going back the way that we came from. Now, we were the last tank. When we ran into another roadblock, they turned around, and now we were the lead tank again. By this time, the commander decided that he was going to pull up to a farm and put out guards and study the situation and find out what we could do. In the meantime, it starts to get light, and he's of the opinion that he doesn't have enough gasoline to get back, so he orders his men to drain gasoline from half of the tanks and half-tracks, put the gasoline in the others, and we are going to go with a half column. Then, as we were all getting ready to go and getting loaded up, all hell broke loose, and we got fired on. Well, it was the biggest firefight I was ever in, because a German paratroop division, which was headed for the front, was stopped and told we were trying to break out. They had us surrounded, so we were recaptured and taken back to the prison camp. We were put in a big auditorium, given some boiled potatoes and a piece of meat and a piece of bread. Then they loaded us on boxcars, but this time more comfortably so, like twenty in a boxcar, and taken to Nuremberg.

At that point, did you think you would ever get out of there?

I don't ever remember thinking, it's all over. And there were so many things that happened during these times we were talking about, like when I got captured the second time. These Panzer SS troops, they didn't care who they killed. They were just firing, and you knew that it didn't make any difference to them. You wonder, how do you still keep going through this? When we got to Nuremberg, they took us off the trains, gave us some hot soup, and then we started marching south. When we got to the

Danube River, Reed and I escaped. We thought, we've got to get out of here, they're taking us to the Alps. Well, we were free about two hours and got caught again. They got us back to the column and took us all to Munich, where we boarded trains and ended up in a place called Nussberg, to a prison camp, which I learned later had 27,000 prisoners there. I remember seeing POWs just by the thousands, and they put us in a shed, and by now I was really sick and weak. We were there two or three days, and on the 27th of April, we heard small-arms fire, and the Air Corps was circling around and they told us the Americans were here. I thought, "Well, we've gone through this before." But we went outside, and I saw a GI with the 99th Division, and he gave me a K-ration box which was wrapped in cardboard with wax on it and a pen that didn't have any ink in it. So I scratched my name on it and drew a picture of where I was. I said, "Can you remember the name Kriz?" He said, "Yeah, I know about him." I said, "If you can get this to him, tell him where I am." I figured that was a waste of time, but the next day we were in this hut, and somebody was calling my name. I was nauseated, but I went to the door, and there was Kriz. He said, "Get in the Jeep," and we took off. So we eventually got back to Regimental Headquarters, and they got some chicken soup for me. I started to eat it, and I was throwing it up, so they called the regimental surgeon, Dr. Gillespie. He looked at my eyes, pinched my fingers, and said, "Get him in an ambulance, and get him out of here." He said, "You've got hepatitis." So I was evacuated through several hospitals and started getting some food I could handle a little at a time. I eventually was evacuated back to the States and wound up at O'Reilly General Hospital in Springfield, Missouri. I spent a year there recovering.

What sort of lessons did you learn from your experiences that you carried forth?

Well, I guess to do all you can each day and never give up on anything. I think all of us go through parts of life that aren't too much fun, and we all have to make decisions to continue on. Some people bear it out and continue on, while others fold and buckle up. You try to stay mentally and physically as sharp as you can. Be fair and honest, and pursue something in life that has meaning.

Paul Neuhoff

Date of Birth:
1922

Place of Birth:
St. Louis, MO

Military Assignment:
35th Infantry Division, 134th Infantry Regiment

Highest Rank Achieved:
First Lieutenant

Postwar Occupations:
Design Engineer, Instrument Engineer at Monsanto

Paul joined the Enlisted Reserve in June of 1942 and was called to active duty in July of 1943. He attended Officer's Special Basic in the Infantry at Ft. Benning, Georgia, and spent sixteen weeks at Camp Wheeler, Georgia, teaching infantry tactics to draftees. Paul went overseas on the *Saturnia* in late October of 1944, landing in Southampton, England. In mid-November, he joined Company I of the 334th Infantry Regiment near Morhange, France. He was injured three days before the Battle of the Bulge near Frauenberg, France, and was evacuated to a hospital in Nancy, France. After the Bulge started, he was evacuated to England. After he recovered, he rejoined his unit at Rheinberg and fought with them until the war's end. Paul earned the Combat Infantry Badge and was awarded the Purple Heart, American Theatre Medal, European-African-Middle Eastern Service Medal with two Battle Stars (Rhineland, Central Europe), World War II Victory Medal, and Army of Occupation (Germany) Medal. Paul returned to the United States in August of 1945, was separated from active duty in June of 1946, and pursued a career as an engineer at Monsanto.

How did you get wounded?

We were at the Blies River, which was the German border, and one afternoon about four o'clock on the radio they said, "Secure the other end of town; put an outpost down at the end so they can't attack us without us knowing about it." So I stepped out the door and across the street, about twenty feet away was an orange flash, and a piece hit me on the bone right here—a half inch over and I'd be blind in one eye. Another piece hit me in the Adam's apple. Then there was a little, one-eighth-inch piece in the side of my leg, and I've got a mortar fragment about the size of my fingernail between the two bones of my left leg. I got a ride on a Jeep back to the Army aid tent and wound up in a hospital back in Nancy, France. They x-rayed my leg and gave me a shot of penicillin and said it would do more harm to take out the shrapnel than to leave it in, and so it's still there.

Three days later, the Battle of the Bulge started, and all the convalescent hospitals became evacuation hospitals. So maybe in seven days I went across to England, where I was in a hospital, and it took a while through the Replacement System to get back to the front. I read books and played cards, I can remember that this was right around Christmastime and the Red Cross gave us a little package. That was one of the nicest Christmas presents I ever had. At home I'd always been showered with a whole lot of gifts and stuff, and this was just a deck of cards, a pack of cigarettes, and I think some M&M's, some chewing gum, a little address book, and a pocketbook, and Ogden Nash's *Book of Treasury* or something like that. And then there was another book of famous poems that I brought home.

I had to go into rehab while at the hospital, and I can remember we went out in the back, and they almost never have snow in England there, but they had eight inches of snow. They had a courtyard with a track, and we were out there running around to get in shape again. Then we went back to Litchfield Barracks, and there I met a number of fellows from school who got hit or were being sent back to either the front lines or back to the States.

Joseph Potter

Date of Birth:
February 1924

Place of Birth:
East St. Louis, IL

Military Assignment:
First Army, 38th Cavalry Reconnaissance Squad

Military Duties:
Reconnaissance Squad

Highest Rank Achieved:
Staff Sergeant

Postwar Occupation:
National Auto Supply

Joe was drafted in 1943 and took his basic training at Camp Maxey, Texas. He landed in Exeter, England, in September of 1943. Joe crossed the Channel on D-Day (3rd Wave) and landed at Omaha Beach. He served with the 1st Army in the Normandy, Northern Europe, Ardennes, Rhineland, and Central Europe campaigns. Joe earned the Combat Infantry Badge and was awarded the Purple Heart, the Presidential Unit Citation, and the European Theatre Service Medal with five Battle Stars. Joe returned to the United States in November of 1945 and pursued a career with National Auto Supply.

When did you leave England to go over to Europe?

When I was in England, I got transferred into the OSS, they call it the CIA now. Well, that was good duty because I had to go to work at six in the evening and worked until eleven at night. That's all I did, and I didn't do any other thing; it was kind of a special treatment, you know. I'd come back to the barracks, and maybe the guys would be out doing their training, and I could sleep. In fact, all I had to do was walk around in the pubs, and if a guy was mouthing off too much about "they was just out there and they got a bunch of new tanks or something," I think I'd have to shut him up. I only had to pull one guy in. In fact, I was working with the OSS when the Invasion started. I came back to the barracks, I guess it was the night of June 5, and all our equipment's gone. My barracks mate was there, but everybody else was gone. The next morning I went up to the chow hall; hell, there's nobody there. And Major Rusack says, "Potter, what are you doing here?" I said, "Where's everybody at?" He said, "The invasion started. Get your barracks bag and get in the Jeep." And so I didn't go with my outfit; I went in with a bunch of guys who were just making the Invasion. I got on a troopship at night, and we went over to Omaha Beach the next morning.

I was on the third wave and didn't go in till ten o'clock. The other guys went in at daybreak. But I'm standing on the ship—it could only go in so close—and I'm watching everything. All the guys went in on these LCIs. They would hold forty men, and I kind of like to remember the funny parts, but they broke out a barrel of crackers, I'm talking about a barrel of crackers, and they had some orange marmalade. It was so bitter you could hardly eat it. I was on a British ship, and we got tea, no coffee. And so a lot of those poor guys, that's the last meal they had. So I'm watching this, and they had the big battle wagons pulled up alongside of the shore, and they'd fire their guns, and then it was our turn you know to get, this old British officer, he said, "All right Yanks, now's the time." I didn't think too much of it. I was nineteen, and they had a canvas chute they used to get you down into the LCIs, and one of them eggheads before me put his bayonet—we used to have big old long bayonets on the M1s—he put his bayonet down there and ripped it apart. This British officer, he was going nuts. And so I had to go down on a damn rope ladder. I'd never done that before, and here you got a beltful of ammunition this way and you got a bandolier over this way, and you have two grenades, and you have a gas mask, and we had protective clothing for mustard gas. Then they give us a life belt, so you put it around your waist, and I was real skinny then. I only weighed 130 pounds then.

Do you recall what your first battlefield engagement in the Bulge was?

I sure do. I can tell you right down to a T. There was three of us, we had a .30 caliber air-cooled machine gun set up in an old warehouse. It was in no man's land, and we got there in November, so we were well set up, all of our guns were set up. I had three guys, and so I said, "Now two of you stay on the gun, and one of us will sleep." Well, it was my turn to sleep in, at daybreak December 16 I think it was, and boy, you're dying, you want some sleep, and it's my turn to sleep. I'm dreaming they were shelling us. They didn't shell us, but I'm dreaming that they're shelling us. And finally a shell hit right beside the old warehouse. But I had sandbags up, thank God. Woke me up, and I told the other two guys, I put one guy on the gun, and the other guy feeding it. I had plenty of ammunition, I was a scrounger, I must have had two thousand rounds, and I had two extra barrels 'cause you had to take the barrels out if you fired too much. They would get too hot, they'd warp. So I said, there's something going on, I said, Taylor, boy he was a good soldier, crazy, but he was good. And Mapes, yeah. So I had Mapes feeding the gun, and I said now don't shoot, it was all real foggy. There was a field out in front of us, and I'll fire the first shot. And when I start shooting, you guys shoot; don't shoot before that. They were nervous, too, you know. And the Germans come across that field like they were just going to a restaurant. They were in formation, and I thought, good God, there was forty or fifty of them, or about sixty, I don't know. I thought, God Almighty, they were just walking to their death. We killed every one of them, so I shot the first one, I let them get up, and we took that air-cooled and run a belt through, and then I took the barrel off, put a new barrel in, and any that was standing, why we shot them down, then we just fired wherever they were lying. We didn't want anybody to get up, and that happened all up and down A, B, and C line. And poor buggers, they just walked right to their deaths. They should have known better; somebody should have trained them better.

Stanley Gibson

Stan was drafted in June of 1942 and took his basic training at Camp Walters, Texas. He spent some time as an aviation cadet before being transferred to the 86th Infantry Division and was sent over to England in that division. He was transferred to the 99th Infantry Division in November of 1944. Stan and six others from the 99th survived in the Ardennes from December 16, 1944, to January 4, 1945, after their company was devastated at the onset of the Battle of the Bulge. Stan earned the Combat Infantry Badge and was awarded the Bronze Star for capturing forty German soldiers, as well as the Presidential Unit Citation. Stan returned to the United States in July of 1945 and worked as an auto parts distributor.

Date of Birth:
February 1924

Place of Birth:
McClure, IL

Military Assignment:
99th Infantry Division, 393rd Infantry Regiment

Military Duties:
1st Gunner in a Machine Gun Squad

Highest Rank Achieved:
Sergeant

Postwar Occupation:
Automobile Parts Distributor

Where did you go with the 99th Division, and what was your first action?

I think about December 14, there were four or five of us on an outpost in front of the main line, and it was just sort of a holding position, waiting for Christmas. We were just at the international highway and probably the farthest point of the 99th Division into Germany at that particular time. So when the Bulge started, the German tanks and so forth came by and didn't bother us at all. So it's daylight, and the next thing we're going to go back, but there's a German tank setting probably fifty, sixty yards away right in front of our hole, so we stayed there until dark. Then we started following buzz bombs. We thought they were going to England, but they were going toward Liege, Belgium, which threw us off kilter. So we started back, and then somewhere in this line we began to make contact with some German troops. So we had some skirmishes, and we decided we'd better bust up in twos. Some of 'em would make it through, I guess. So now I don't know what happened to the other four.

Back in the woods, no compasses, overcast, so you didn't know north, south, east, or west. We get into this wooded area, and we come across a house. So I made it to this particular house, and a Belgian girl was there with her grandmother. They didn't have any idea that the war was coming into Belgium again. Of course, there were Germans in the area, the same as American troops. So I got into a shed in the yard area, and she locked the door, in case the Germans came by I would have some time to figure out what to do. But you don't always think about everything you should think about. We left footprints in the snow going to the building, but there weren't any footprints coming back. So the Germans saw the footprints to the building, and the girl was told to open the door. She didn't have the key or whatever it was so they shot the lock off the door, and I'm squatting down on the inside. They shot the lock off the door, pulled the door open, and I shot both of them bang bang with a .45 pistol. If I hadn't done that, they would have killed me and probably killed her and her grandmother for hiding me.

I was behind the German lines from December 16 until January 4 eating K-2 biscuits and chocolate bars and what you could scrounge out of every foxhole that we could find. You could always find some K-2 biscuits. These are like the little lunch packs with about six crackers in them. The white one was K-1, the other was K-2. K-2s, nobody would eat those. They were cruddy so they were always available any time the snow had not covered them up. So we scrounged some of the K-2 biscuits, and I think I had about six chocolate bars and about three to four—I don't remember the name of the lunch—it looks like a Cracker Jack box. And like potted cheese, potted ham, cheese, four cigarettes, maybe some other stuff, I don't recall exactly what we had. I'd be able to survive with that till I got back on the line.

Is there a particular combat engagement or experience that stands out in your mind?

One time we were marching from one area to the other, and we went through a section where there's a railroad gun on the track. This gun had already been destroyed, but it looked like it had been moved out of this tunnel on the track. So Jake and I and Van Maas went into this tunnel, and when we got on the other side, it was just going down the ravine, but there was a building sitting out pretty much in front of us. A stone building and to the right of me, there was about forty Germans. In uniform, standing in formation, just like we would have to do when we would get a ten-minute break. So I set the gun up, and I'd carry tracer rounds of ammunition, most of them would be ball rounds. But when I got in a situation where I might be capturing people without having to shoot them I'd use the tracers. And so when I did that, I shot between a group of people and the building with the tracer rounds up and down so they could see the tracers coming by. And they knew I wasn't shooting at them so it gave them a chance to surrender. But some decided (this is pretty difficult) to make a run for the woods. And I machine-gunned them. The rest of them gave up pretty fast. By that time, our other troops heard what was going on, so they ran into the tunnel and went down, got these Germans, and they come up the hill by our machine, and you could see the expressions on some of these guys' faces. Some said, "Thank you." If I'd been a mean fellow, I could have shot up a helluva lot of Germans. I never did do it that way.

Is there anyone that you haven't mentioned that you would like to pay tribute to now?

I never did get acquainted with my own people. I was a machine gunner, and nobody wanted to associate with me 'cause you draw enemy fire. Every time you'd fire the gun, it would make a big black teardrop in the snow, turn the snow black out in front, which means anybody on the other side, they see the snow turn black, they know I'm there. So I developed an extra spring in my belly. I would sit in one spot for a period of time, and then I'd move to a different spot. Sometimes I'd move forward, sometimes I'd move left, move right, sometimes I'd move back.

A number of times shortly after I moved, there'd be mortar shells hitting right where I was sitting. So I survived it. I would carry about one thousand rounds of ammo when we moved out for combat, and that's a lot of bullets. In normal times toward the end of the war, instead of a tripod gun, I got a bipod, so one guy could carry that. You could fire standing up, lying down, squatting down, anyway you could when you had to do it. And you always tried not to have to do much shooting standing up. I helped two other fellow GIs; I helped 'em, I helped 'em die. They were shot up so bad they couldn't survive; so they were just gonna die in misery. So I felt bad about doin' that, but I also felt good. They would have had a terrible death just lying there dying by themselves so I assisted them to die. It was bad.

I think they would thank you if they could.

I hope. You try to think that way. But some of that stuff pops back up every once in a while. I meet every Monday with about twenty-five, thirty guys like me down in Jefferson Barracks. We're in the PTSD Program, and you get along pretty well, but every once in a while something pops up, opens the safety deposit box in your brain. Just like this; I wouldn't have done this interview six or seven years ago, but the group encourages each other to get it off your chest a little bit.

Anything else you'd like to add?

During one continuous deal, there was no lapse at that particular time. It was constant. We fought from December 16 through January 28. Somebody was shooting at you basically twenty-four hours a day. If you'd have nighttime, then you'd have patrols that would come into your lines. Of course, you had patrols going in their lines so it turned out to be a very nasty game of hunting. When you start hunting for people to kill, that's a bad hunt. And that's what we were doing, and that's what they were doing. We were trying to take their ground; they were trying to keep it. It would be like somebody comin' in your home, somebody tryin' to take your home; and you tryin' to keep it. Hell of a conflict that way.

James Johnson

Jim was drafted in June of 1943 and took his initial basic training at North Camp Hood. He spent time in the ASTP until March of 1944, when he was sent to Camp Maxey, Texas, to complete basic and was subsequently sent overseas, leaving from Boston and arriving in Plymouth, England, on October 10, 1944. He crossed the Channel on November 1 and landed at Le Havre, France. Jim fought with the 99th Division through Belgium and Germany. He earned the Combat Infantry Badge and was awarded the Bronze Star, Good Conduct Medal, and the European Theatre Service Medal with three Battle Stars for the Ardennes, Rhineland, and Central Europe campaigns. Jim returned to the United States in March of 1946 and pursued a career in engineering management.

Date of Birth:
June 1924

Place of Birth:
St. Louis, MO

Military Assignment:
99th Infantry Division, 395th Infantry Regiment

Military Duties:
Machine Gunner

Highest Rank Achieved:
Technician Fifth Grade

Postwar Occupation:
Engineering Management

Where were you when the Germans launced their offensive?

We went on the front lines on the 8th of November, just outside of Kalterherberg, Germany. On December 12, we became part of a Regimental Combat Team attached to the 2nd Infantry Division, and we started an attack on the 13th of December for the Wahlerscheid Crossroads, which was a customs station on the border between Germany and Belgium. We had eight German pillboxes to take on December 13, and we took them and stayed in the woods that night. The pillboxes were all out in a clearing, and the Germans reoccupied them that night. On the morning of the 14th, we called for artillery fire on the pillboxes. Instead of hitting the pillboxes, the shells hit the trees above us, and we had shrapnel flying all over the place. Eighteen men in our company got hit by friendly fire. Three of them were killed, and one guy not far from me was cut in half by shrapnel.

On December 14 and 15, the engineers came in and blew up the pillboxes, but we stayed there because the 2nd Division had not yet taken the customs station. So on the 16th, they were in action on the customs station, and we were directed to move down to reinforce some of our units to the south. I was in the 395th Infantry Regiment, and we were on the northern part of the sector that the 99th Infantry Division had occupied. To the south of us was the 393rd Infantry Regiment, and the 394th Infantry Regiment was in reserve. Those were our regiments, and we covered about a twenty-mile front, so we were spread out pretty thin at that point. We set up a defensive line along the Hasselt Pass Trail, and the 2nd Division withdrew from Wahlerscheid Crossroads to Krinkelt, which was being severely hit by the German 6th Panzer Army. Our K Company of the 393rd was really brutalized. The 2nd Division went in to Krinkelt to reinforce them, and we had set up a protective front, right at the Hasselt Pass Trail and the Wahlerscheid Crossroads. On the night of the nineteenth, we withdrew to Elsenborn Ridge, arriving sometime during the night, and they said, "Dig in." Well, we didn't dig in. We were so tired from what we'd been through, and we were cold and hungry because when we pulled off of Hill 621, we dropped everything. All we had was what we could carry, and I happened to be in a light machine gun squad, so I had a forty-two-pound air-cooled machine gun with me. The Germans had followed us up the ridge with tanks, and they started shelling us, so wherever a shell hit, that's where we start digging in deep. Fortunately, our artillery was set up behind us, and they started counter-fire.

Could you describe the role of the weather during the Battle of the Bulge?

Well, Hitler picked the date based on weather conditions. He wanted it to be foggy and snowy so our ground troops would have no air support. And it stayed that way until December 23, when it cleared, and we started getting more snow on the ground. By early January, the snow was a couple of feet deep. On Elsenborn Ridge, we were able to get dry clothes, and we were able to get warm clothes, where we didn't have them when we started out, so that was a plus for us. We got snow packs to replace the boots we had, and that was an improvement. We were able to leave our foxholes and go back to the kitchen and get some hot food, which was a real plus. You didn't stay in the open, because if there were more than two guys close together, you were good for a mortar shell or a sniper. The snipers every now and then would shoot at you if you got out in the open too much. And I had one incident occur, during the early part of January. I was over in my buddy's foxhole, and it started snowing heavily. I decided I'd better get back to my own hole, but due to the conditions, I lost my bearings on the way back. I knew if I went down the hill, I was going toward the German lines, and if I could stay on the level I'd be okay. Well, I roamed around for thirty minutes or so before I found my way back to my foxhole. When I got inside, I took off my clothes and wrapped myself in blankets to warm out, and for a while I thought I was going to freeze to death. Another time, we went out on patrol to find out where the German positions were. While I was crossing a creek on the way back, I went through the ice all the way up to my waist, and I couldn't get out. My buddies finally were able to pull me out, but my clothes froze on me so I went to the aid station. They gave me some blankets and had me go over to the basement of a house to change my clothes and warm up.

The 99th Infantry Division was one of four divisions (the 99th, the 106th, the 28th, and the 4th) that were attacked in the initial breakthrough. We were fighting the 6th German Panzer Army, and their objective was to come over Elsenborn Ridge, because that was the shortest route to Antwerp. The battle started with four divisions in the area, but before it was over, there were over 32 Infantry Divisions and 12 Armored Divisions; 600,000 Americans versus 400,000 Germans. It was a million-man battle.

Wilbur Cruse

Date of Birth:
October 1922

Place of Birth:
Odin, IL

Military Assignment:
*First Army, VIIth Corps
Headquarters*

Military Duties:
*Driver for G2 (Intelligence)
Officer*

Highest Rank Achieved:
Corporal

Postwar Occupations:
Baker; Truck Driver

Wilbur was drafted in 1943 and took his basic training at Camp Wallace, Texas, with additional training at Ft. Bliss, Texas, and Camp Carson, Colorado, before going overseas in July of 1944. He landed at Liverpool, England, and crossed the Channel on August 10, landing at Omaha Beach. Wilbur served as a driver for several intelligence officers in the VIIth Corps through Germany, Belgium, and Luxembourg, in the Rhineland, Ardennes, and Oder River campaigns. He received the Good Conduct Medal, European Theatre Service Medal, and World War II Victory Medal. Wilbur was discharged from service in July of 1945 and pursued careers as a baker and a truck driver.

Could you talk about your duties at the start of the Battle of the Bulge?

I was in G2, the information section, and I drove a first lieutenant. At that time we were in the Hurtgen Forest, and we were losing better than one thousand men a day there. We gathered information from the units and also delivered the orders for the day—what the troops were supposed to do. I was driving one of our Jeeps, and I drove the same Jeep all the way through until the end of the war. We received orders about four o'clock in the afternoon of December 16 to proceed to Army Headquarters, which had moved at that time from Spa, Belgium, down to Chaudfontaine, Belgium. So while my officer went in to get our orders, I stayed outside and watched the V-1s plop in. So that was exciting. During the day of the 16th, there was fog hanging over the whole area, and it was two to three feet off the ground, solid fog, and the whole day was like that. At that time of the year, it only got light about 8:30 or 9:00 in the morning, and it was dark at 3:30 in the afternoon, so there was very little daylight. After we got our orders, we went to the 1st Army Headquarters in Liege, and later on we headed out. Sometime around six or seven in the evening, it started sleeting and snowing and raining. So that was the first night we put in. It was complete sleet and snow and ice, and we went from the Army Headquarters and entered what probably could be called no man's land at Stavelot, on the Ambleve River. We redirected the troops for the next day or two. The first night was hectic. I remember we were up all night in the sleet and the snow, and one boy came up to me as his convoy was passing; they were coming back from leave. He wanted to know whether they would see any action. He was ready for action. I never have forgot it. He was from the 99th Division, and they ended up getting hit really badly in the first couple of days.

Was there ever a time when you went through some battlefield conditions that made you more determined to defeat the enemy?

Probably the moment would be when we ran across Camp Dora at Nordhausen, where they made the V-2s and killed all those people. We buried somewhere in the neighborhood of four thousand in a common grave there. Most all of them were disabled in some way, or had died of starvation, so that was probably the hardest. I have some pictures with me that I took, four of them that I took after I went back the second day with an AP photographer. We took a lot of pictures that day, and some of them made it into the photo section of the *Post-Dispatch*, on approximately April 15, 1945. After I took the photographer in there, I was free to roam, and I went in the side of the cliff where they had the underground factory where they built the V-1s and then started the V-2s. They manufactured them there, and I got to see where these fellows were in the straw hut beds, and the ovens. You name it, I got to see it.

Lloyd Stephens

Date of Birth:
August 1914

Place of Birth:
Flat River, MO

Military Assignment:
*Third Army, Attached to 4th &
6th Infantry Divisions*

Military Duties:
*Head of a Forward Observation
Battalion*

Highest Rank Achieved:
Lieutenant Colonel

Postwar Occupation:
Teacher

Lloyd was drafted in October 1941 and took his basic training at Ft. Shell, Oklahoma. He went overseas on the *Tarawa* in September of 1944, landing in Glasgow, Scotland, and was taken by train to Wimbourne, England. Lloyd crossed the Channel on December 10, 1944, and landed at Le Havre. He served with the 3rd Army through France, Belgium, Luxembourg, and Germany and was awarded the Good Conduct Medal, World War II Victory Medal, Pre-Pearl Harbor Medal, Sharpshooter (.45 and M1), and the ETO Ribbon with three Battle Stars (Ardennes, Rhineland, Central Europe). Lloyd returned to the United States and pursued a career in education at Ritenour High School.

Describe your first battlefield engagement.

Engagement sounds like infantry, and I wasn't infantry. My battalion consisted of two batteries. We got to Arlon and then headed north to Bastogne. I was sent out with half a platoon that was part of the battalion going to Bastogne. We were in a convoy of three trucks and two Jeeps, and the MPs stopped us. I got out to see what the holdup was. We were coming to a crossing that the Germans were shelling. The

MPs said the Germans would fire every thirty minutes and then fire again in twenty-five minutes. So we needed to get out of there. This was about ten miles south of Bastogne, so the rest of the convoy broke off after about twenty-five minutes before the second set of shelling. The Germans also fired on Bastogne every day at three different times so everybody just got out of their basements and let the Germans fire. When I got into Bastogne, I went in and reported to the commanding officer that I believe at that time was McAuliffe [General Anthony Clement McAuliffe], and he told me to go out to a little village just southeast of Bastogne. So I went out there and reported in to some colonel who told me just pick out a house and take over and that we would help with the perimeter defense.

Describe the role the weather played during your time in Bastogne.

Well, we went up there in the fog. It was foggy for at least ten days, and I believe I was in Bastogne about fifteen days in all. And you just couldn't see one hundred yards, especially not in the transit that we used mostly. The transits were our mode of bringing control to the division, and that was really our mission, to bring surveying control to the artillery so they could fire accurately on enemy installations.

If the weather prevented you from spotting artillery, did you serve as a rifleman then?

No, there was no in-city fighting in Bastogne. The Germans did not come into town; they just fired artillery in there. We did set down a sound base and a flash base, but we had to be able to see the enemy territory to see the flashes. You could see the German artillery flashes, but it was hard to pin-point them through your transit, so we had maps of the area. I had several observers who could pick out the place on the map. So by studying the maps, we located an area where we thought the Germans were firing from. So I went to the G3 of the 6th Armored and told him that I had located an area from which the Germans were firing at us. It looked like it was two to three hundred yards, so we planned to use all the artillery and tanks in Bastogne and to block out areas for the different battalions to fire upon. We took four grid squares, a thousand meters each, and covered that four thousand meters; every gun in Bastogne was aimed at their relative position on the grid square. I had observation posts up there who were going to see if we'd covered the area. And when the G3 told me that all the guns were ready to fire, so I gave the order to fire. The observation posts said they never seen so many flares before, and that every gun seemed to hit the target. So that was the highlight of my career in the Army.

Richard Swatske

Date of Birth:
February 1924

Place of Birth:
St. Louis, MO

Military Assignment:
86th Infantry Division, 404th F.A.; 6th Armored Division, 15th Tank Battalion

Military Duties:
Assistant Driver, Bow Gunner, and Loader in a Tank

Highest Rank Achieved:
Private First Class

Postwar Occupation:
Jeweler

Richard was inducted in January of 1943 and took his basic training at Camp Howze, Texas, followed by advanced training at Ft. Livingston, Louisiana, all with the 86th Infantry Division. He went overseas on the *Mariposa* and landed in Scotland in mid-June of 1944. He crossed the Channel in the fall of 1944 and landed at Omaha Beach. Richard was transferred to the 6th Armored Division and served with them through France, Belgium, and Germany. He earned the Purple Heart, Good Conduct Medal, American Campaign, World War II Victory, European-African-Middle Eastern Campaign Ribbon, and the European Theatre Service Medal with three Battle Stars (Ardennes, Rhineland, and Central Europe). Richard returned to the United States in February of 1946 and pursued a career as a jeweler.

Describe your functions on a tank.

I was an assistant driver, bow gunner, and loader. I was on the right side of the tank, and there was a .30 caliber machine gun sticking out, which was called the bow gun. One time we had stopped in this field at night with our tank, and whoever was on guard had to load the gun and put the shell in, and then you had to fire it at intervals, always odd times, eighteen minutes till, eighteen after, ten after, like that, so the enemy didn't know when the shell was coming. So one time I put a shell into these 105s, and I could not get it in the breech; couldn't get it out, and I called for help. Turns out it took two or three of us to finally get the shell out, because the shell casing was crimped, wouldn't work.

A 105mm shell must have been very large and very heavy?

Yes. They were anywhere from two or three feet long, and they had something on the front of the shell. You had to unscrew that and then screw a fuse into it. My job was to put the fuse in and set the time for the firing sequence, when they wanted the shell to explode. It could go for maybe a mile up to twelve miles, depending on how it was set. And then when I gave the signal, two or three other guys put the shell on the platform and shoved it into the breech. We were used as artillery support for the infantry. We had to fire our howitzers over them at times to clear a path so they could go forward. And in the Bulge we had to be careful about firing because we had lost contact with the infantry. We did not know where they were, so we would not fire in the fear of hitting them instead of the enemy.

Do you recall where you were when the Bulge started?

We were at the Saar at the time and were ordered to go up to Bastogne. Well, we went in there, and it was awful. It had snowed badly, and we slipped and slid getting into there. And then we got into these woods on just a narrow pathway, just wide enough for the tank. Snow was all over the trees, and as we were going through there we knocked the snow loose and it covered our periscopes in the front, so we couldn't see where we were going. Somebody had to get out and clean them off, 'cause we couldn't open the hatch and clean them off. We were stopped and being fired at with small-arms fire and machine gun fire. What are we going to do? So one fellow had some grenades, and he was able to toss the grenades into where the firing was coming from, and after a short while we didn't hear any more fire. So the commander of our tank climbed out and cleared the snow away. But then the firing started again, and the poor guy was on the front of the tank, holding on for dear life. He couldn't move. He wasn't about to get up and get shot, so he hung on for a while until we could finally get him back inside.

James McCulloch

Jim was drafted in January of 1943 and took his basic training at Camp Maxey, Texas. He landed in England in March 1943 and fought with the 158th Combat Engineers through France, Belgium, Luxembourg, Germany, and Holland. Jim was awarded the Purple Heart, D-Day Invasion Medal, and the European Theatre Service Medal with five Battle Stars (Normandy, Northern France, Ardennes, Central Europe, Rhineland). Jim returned to the United States in November of 1945 and pursued a career with the U.S. Post Office.

Date of Birth:
November 1924

Place of Birth:
St. Louis, MO

Military Assignment:
VIIIth Corps, 158th Combat Engineers

Military Duties:
Combat Engineers, Mine Detection and Placement

Highest Rank Achieved:
Private First Class

Postwar Occupation:
Post Office

Do you remember where you were when you heard about the German breakthrough on December 16?

We were right up there, on the outskirts of Bastogne, and a German plane attacked our chateau the night before and dropped a bomb and wounded the sergeant, took his leg off. That's when they told us to pull out of the chateau, because German tanks were coming. It was at midnight, and they pulled us all out and took us down towards Bastogne and put us on a skirmish line. They used us as infantry, took about four or five of us at a time, and dropped us off at different places. They put four of us on a bridge and said stop anything that comes through. Of course, I figured I had no chance to stop a tank, but that's what they told us, to stop it. Even though we had bazookas with us, you had to get pretty close with a bazooka to get a tank. We had a machine gun, a bazooka, and a rifle on the bridge. The way those German tanks sounded, you could hear them all night running their motor 'cause it was cold. Sounded like there was a whole column of them. So I knew we couldn't stop all them. And we had a machine gun, but every third bullet was a tracer and that'd give away our position when we were shooting the thing. Well, I know my feet got frozen. It was wet and cold, and the town next to us was abandoned. It was the same name as the bridge: Ortheuville.

And were you relieved from your post at this bridge?

No, when we were shooting that machine gun, every third bullet was a tracer, and the German tank came up there and started firing on us, 'cause he could see our bullets. All he had to do was follow our tracers, and he lobbed a big shell in there, and shrapnel flew in all directions when that thing hit, and I was all bloody in the face, in the arm, and the back. Shrapnel was all over us. I don't know if he was lost or what, but an ambulance picked about four or five of us up and took us to the nearest first aid area. But after we were there a few hours, they said the German tanks were coming, and we had to abandon the hospital, which was all tents. It was a tent outfit. And then they took me to the other hospital in Belgium and then from there to Paris, and there they found out I had frozen feet. I knew that; my feet were frozen stiff as a board, so they said, well, he goes over to England 'cause I couldn't walk very well. So they sent me to England for about two or three months. I had my feet in a birdcage-like thing, so no blankets would touch them. They had that rigged up that way. I just lay in bed there with my feet in that cage, and I was off my feet then for a while. Then they got better, I guess, but they never did get real better, but they were good enough so I could walk on them awhile.

James Leahy

Jim was drafted in April of 1943 and took his basic training at Camp Mackall, North Carolina. He went overseas on the SS *Mount Vernon* and landed in England in August of 1944. He served with the 17th Airborne Division through France, Belgium, Luxembourg, and Germany. Jim was awarded the Good Conduct Medal, World War II Victory Medal, American Service Medal, Service Arrowhead, and Europe–Africa–Middle Eastern Service Medal. He returned to the United States in January of 1946.

Date of Birth:
November 1924

Place of Birth:
Kirkwood, MO

Military Assignment:
17th Airborne Division, 155th AAA Battalion

Military Duties:
Bazookaman

Highest Rank Achieved:
Private First Class

Postwar Occupations:
Machinist; Molder

Where were you on Christmas Eve 1944?

Well, I was sitting in the airport in England. They gave us a Christmas dinner and then put us on a plane, and I flew over Paris, which I was surprised to see was lit up like a Christmas tree. So we landed on the other side of Paris, and then on Christmas Day we started going up towards Bastogne. And we'd walk, and then they'd pick us up and they'd transfer us. They'd shuttle you so far and then you'd start walking, and then they'd go back and get some more and then they'd bring them up. That's the way we got up there. So I don't know where I was at exactly and I don't even know when New Year's came in. I don't remember it. I don't think about it, 'cause I was somewhere between Paris and Bastogne, going into Belgium in the snow in the mountains. The only thing I was thankful for was that I wasn't the man in the lead. He made the path, so that's the guy who had the trouble. We just stayed behind him. I was the 3rd Platoon. First Platoon was there, then the 2nd, and then the 3rd, so I was way back. We were assigned to Patton's 3rd Armored tanks, and we broke in. The tanks could hardly fight because it was tank against tank, and it was pretty hard, so we had to really take it on our own, and we did. We had a little trouble at first, until we started getting them on the run. But it took a while to get them on the run. They were pushing us back, but we kept going until we got up to Bastogne. We broke the pocket through, 'cause the 101st Airborne was in there surrounded, and when I walked in to relieve those guys, they looked pretty rough. I mean they were in there a couple of weeks before we got to them and they had beards on them that was rough and their face was rough and they were just rough all over. 'Course there for a while they couldn't get any supplies or ammunition. The airplanes couldn't fly because it was cloudy, so they couldn't drop or parachute anything in. And then it got clear, and they dropped some stuff in, and then they were able to fight their way out to us, too. So between the two of us we closed it in and broke through. There were some 82nd Airborne in there, but I think it was mainly the 101st.

There must have been bodies just everywhere by the time you got there.

That's why I don't talk about it much. When the snow started melting, all these bodies started showing up, so that made it hard. My wife wants to go back over there, and I don't want to remember that. I'm sorry. At my old age, it just seems like the more it bothers me. Maybe I should have talked about it a long time ago and got it out. I never did. I can still see them and smell it. It's not a nice smell. And it was Americans and Germans both. The ones that's over there, that's the ones that ought to have the glory. Not me. I came back to enjoy life. They didn't.

William Keenoy

Date of Birth:
October 1924

Place of Birth:
St. Louis, MO

Military Assignment:
84th Infantry Division, 335th Infantry Regiment

Military Duties:
Rifleman, Jeep Driver

Highest Rank Achieved:
Sergeant

Postwar Occupation:
Truck Driver

Bill was drafted in March of 1943 and took his basic training at Ft. Butner, North Carolina. He earned the Combat Infantry Badge and was awarded the Purple Heart, American Theatre Campaign Ribbon, World War II Victory Ribbon, three Overseas Bars, and the European–African–Middle Eastern Theatre Campaign Ribbon with three Battle Stars (Ardennes, Rhineland, Central Europe). Bill returned to the United States in January of 1946 and pursued a career in trucking.

The replacement depot didn't return you to your unit, but rather they assigned you to a new one?

Yes. The 84th Infantry Division. They were in some town in France when I came back over again. And our baptism of fire was that night. Well, it was the trees that they hit, the shells would go off at the top of the tree line. So we dug foxholes and laid in them, but the thing was, the shell fragments would come down after they burst. We didn't know where to go then, so I took a tree and moved over and got under some of the branches so the shells would ricochet off of the trees. A lot of the limbs got cut off the trees by the artillery fire.

Do you recall where you were when the Germans launched the offensive that would be called the Battle of the Bulge?

We were up with Montgomery in the 1st Army, and they wanted somebody that could get down to the Ardennes Forest. So we got with Patton, and he said he could get us there in two days. That's when we left with the 3rd Army.

You were transferred to Patton?

Yes. We went down with the 101st Airborne. So most of the guys that were with our division were from the 101st. But we made a lot of friends there and lost a lot of friends. And they left us off these trucks, out in the woods. We didn't know where we were, and we said, man, my feet are cold, it's cold here. That's when the weather started changing, and we were still dressed in regular clothes, nothing warm. No jacket, coats, or anything like that. You were in your foxhole, which always had water in it; couldn't get out of that 'cause they'd zero in on you. But we had these old salamander heaters, where you'd warm up coffee, so we put that in the hole and warm up about four or five guys that way.

Did you experience a German assault during the Battle of the Bulge?

Oh, yeah. We were in Bastogne itself outside say about a quarter of a mile, and there was a big roundabout with a signpost and a water fountain in the middle, and we got in that. We just stayed right around there, and at night we'd pull out our daisy chains. You know what a daisy chain is? It is a land mine on a chain or a rope, and there would be a man over on that side of the roadblock and one on this side of the roadblock. And if you came and didn't give the countersign, you know like, Baby . . . Ruth. Well, if you didn't give it, we'd pull this daisy chain up across the road, and when they'd come up, they'd hit it and blow them up. That happened once, and it was a British vehicle, and they didn't know the countersign, so their half-track got blown up.

I understand that you actually saw, or met, Patton once?

Well, his Jeep driver fell asleep at the wheel when we were moving down to Bastogne, and I was standing there, and he just said, "Come here. Drive this Jeep." So I did. I didn't know the man from Adam. I knew him, but I didn't know that that's who I had met. What was it he always said? Blood and guts. Our blood and his guts.

Harold Shapiro

Date of Birth:
April 1924

Place of Birth:
Boston, MA

Military Assignment:
26th Infantry Division, 104th Infantry Regiment

Military Duties:
Regimental MP

Highest Rank Achieved:
Corporal

Postwar Occupation:
Salesman

Harold was drafted in August of 1943 and took his basic training at Ft. Benning, Georgia. He served with the 26th Infantry Division through France, Germany, Belgium, Austria, and Czechoslovakia. Harold started out as an assistant BAR man but was later transferred to Regimental Headquarters as part of a three-man team who evacuated enemy prisoners of war away from the front lines for interrogation, based on his ability to speak German. He earned the Combat Infantry Badge and was awarded the Purple Heart, two Bronze Stars, the Good Conduct Medal, Army of Occupation and World War II Victory Medals, the French and Belgian Croix de Guerre Medals, and the European Theatre Service Medal with three Battle Stars. Harold returned to the United States in March of 1946 and pursued a career in sales.

Could you describe your first battlefield engagement in the Bulge?

Well, I think it was Christmas. The 26th Division was one of the three divisions that Patton rushed to the Bulge before anybody else did. At that time, we were moving east towards Germany, and some of us had already entered Germany when they realized how serious the Bulge was. The three divisions were the 4th Armored, the 26th Infantry, and the 80th Infantry. Our objective was the city of Wiltz, was to the east of Bastogne. So we came into this small town in Belgium, and there was snow everywhere. As we entered the town, there were dead Americans and dead Germans on both sides of the road. They were just lying all over the place. Right behind us came a Graves Registration team. These were the guys who picked up the bodies, and they were loading the dead Americans in the truck. They were frozen stiff. They were like stacking cordwood. And they were putting the dead Germans in a trailer that the truck was pulling. We had just retaken that town, and these troops were killed when the Germans first overran the town. We got our first hot meal in a week or so that day.

Where were you at the time you were moved to the Bulge area?

We were in Metz, France. The 101st Regiment of our 26th Division was taking Fort Jeanne d'Arc, which was the last fort in Metz. It was a big fort, and my regiment was held in reserve at that time. We had taken over a French army barracks; there were no beds or anything. We had no bedrolls and were sleeping on the floor. And they told us we were going to be there for two weeks, for rest and recreation. Then one morning the sergeant woke me up and several other guys and said get your gear together, we're moving out. Well, what they did is they loaded about a couple dozen, twenty, twenty-five of us on a truck with our gear, still black outside, and we had a bulldozer to lead the truck for short distances opening up a path through the snow until the truck was able to go on its own. And we were gonna be road guys. We didn't know what was going on, that the Germans had broken through. And they started dropping us off at different intersections, telling us which way to direct the regiment when it started moving up. I was next to the last man dropped off, in this little town in Belgium. The road junction was like the letter Y. I had come up from Metz on the tail of the Y, and I was supposed to direct the regiment up the right-hand road and the only support I had were the people in the town. There was a Belgian policeman, and he had a Springfield '03 rifle from World War I. And there was a kid about twelve years old, went in his house, he came out with an American .45 pistol, and I said, "Where'd you get that thing?" And he said it was World War I vintage. And me. We were the whole firepower. And about ten o'clock that morning, here comes a convoy of about ten, twelve American trucks tearing down the left-hand road, moving towards me. Not the road I was supposed to direct the division to, but the other road. And in the first truck there's a lieutenant sitting next to the driver and he says, "What are you doing here, soldier?" So I said I'm a road guy, my division's moving up. He said, "We're pulling back." They were actually retreating. He said, "If I were you, I would get on one of the trucks." He also said, "We don't know where the 'H' the Germans are." And being a naive gung-ho soldier, I said I can't leave, I've been posted here. And that's a funny feeling when you're standing in the middle of the square in this town and seeing this convoy of trucks tearing down the road you just came up, knowing that you don't know how far behind the Germans are. I had a box of K-rations with me, and the police-man had a metal police hut on the side of the square. So I went in there around noon and sat down on a bench and opened up my K-ration. The policeman said something to the young boy, and the kid came back with a cup of warm milk for me. And then this short man, dressed in a suit with a shirt and a tie approached me and invited me to have lunch with his fam-ily. It would do him great honor; you know I spoke German.

So I thanked him, and I said I can't leave my post. The units will be coming up shortly. So the policeman says, see that house right on the square? That's the mayor's house. The windows face out on the square, he said. I can see down the road, and if I see anything coming, I'll rap on the window. So I thanked the mayor and went in his house, and I took off my helmet and my backpack and my weapon and all, and I sat down at the table with his family, and his wife brought boiled potatoes and slices of cold meat which was like eating at the Ritz. I don't think I took four or five bites of food, and there's a rapping on the window. So I grabbed all my gear, and I come running out the door and this captain in this Jeep comes zooming by and tears up the road that I was supposed to direct. And I said to the policeman, I'm in trouble. I said would you please go back in and tell the mayor, pay him my respects, tell him I can't come back. I thanked him again, and I thought that I better stay here because he'll be back shortly. And about twenty minutes later here comes the cap-tain coming tearing back down in the Jeep, and he starts cussing me out. Where in the "H" were you? Blah, blah, blah. Well, I won't use the lan-guage I told him, but I'll tell this way. I said, "Captain, I had to go to the bathroom. And I was behind that stone wall, and I saw you coming, but I couldn't get my pants up fast enough." So he said to me, "I don't care if you have to, right in the middle of this square, you don't leave, because the regiment will be up shortly." And sure enough in about three-fourths of an hour, here they come. And boy, it made me feel good when I saw them coming, you know, and I directed them up the road. Here comes roughly two thousand, twenty-five hundred men, and I could see their vehicles coming and all that. And here I see M Company. I recognized M Company because they were the weapons company, and they had lost most of their vehicles in one of the attacks. The captain was driving a German Volkswagen, an open type, an army vehicle. And they had a German half-track, which they had repainted in olive drab with a white star on the side, you know, American colors. So they were using German equipment. They had lost their equipment.

So they had just confiscated what they found?

Yeah. Well, we found out that the German switchboards were better than the American switchboards, so we dumped our switchboards and started using the German ones. And they did that on certain things they found, better equipment. I mean it made me feel good, and then as I say, I got on the last truck and that night I remember sleeping in a one-lane bowling alley in some town in Belgium. They had us lined up lying the length of the bowling alley, and they told us that if there's any light shining through the curtains from some of these houses, don't do anything. Let the Germans think that the civilians are still there and there's no troops there or anything like that. Just let things be, and then the next morning we moved out. We sent scouts out, but we had no idea where the Germans were. We were just supposed to keep walking until we made contact.

Joseph Venverloh

Date of Birth:
August 1923

Place of Birth:
St. Louis, MO

Military Assignment:
2nd Armored Division, 41st Armored Infantry Regiment

Military Duties:
Rifleman

Highest Rank Achieved:
Private First Class

Postwar Occupations:
Accountant, Purchasing Agent, Sales Representative

Joe was drafted in March of 1943, took his basic training at Camp Campbell, Kentucky, with the 20th Armored Division, and was assigned to Battalion Personnel until he was sent overseas as a replacement. He arrived in England on June 3, 1944. He crossed the Channel in July and was assigned to a rifle squad with the 2nd Armored Division in an area close to St. Lo, France. Joe fought with the 2nd Armored Division through France, Belgium, Holland, and Germany. He earned the Combat Infantry Badge and was awarded the Purple Heart, Belgian Fourragere, Unit Citation for action on an antitank position east of Puffendorf, Germany, and Marksman Badge with the Carbine and five Bronze Battle Stars (Normandy, Northern France, Central Europe, Ardennes, Rhineland). Joe returned to the United States and was discharged from the service on December 3, 1945. He enrolled at Saint Louis University School of Commerce and Finance under the GI Bill and eventually received a degree in marketing. Over the years, he pursued careers as an accounting clerk for Lincoln-Mercury, then as a purchasing agent for Parke Thompson Associates, and later as a sales representative for Calgon.

What was your experience during the Battle of the Bulge?

Our whole division took off on a hundred-mile road march. We were slipping all over the place. By that time it was raining and slick and sleeting really badly. Vehicles would slide off the road, but we made it down there and eventually made our contact on Christmas Eve. Our company was walking down both sides of the road at night. We heard a convoy coming in our direction, so the word went down, hit the gulleys on the sides of the road and wait. Let the convoy come through. So it began to come through, and you could hear them getting closer and closer. And eventually the motorcycle that was leading the convoy stopped right where I was, and I could see in the shadow, the guy putting his foot down, and the handles of the motorcycle move to the right, and the light shone on the embankment right above my head. Then he started up, and it seemed like an eternity, and then the firing started in back of us, and we all opened up and just completely destroyed the convoy. So a lot of Germans died that night.

What was in the convoy?

I saw one big long gun, so I guess it might have been an artillery outfit. But there was just a mix of everything in there; even, I think, one of our own ambulances. We had pulled up on the hill that night and set up a perimeter, a defense line. Next morning, we waited, and we could look down at the road and see this whole convoy, and sometimes here and there you'd see a German soldier lying around. I don't know how many we killed that night, but there were a lot of them. Then about the time we moved out, two P-38s came over, and that's the first time we'd seen any planes for a long time. It had been bad weather for a long time, but now the sun was out and then they started firing at some targets ahead of them, which was a nice feeling. So that was my first experience, as far as the Bulge was concerned.

Did the weather affect your weapons or your abilities as a soldier?

Not so much the weapons, but our gear. We weren't really prepared with clothing to fight in that kind of weather. It got pretty cold; down into the zeros and below. You put on everything you had to keep warm, and eventually they came up with something, not boots. I don't know what you'd call them; they were a heavier kind of a boot that was insulated. But the only trouble with that is, being insulated, when you were in them and your feet sweated, at night they'd get cold, and I think that's where a lot of the trouble with the frozen feet took place. Myself, I kept extra socks close to my chest, on little pins or something to hold them in place. That would dry them out. Then I'd change my socks as much as possible, so I was never affected as far as frozen feet. They did get winter clothing and gear up to us eventually, though.

Sheldon Tauben

Sheldon was drafted in April of 1943 and took his basic training at Seymour Johnson Field, North Carolina, with additional training at Camp Polk, Louisiana, and Camp Breckinridge, Kentucky. He arrived in Wales in October of 1944 and crossed the Channel a month later, landing at Le Havre. Sheldon served with the 75th Infantry Division through France, Belgium, Germany, and Holland. He earned the Combat Infantry Badge and was awarded the Bronze Star, the Good Conduct Medal, and three Battle Stars (Ardennes, Rhineland, Central Europe). Sheldon returned to the United States in January of 1946 and pursued a career in education.

Date of Birth:
January 1925

Place of Birth:
New York, NY

Military Assignment:
75th Infantry Division, 289th Infantry Regiment

Military Duties:
Wireman/Lineman, Communications

Highest Rank Achieved:
Private First Class

Postwar Occupation:
High School Teacher

Please describe your experiences during the Battle of the Bulge.

I think we were at the southern end of the line, and it was kind of an emergency situation because they stopped us en route. We were issued hand grenades and live ammunition, and everybody was ready to go. The weather was still pretty nice, and it didn't dawn on me that we were not really well equipped. I had a pair of galoshes; I was fortunate. A lot of the soldiers didn't have galoshes; most of us had gloves. None of us had the equipment that should have been issued to us, considering where we were headed, into the Ardennes Forest with bitter cold weather, deep snow, and as a result we had more casualties from frostbite than from anything else. And we were put in this position I remember, the division was committed on Christmas Day, because Christmas morning the weather broke for the first time, and you could see the vapor trails from the B-17s overhead. And one incident I remember was that one of the planes was hit, five or six, maybe ten miles ahead of us, and we were counting the parachutes coming out. We knew there were ten in a crew, but we only counted about four chutes. About two days later we caught up to the spot where that plane had crashed. It hadn't burned, they must have turned the ignition off and gone in. The plane crashed, and we were able to extricate the airmen's bodies. A Graves Registration team came up and the bodies were put in bags, some in grotesque positions, frozen. The fur-lined or sheepskin-lined boots and jackets were liberated by some of the American troops, 'cause it was cold, and these guys couldn't use them any longer, so no one objected to that, but I felt sorry for those guys.

The first casualty in our company was, unfortunately, one of our own men. We were walking up the side of a ravine, and some guy had a BAR with a round in the chamber and his finger on the trigger guard, and he tripped and let go a burst, and he got the guy in front of him. It's too bad. That was our first casualty. The following few weeks was spent mostly outdoors in the Ardennes in deep snow. But one night I remember we were called out, there was some tanks that were maneuvering in front of us, and one of my buddies and I were assigned to a bazooka squad. He carried the bazooka, and I was the ammunition carrier and the loader. When we had the thing loaded and ready to go, we marched out into this area. We could hear the tanks, but we couldn't see them, and after a while they went away. They just kind of disappeared, and we went back to where we were and unloaded the bazooka and went back to sleep. The main responsibility I had at that time was sharing a responsibility to be the communication liaison between Regimental Headquarters and the 2nd Battalion Headquarters. And this consisted of making a daily trip by

Jeep back to headquarters and picking up some urgent supplies, radio batteries, maybe some water, some rations and ammunition. And we made this run daily, depending on where we were.

One time we were driving a Jeep back to Battalion Headquarters, and you couldn't put any lights on. The road was really a wide path, and the only way you could tell where you were going was by looking up. You could look up and drive this way, because the starlight or whatever would come through the treetops and you could follow the route without knowing the road. It was pitch dark, and we made our way back to headquarters, and Battalion Headquarters consisted of about a three-foot-deep, ten-foot-square foxhole, if you will, covered with a big tent. And that was headquarters for the battalion commander, the medical office was there, the battalion switchboard operator, and the radio operator. So we made our way back there, and we're kind of relaxing a bit afterwards, it was kind of a harrowing trip. I don't know how long it took us, seemed like it was twenty miles, although it couldn't have been more than four or five miles. Then directly on the path to come back, we heard some M1 fire—boom, boom—and we heard some chatter of machine guns; it sounded like German machine pistols. Some hand grenades were there, muffled 'cause the snow was heavy on the trees, and it muffled the sound a lot. But there had been a small firefight just over the road where we had just passed. Because about fifteen minutes later, five or six soldiers from one of the companies followed the road up. No one was hurt, and they told us what happened. They ran into a German squad, and there was some fire, rifle fire, machine gun, apparently no one got hurt. They disappeared off into the snow somewhere, but what dawned on me the next day, actually I didn't think about it. Edwin Trahee was my buddy from Detroit, he was the Jeep driver, and I was the shotgun, actually it was a carbine, and we had just passed through this road within that same period of time, and we heard the shooting afterwards, so it appeared to me that we had driven that road under the observation of this German patrol. And they didn't shoot at us, they let us go. They were probably looking for the Battalion Headquarters, and a couple of guys in a Jeep didn't mean much to them. But it meant something to me because, I wrote this at the time, "We had passed unscathed, probably because some German trooper had his white-gloved hand up like this, restraining the machine pistols from shooting until we had passed. I often wondered who he was and whether he survived the war or not."

Billy Stiegemeier

Billy was drafted in June of 1942 and took his basic training at Camp Wheeler, Georgia. He went overseas in early December of 1944 and landed at Glasgow, Scotland. He joined the 87th Infantry Division as a replacement, joining them in Metz, France, shortly thereafter and stayed with them through France, Belgium, Luxembourg, and Germany. Billy was the head gunner of N Company, with a 30-caliber water-cooled heavy machine gun. He had no bed or bath for fifty-four days, and the only clothing he had was on his back. Billy participated in the Ardennes, Rhineland, and Central Europe campaigns. He earned the Combat Infantry Badge and was awarded the Bronze Star and the European Theatre Service Medal with three Battle Stars. He returned to the United States in July of 1945 and pursued a career as the owner of a lumber and hardware operation.

Date of Birth:
December 1925

Place of Birth:
Staunton, IL

Military Assignment:
87th Infantry Division, 347th Infantry Regiment

Military Duties:
Heavy Machine Gunner

Highest Rank Achieved:
Sergeant

Postwar Occupation:
Owner, Retail Lumber and Hardware Business

Did the training give you a good idea of what to expect as far as weather conditions or battlefield conditions?

Weather conditions and battlefield conditions I would say did have some resemblance, but in my case, I was out of basic training in thirteen weeks and then from there went right overseas as a replacement. I didn't train with a division. I trained at Camp Wheeler, Georgia, shipped out of the port of embarkation at Boston. It only took four days to go over. I left the States about the 3rd of December and about four days later was in Glasgow, Scotland. I went over on the *Aquatania*, which was a luxury liner converted to a troop ship. We had fifteen thousand individuals on that ship, and a bunch of us got sick. Being eighteen years old, you don't consider we had no idea of what war was all about. We landed at Glasgow, Scotland, and then from Glasgow went by train to Southampton, England. We crossed the English Channel in an LCT, boarded a 40 & 8, and rode the boxcars for a couple of days. Just at that time is when they were needing manpower, and I wound up with the 87th Division, in the heavy machine gun outfit. I never will forget the first day in combat when I didn't think that a Screaming Mimi would hurt me if it didn't hit me point-blank. I remember my sergeant hollering, "Stiegemeier, get your butt down." He didn't use the word butt either, and I had no idea that I was that close to being hurt under those conditions.

As you went along during the Bulge, were there things you learned on how to survive?

Yes, I guess the fear was the thing that made us survive, and you learned as you went along to be careful walking and what have you. We had to be alert for land mines as well as any overhead fire, any snipers, things of this nature that you had to be careful with, and this is where we lost a lot of our second lieutenants. They'd get out there and get sort of anxious to go. They had a perfect target on their helmets with the gold bar, and many of them didn't last long. The turnover in general was so large that you really didn't get acquainted with one fellow or another. I think our division had a total of something like nine thousand either wounded, killed, or frozen. The only ones that really stuck around were some of our platoon sergeants. And our medics weren't equipped with any kind of firearm. They had to survive the best they could, and I think they did a tremendous job trying to handle the injured and those who were dying. I think they along with the infantry were two of the groups that were the least recognized.

Can you talk about the role that the weather played in the Battle of the Bulge?

That was a problem, and we weren't equipped for it. It was a point of not being able to get it to us, and all I had in my possession was what I had on my back, and I wasn't equipped for the weather conditions that we didn't know we were going to run into. But it was a situation that we did their best with what we had, and ammunition was the thing that saved our lives, more so than our clothing. I didn't have a pair of boots until I was able to get a pair off a frozen soldier. Occasionally, we would get into a hayloft or a barn or residence of some type where we might have captured the town. We had snow that was knee-deep. I did freeze my feet and wound up one night in the field hospital at Luxembourg City. Today, the nerve endings are gone in my feet. My feet right now feel like they're in ice water.

What was the most intense battle or firefight you were involved in during the war?

I think maybe when we tried to cross the Rhine River. We had set our guns up on a railroad track that ran along the Rhine River. We had set eight guns from the company up on the track, and we were going to support our rifle troops crossing the Rhine River in a rowboat because the bridges were all blown up. And about quarter to twelve at night, the order came down to commence firing. We were firing tracer bullets every twenty or twenty-five rounds, and we fired constantly for ten to twelve minutes. An order came down to cease-fire, and the troops were going to load in the rowboats. Unfortunately, it was just about the time they got set in the rowboats that flares went up on the Rhine River by the Germans on the other side and it lit up like Las Vegas, and then all hell broke loose, pardon the expression. They threw everything but the kitchen sink at us that night, and we lost a lot of soldiers. The next day, the Air Corps came in and strafed the side of the hill on the other side. We were able to get out of there, but it was a terrible night, which was around March 24 or 25. We walked from Metz, France, almost all the way to Berlin. You wouldn't think the human body would take that kind of treatment, but it can. I think I weighed 205 pounds when I played football in high school, and when I came out of the service, I was at around 167 pounds.

Gerald Riechmann

Date of Birth:
March 1925

Place of Birth:
Centralia, IL

Military Assignment:
35th Infantry Division, Heavy Weapons Company

Military Duties:
Infantryman

Highest Rank Achieved:
Private First Class

Postwar Occupations:
Teacher and Counselor

Gerry was drafted in November of 1943 and took his basic training at Camp Blanding, Florida. He landed in Glasgow in July of 1944 and joined the 35th Infantry Division on the battlefield on December 24. Gerry was wounded in Bastogne shortly thereafter and was sent to a general hospital in France. After he recovered, he went back to his unit and served with them until the end of the war. He earned the Combat Infantry Badge and was awarded the Purple Heart, Bronze Star, the Good Conduct Medal, World War II Victory Medal, American Campaign, Army of Occupation Medal, and the European–Africa–Middle Eastern Service Medal. Gerry returned to the United States in January of 1946 and pursued a career in education.

When were you sent to the Bulge area?

We got up there about the day before Christmas, and I was an ammunition bearer for a machine gun. The next day the sun came out, and then our aircraft came out. We didn't know anything about the battle; they didn't tell you anything. We knew we were in Belgium someplace, but we didn't know how bad the battle was. But all day they bombed and strafed, and then the next day the Germans attacked, and all day long we were just holding our position, firing that machine gun. We were behind the machine gun, and I was called up there once to bring ammunition, one time. Now, I didn't see it, but I heard that the machine gun got real hot and jammed on our machine gunner, and he jumped out of the foxhole and got killed. So the lieutenant said, "We need another machine gunner up here, are there any volunteers?" We had one guy, I think his name was Shaw, and he was kind of an aggressive kid, and he volunteered. So we held our position all day long, and I saw one German soldier all day, and he was a kid. We were all kids, but I would say he was about sixteen, and he came running out of the woods and got behind the line somehow. He held his rifle over his head to signify that he'd surrendered and so they took him to the tent that they had set up for wounded soldiers. I don't know what happened to him, but we just said, go back there.

Can you describe your first battlefield engagement?

I just remember that we naturally stayed in our foxholes all night. Early in the morning we heard firing, and we thought there must be a lot of Germans around someplace. So we stayed right there all day long, and that was in, I guess, Bastogne, holding our position the whole day, and they were driving towards us. We didn't give up an inch, we just held them all day long, and the next day we were going to take off early in the morning, when this mortar shell came in. We were standing along the roadway there, and I don't know how many got hit by that mortar shell, but the Germans had some good equipment, and they were accurate. We shouldn't really have been standing along the road, but we were going to move out, and all of a sudden a round came in and hit right between us, and I felt something hit my foot. Since there weren't medics there, and I had been protected by some of the other soldiers from the shrapnel, I just reported to first aid. When they saw me hobbling in, they took one look at me and put me on a bus and then on a train, and we went down somewhere in southern France to a general hospital. I didn't think there was any metal in my foot. In fact I don't even have a scar from it today. But the shoe helped, and there was just kind of a big burn, didn't break any bones or anything. So finally a doctor got around to looking at it, and I remember him saying, "Is this all you got?" And I said, "Well, that's it." He says, "Send him back." So the next day or two they put me on a train, and I was headed back to my outfit.

Harold Mueller

Date of Birth:
March 1923

Place of Birth:
St. Louis, MO

Military Assignment:
First Army, 110th AAA 90 mm Mobile Gun Battalion

Military Duties:
Driver for a 90 mm AAA Battery

Highest Rank Achieved:
Corporal

Postwar Occupations:
Tool-and-Die Designer; Salesman

Harold was drafted on his twentieth birthday in March of 1943 and inducted into the Army at Jefferson Barracks, Missouri. After two days of indoctrination, he was sent to Camp Edwards, Massachusetts, for artillery training, first with the 40 Millimeter Gun Battalion, and later with the 110th Antiaircraft artillery, 90 Millimeter Mobile Gun Battalion, Battery C. He went overseas from Camp Kilmer on the *Queen Mary,* leaving on December 23 and landing January 1 in Glasgow, Scotland. He crossed the Channel on D-Day, landing at Omaha Beach, and fought with the 110th AAA MGB through France, Belgium, Luxembourg, and Germany, returning to the States after the war in December of 1945. His decorations include the Invasion Arrow with five Battle Stars (Normandy, Northern France, Ardennes, Rhineland, Central Europe), and the French Croix de Guerre citation.

Describe the role of your gun battalion.

The 90 mm Mobile Gun Battalion's job was to support the 29th Division by keeping the German planes from bombing and strafing the troops. During the day we fired antipersonnel shells when requested by the 29th Division, for added artillery. We also carried armor-piercing shells for antitank duty when we were involved in the Battle of the Bulge. I drove a CAT, which was a ten-ton bulldozer-type tractor with a cab in the front for the drivers. It had storage for three hundred gallons of gasoline, and it carried fifty-two 90 mm shells. It also towed a 90 mm gun, weighing ten tons.

Where were you when the Germans broke through on December 16?

We were in Malmedy on antitank duty at the time. That was the first time we ever were on antitank, and by the night of the 18th I hadn't slept for three days. We had been taking pills to keep awake. We were sound asleep when our building was hit with an 88 shell. There was a two-and-a-half ton truck setting outside, and the bricks smashed it down to about two feet high. Luckily nobody was in the truck. But on the gun, one fellow got wounded, and he almost got his little finger cut off with shrapnel. We were sleeping inside, and the flue tile came down between myself and another fellow that was sleeping face to face, and a good thing we were because if we had slept back to back we would have been crushed with the big flue tile. The six fellows that were sleeping on the other side of the room had their shoe soles ripped off from the toe back to the instep from the concussion. So we always wondered with a concussion like that how come our lungs weren't hurt. We woke up enough to push this flue tile down to our feet 'cause it was hot, and so we pushed it back to the center of the room and all went back to sleep. When we woke up in the morning we found out all this other business with the truck outside.

Where was your combat division stationed, and where did you serve in the Battle of the Bulge?

My first position was in Malmedy. We got knocked out of there after the second day of the Bulge, and we got orders to move up on a hill right outside of the town. Our job was to protect that road from any enemy coming up there trying to get through. There was a two-million-gallon gas dump which was not too far from us, which one of our other batteries was guarding.

Do you recall where you were on Christmas Day of 1944?

I was with my gun crew, sitting on a hill there out of Malmedy, freezing. On Christmas Day, the Germans cut us off, and our gratitude goes to the 82nd Airborne. They opened out the route which brought our food up. We didn't get any Christmas dinner like was supposed to come, and it was the next day when we got food. But that was quite scary when we thought we were going to be the next prisoners of war, and we got ready to blow our gun up, but it didn't come to that. For a while we were cut off from the rest of the unit that was supplying us. So that was one of the more stressful days of my life.

Courtesy Marvin Cox

Crossroads near Bastogne just prior to the Battle of the Bulge. Courtesy James Darmstatter

Courtesy James Darmstatter

Christmas, Lierneux, Belgium. Courtesy Robert Gravlin

Courtesy Rusty Pendelton

Courtesy Glenn Hillgartner

Courtesy Ed Bronenkamp, at far left

Leaving Pinton outside of Paris. Courtesy Harold Mueller

John Seesock in Weilmunster. Courtesy Harold Mueller

Charlyville. Courtesy Harold Mueller

France, summer 1944, C Company, 2nd Rangers. Courtesy Charles Ryan

Courtesy Rich Maskell

Courtesy Charles Ryan

Courtesy Ed Bronenkamp

The Road to Bastogne. Courtesy Rusty Pendelton

Remagen Bridge from East Bank of Rhine River, March 13, 1944. Courtesy Charles Ryan

Charles Ryan in Hurtgen Forest

American tanks in the snow. Courtesy Robert Gravlin

Ardennes, winter 1944–45. Courtesy Robert Gravlin

Courtesy Vincent Kemper

Some outfits had mascots
here is one belonging to
Headquarters Company - -

George Kottwitz in a half-track, April 1945   Courtesy Ed Bronenkamp

Omaha Beach, June 6, 1944. Courtesy Charles Ryan

Mass before D-Day. Courtesy Charles Ryan

Unloading 6 x 6 from boat. Courtesy James Darmstatter

Courtesy Roy Lynch

Moving past a German Mark IV. Courtesy Robert Gravlin

Karl Das at Jefferson Barracks

France, October 1945. Courtesy Gerald Riechmann

Courtesy Lyle Bouck

Meade "Bud" McCain

Date of Birth:
March 1926

Place of Birth:
St. Louis, MO

Military Assignment:
83rd Infantry Division, 331st Infantry Regiment

Military Duties:
Infantryman

Highest Rank Achieved:
Second Lieutenant

Postwar Occupations:
Retail Shoes; Residential Real Estate

Bud enlisted in January 1944 and took his basic training at Camp Roberts, California. He went overseas to Southampton, England, in November 1944. He crossed the Channel on December 25 and landed at Le Havre. Bud served with the 83rd Infantry Division through Belgium, Holland, Germany, France, and Austria. He earned the Combat Infantry Badge and was awarded the Purple Heart, Bronze Star, the Good Conduct Medal, World War II Victory Medal, and the European–African–Middle Eastern Service Medal with three Battle Stars for the Ardennes, Rhineland, and Central Europe campaigns. Bud returned to the United States in April 1946 and worked in the family shoe business and real estate.

Describe your first combat experience.

I arrived as a replacement on January 1 with the 83rd Division. They'd been in the Hurtgen Forest battle and lost a lot of people. The first thing I saw as we were going to our platoons was a soldier lying on the ground with a red cross on his back. He didn't look too alive, and they said it was from mistaken, friendly fire; somebody had accidentally killed one of our aid men. That was my introduction to combat.

The Bulge had been going on two weeks, and the Germans were into Belgium as far as they could go. We were on the southern end of the Bulge, and the British were on the north. We just closed up the curtain, and the Germans were stuck in Belgium and couldn't escape into Germany.

It was extremely hot fire. We dug two-man foxholes in a forest of pine trees, which we cut and then fashioned into a roof over our foxholes because the tree bursts were causing most of the fatalities rather than direct fighting. In reconnaissance we ran into pockets of either very young or very old German infantrymen who weren't overly enthusiastic about their positions; if they got injured or "felt" surrounded, they'd surrender. Sometimes they'd sit around our foxholes at night because they had given up. But there were still a lot of fatalities and injuries.

I got a severe case of frostbite, and when someone jumped me and hurt my neck, I went to an aid station, but there were so many injuries. This was only my second week in that unit, but they were concerned about my neck and frostbite so they sent me to a hospital in Le Havre. They quickly patched me and sent me back to my unit, now near the Rhine River.

The next campaign was called the Central European Campaign where we went town to town. There wasn't much German air power then, but they still had a lot of artillery and ground troops. We'd go house to house, securing these towns. Fortunately, the civilians were not hostile, but there were still plenty of Nazi soldiers around so we had many fatalities. We were attached to the Second Armored, which was the ground force strategy—pairing an infantry and a tank division. We actually rode the tanks when we were moving to a town until we started getting fire, then we'd get off the tanks, spread out, and walk. So we worked as a team.

Did you have much contact with the German civilians?

Not in combat, but we didn't stay put. Once we got to Central Europe, every day we would take towns, moving very fast. It was early May and getting warm, and there wasn't as much enemy fire then. We were still getting hit, but it wasn't like D-Day, so we could thoroughly search the houses.

We didn't fraternize much with the civilians, but they weren't hostile. Usually our division would move through two or three towns with a frontal attack, then A Company would go into the town and see the burgermeister. We'd ask him to have the citizens bring any guns to the city square, and they'd bring these gorgeous engraved shotguns used mainly for hunting. And then we'd run the tanks over these gorgeous shotguns, because you didn't want just anybody having a gun.

Laverne Ilges

Date of Birth:
November 1924

Place of Birth:
Breese, IL

Military Assignment:
101st Airborne, 755th Field Artillery Battalion

Military Duties:
Forward Observer for Howitzer Crew

Highest Rank Achieved:
Technical Sergeant

Postwar Occupation:
Painter

Laverne was drafted in June 1943 and took his basic training at Ft. Sill, Oklahoma. He arrived in England in August 1944 and crossed the Channel a few weeks later. He served with the 101st Airborne in the Ardennes, Rhineland, and Central Europe campaigns. Laverne was awarded the Good Conduct, WWII Victory, and American Campaign medals; three overseas bars; the Distinguished Unit Badge; and the European-African-Middle Eastern Campaign Medal with three Battle Stars. He returned to the United States in February 1946 and pursued a career as a painter.

Where were you stationed during the Battle of the Bulge?

We were just outside of Bastogne. As we crossed the river there, American engineers blew up the bridge; we couldn't get back! We felt like guinea pigs, and we lost everything—the Germans took over the Howitzers and everything we had. When we got back, there was actually more artillery there than when we left. Where the Germans got it, I don't know. And the fields were covered with bodies.

How did you cope with the weather?

You didn't. Your feet were cold and wet, and we had no socks. You wore the same clothes for about thirty days. One day Captain Ferris, who was in charge of the forward observers, saw that I was shivering from the cold so he gave me his coat. We got in the command car and moved on, and everybody was saluting me. He says to me, "You have to salute back." I said, "What for?" He says, "You have captain's bars on." That guy was really nice.

After the breakthrough they brought us portable showers, but you had to strip, run through the snow, take a shower, then run to another tent for clean clothes. It was cold, but we were happy because we had clean clothes and knew we were safe. Looking back you wonder how anyone survived the snow, cold weather, and living outside.

How were the lines of communication during the Bulge?

We had radios and telephone communications with the artillery batteries, and we'd communicate with headquarters if we saw action or Germans. We'd give them the coordinates, and headquarters would get the batteries to fire. The observation planes would also radio us and headquarters what they saw. I really don't think communications could have been improved at all.

Do you recall Christmas, 1944?

To break down our morale, the Germans dropped leaflets on us Christmas Eve that showed how it could be at home with your parents and children. They loudly played "White Christmas" and other songs. That really hit us. Christmas morning, I looked out of my foxhole, and my buddy from home was sticking his head out. I wished him a Merry Christmas. I can't repeat what he said on camera, but it made me smile.

Describe your saddest moment during this battle.

Seeing all the dead guys. A lot of Americans had their hands tied behind their back and were shot. That just breaks you down.

What was your most intense battle during the Battle of the Bulge?

It was the Battles of St. Vith and Houffalize. It was back and forth: We'd take it, and then they would take it. And the dead were horrific. Later, Graves Registration piled up the bodies like cordwood and laid them alongside of the road. At night they'd haul them away.

Anyone you'd like to mention?

A guy from my hometown named Mac McAllister went into the Army with me and fifteen others. We fought together and came home together. That was really something. I'm the only one left now.

Thomas Hancock

Date of Birth:
December 1920

Place of Birth:
St. Louis, MO

Military Assignment:
3rd Army, 452nd AAA

Military Duties:
Section Chief of Antiaircraft Crew

Highest Rank Achieved:
Sergeant

Postwar Occupation:
Education (Harris Teacher College)

Richard was drafted in 1942, took his basic training at Camp Stewart, Georgia, and received additional training at Camp Attebury, Indiana, and Ft. Sheridan, Illinois. He went overseas in late October, landing in England on November 2, 1943. After additional training at Tidworth, England, he crossed the Channel on June 11, 1944, and landed at Omaha Beach. Richard fought with the 3rd Army in the Normandy, Northern France, Ardennes, Rhineland, and Central Europe campaigns. He was awarded the Silver Star, D-Day and Good Conduct Medals, and European Theatre Service Medal with five Bronze Stars. Richard returned to the United States in November of 1945 and pursued a career as a teacher at Harris Teacher College.

Do you think that the training you received before going overseas played a big role in your success on the battlefield?

It played a big success on the battlefield, but I think my best training was after I went overseas to England. We first were in a town called Tidworth, and we set up our antiaircraft guns there. Sometimes German planes would come in our range, and we'd shoot at them. I don't know if we ever hit anything, but they had searchlights looking for them. Then they sent us to Camp Tiffany, and that's where I got my best training for combat because most of the planes were low-flying. We were geared up for low-flying airplanes that hedge hop, so we'd have to learn how to shoot fast and hit those planes. I was the chief of a section of a gun crew, a buck sergeant, and I had about twenty men under me, and two two-and-a-half-ton trucks. One pulled a 40 mm cannon, which you call a Bofors gun, and another one was on a trailer which had four air-cooled machine guns called the M51 mounted on it. And we had mostly British officers. In fact, I guess I was in the British army for a while, assigned to them or whatever. Since they had been training since 1939 shooting at enemy aircraft, they probably knew more about it than our American trainers did. The Bofors gun was for mostly low-flying aircraft, and each round had a tracer on it so it would show where you were shooting. And they showed us how to put leads, so when you saw an airplane coming, you would shoot in front of it so the airplane and the projectile would run into each other.

Do you recall the details of your first battlefield engagement?

Yeah, I was with the 3rd Army, I think the 87th Division. I remember these fellows had acorns on their shoulder. We were not too far from Strasbourg when we got a march order. It was a black tank battalion; I think the 761st, I learned that they were there before. I never saw a black tank division before. But we had to make a strategic withdrawal (never a retreat) in the early part of October because we ran out of ammunition. So we made this strategic withdrawal, and I could see the tanks coming up, and I thought something's going to happen around here soon. I had never seen any black soldiers besides maybe the Red Ball Express, which was mostly black soldiers who brought us supplies, but I had never seen a black tank battalion before.

When was your first Battle of the Bulge encounter?

I think we got march orders on December 17. That's my birthday, so I remember that. We went north, and I thought we were going back, maybe taking a rest because we'd been up front so long. But they had us turn on our bright lights on the cars, trucks, and everything. So we just drove up north, and we ended up in a Belgian town. We still didn't know what was happening yet, so we stayed with this Belgian family overnight. The next day they stationed us in a field, and I found out later it was close to 20 below zero. And that night the Germans shelled us all night long, and so some of us went into these heavy farmhouses to take cover. We stayed in there all night, and the only way we kept warm was we had these bags of artillery powder. If you'd open them up, they don't have powder inside. These little cylinders looked like little pieces of licorice. So we made a little fire inside this dugout using these powder sticks. It's a wonder we didn't blow up.

What would you feel your biggest contribution was during the Battle of the Bulge?

Shooting down German aircraft. Shooting at them. Capturing German soldiers. I think I got pretty good at it. I didn't know anything else but fighting and so forth. You get used to it, just like maybe in civilian life you get used to certain things. It's one of those things you know. I know I could hear artillery shells, I could hear when they shot artillery maybe a mile away, and I could tell almost where it was going to land or if it's coming my direction. I could hear the artillery coming towards me. I said that's going over there. Don't worry about that. But when you don't hear hardly anything, you'd better take cover 'cause it's coming right towards you. I did shoot down five German planes, and my battalion had the highest record for shooting down aircraft than almost anybody in the ETO. I gave them a clip that came out of the *Stars and Stripes,* and it's talking about the 452nd antiaircraft artillery and how many aircraft we shot down, probably somewhere in the eighties. The United States kind of took over the skies since we were superior as far as aircraft was concerned. The main aircraft was the P47. I remember the P47. We called it the Thunderbolt I believe it was, Thunderbird or Thunderbolt. That was one of our biggest workhorses during the invasion, and I think they carried a couple of 500-pound bombs under their wings. That was the main one. And the Germans had the Messerschmitt, and they had the Focke-Wulf. Those were the fighter planes, and I think the Junkers was their bomber. And when we crossed the Rhine River at the main bridge, that's where the Germans brought out most of their aircraft. I guess they were making their last effort. And that's where I saw my first jet aircraft. I said what the devil is that. I had never seen anything go that fast before. We were not used to shooting at anything that fast. But when we got over to Frankfurt-on-the-Main, that's when we saw our first jet aircraft. And that jet aircraft looked like it was going 1,000 miles an hour. It was going so fast. I never saw anything go that fast. And when it came down low enough to shoot at, we shot down one. Not my battery, but one of our other gun batteries. They might have been one of the first ones to shoot one down.

Do you remember what you did on Christmas Eve or Christmas Day of 1944?

Christmas Day of 1944. They always would get that turkey up to you some way. I got tired of eating that turkey, most of the time it made you sick. I don't know what they did to that turkey, but it made you go to the bathroom a lot. So they brought this turkey up and the cranberry sauce. Always tried to do something like that. So part of my crew would go and eat at a time, since we all couldn't eat at once. While we were getting ready to eat our turkey, all of a sudden we got an artillery barrage, and one of those 88 shells came right through that darn mess hall. But it didn't explode; it was a dud. And you should've seen the guys get out of that farmhouse, whatever it was, and take cover someplace. Right during our Christmas meal. That dud came right through that there, luckily it didn't explode. If it had exploded, it probably would have killed a bunch of us. There were a lot of duds. Maybe there was a lot of sabotage going on in munitions plants 'cause a lot of times you may have read about duds right now, they dig up, find a dud, oh here's an artillery thing that didn't go off. So somebody was doing some sabotage within the German army.

Edgar Griesbaum

Date of Birth:
February 1919

Place of Birth:
New Baden, IL

Military Assignment:
80th Infantry Division, 318th Infantry Regiment

Military Duties:
Bazookaman

Highest Rank Achieved:
Acting Regimental Sergeant Major

Postwar Occupation:
Steel Sales

Edgar was drafted in March of 1944 and took his basic training at Ft. Hood, Texas, spending time in Ft. Meade, Maryland, and Camp Kilmer, New Jersey, before going overseas, landing in Southampton, England, in November of 1944. Three hours later, he crossed the Channel and served with the 80th Infantry Division through France, Luxembourg, Belgium, Germany, and Austria. He earned the Combat Infantry Badge, returned to the United States in January of 1946, and pursued a career in sales.

Describe your first engagement in the Battle of the Bulge.

We were transported by trucks to Luxembourg and were dumped on a snow-covered road. The trucks left, and our company was alone in the field. Our regiment's first battle was in Ettelbruck, Luxembourg, where there were supposed to be only a few Germans, and instead there were many Germans with tanks. I was not with the company at the time; I was sent to take a wounded man back for medical treatment. I had been told there would be people to take care of him, but when we got there, the place was deserted. So we went into an abandoned house. While we were looking around the house, we heard tanks, and I ran to the road thinking they were ours, but they were German so I ran back in the house. We had left our rifles behind and decided if the Germans came in the door, we would throw a hand grenade down the hall. But we were lucky, and they did not come in, but instead drove around the back of the house. Later, one of our tanks came along, and I stopped it and got the wounded guy on the tank, and we rode into Battalion Headquarters. Later that night, I got into Ettelbruck with a group of medics, and I finally found my company, platoon, and squad. The Germans were on one side of the street, we were on the other side, and we traded shots all night.

Where did you serve during the Battle of the Bulge?

We were first in Colmar-Berg. From there we moved into Ettelbruck where we were trapped for about twenty-four hours until C Company rescued B Company, but we lost a lot of men. The following day was Christmas Eve, and we were in foxholes. That night we were supposed to sleep in a chateau, so we were pretty happy about that. We got to the chateau and were looking around when they changed our orders. By truck we joined the 4th Armored Division; we were to rescue Bastogne. We were taken to Belgium, got there about midnight, and had to jump out in the snow. The next morning we attacked. The first town we took was Warnach, Belgium.

This past June we returned to Europe for the sixtieth anniversary of D-Day. In Luxembourg City, we were assigned a guide who found out that I was in the unit that rescued his town of Warnach. He insisted that the bus go off the route to Warnach so he could show me the church where he had been hiding when we came into town. He was twelve years old then.

Are there any individuals who impacted you or your company?

Art Groenig and I were a bazooka team in foxholes for five weeks. I carried the bazooka, and he carried the rockets. Going into combat, we'd have to preload the bazooka so if we were going through woods, the other men would drift away because they feared we'd stumble and trigger the bazooka. And when we'd dig in, they'd say, "Well, you two dig in out there by the road so if a tank comes, you can stop it." They would dig in farther upfield, so we'd be by ourselves at night. We became very close.

Art was killed on Christmas morning. We were in the woods under attack and sitting under a huge pine tree when a shell hit the top of the tree and rained shrapnel down. Art was about six, seven feet away, and the shrapnel went through his helmet and killed him immediately. His tombstone said he died on December 27, but I know he died on December 25; they found him on December 27. This summer, we visited and put flowers on Art's grave in Luxembourg and recently went to Iowa and met his son's family and Art's grandchildren and great-grandchildren. It was a very moving experience.

What was your most intense battle?

The campaign to Bastogne was the most intense; we lost many men, and it lasted for days. We went from town to town, clearing the way. Our E Company was the first patrol into Bastogne ahead of the 4th Armored.

When were you most afraid?

In France during our very first battle, ten of us were left in an orchard when the company withdrew. We were under fire all day. That was the most frightening because we were alone and didn't know what to expect. We were veterans after that.

Any moments of comfort or happiness during your tour?

Getting a letter from home was the best. Sometimes you would get mail every few days; sometimes you wouldn't get any for weeks depending on where you were, what you were doing, how much you had moved. When I went to the hospital for pneumonia towards the end of the Bulge, I went without mail or pay for about three months before they caught up with me.

What was your squad's greatest contribution during the Battle of the Bulge?

We were attacking a town and came to a wooded area and a hill. While we were running down the hill, the three men next to me were hit by machine gun fire, but somehow they missed me. When we got to the bottom of the hill, we looked up and saw a German 88 on the hill behind a haystack. They were waiting for our tanks, but they didn't come so our platoon moved towards the German tank. Our lieutenant and three men went to the right and to the back of the tank and captured the men inside. When we were standing out in the open in front of that tank, I was scared, but we made a good move.

We succeeded in taking the town, but my squad leader and I were separated from the squad. He said, "Let's go into this house and check it out." So we went in and found no one on the first floor. Then we opened the basement door, and I said, "*Kommen Sie raus.*" Come out. We heard a shuffling, and I hollered a couple more times. Finally, German soldiers started coming up the stairs. As they came up the stairs, we told them to put down their weapons and equipment. They piled them on the floor. They kept coming, and soon the hall filled. We captured twenty-five soldiers from the 5th German Parachute Division in that house, all ready to surrender.

Robert Gravlin

Originally deferred from service because he was working at McDonnell Aircraft Company in 1943, Bob convinced his draft board that his work there was not essential, so they let him sign a Voluntary Induction paper. He took his basic training at Ft. Leonard Wood, Missouri, as a combat engineer. Bob went overseas in a large convoy on the *George Washington* and landed in England in early June of 1944. A few weeks later he crossed the Channel and landed on Omaha Beach. Bob fought with the 3rd Armored Division through Normandy and Northern France, and participated in the Normandy, Northern France, Ardennes, Rhineland, and Central Europe campaigns. He was awarded the Presidential Unit Citation, Belgian Fourragere, French Croix de Guerre, five Battle Stars, World War II Victory Medal, Rifle Sharpshooter, Army of Occupation (Germany), and the Good Conduct Medal. Bob returned to the United States in February of 1946, went to college, and afterwards pursued a career in engineering at the McDonnell-Douglas Corporation.

Date of Birth:
July 1922

Place of Birth:
Belleville, IL

Military Assignment:
3rd Armored Division, 23rd Armored Engineer Battalion

Military Duties:
Combat Engineer

Highest Rank Achieved:
Private First Class

Postwar Occupation:
Engineering

Where were you when the Battle of the Bulge started?

We broke through the Siegfried Line and had captured Aachen and Stolberg. We were dug in on a hill outside of Stolberg, but then the Bulge started. So we were told to pull back and attack the Germans around Liege, Belgium. When we first went into the Bulge, the weather was not cold yet, but it was foggy and rainy. As we pulled onto the road, mortars, shells, and artillery shells were dropping. So we tried another road. The Germans were there, but I'm not sure if they knew where we were. It was a hodgepodge—the Germans were pushing through, and we were trying to push them back. So we got into one section and established a line: put in mines, booby traps, and concertina (a very sharp razor wire). We cut down large ash trees and laid them across as roadblocks because we knew the Germans would attack through there. Eventually, the Germans did attack through there. Their tanks hit the mines, and their infantry got tangled in our concertina and booby traps. We then raked them with machine gun fire and stopped the attack.

Tell us your story about the loft.

It was shortly after Christmas. It was so cold you had to move your feet around or massage them, or they'd freeze. Quite a few got trench foot and had to have their feet and legs amputated. I was by myself and saw a hayloft so I climbed up and got under the straw. I took my shoes off and massaged my feet. I heard a sound. It was about ten o'clock at night and pitch-black. I heard another sound. (The Germans had a generator-type flashlight that made noise when the light was pressed.) I identified this noise and knew immediately the Germans were down there. I could speak German, and I heard a sergeant say in German, "We will sleep now." Then the Germans came up the ladder to the hayloft and got under the straw. I heard the sergeant say, "Sleep fast." One of the Germans bumped up against me in the straw, but it was real dark. Fortunately, they didn't turn on their flashlights to look around, or they would have seen me. There were probably about a dozen of them, and they all got under the straw. I could hear them starting to snore. There was no way I could leave after they were asleep because the ladder was on the other end and I would have had to cross over them to get out, which would have woken them. They were SS, and at that time they were not taking any prisoners, so I knew it was either them or me. If they discovered me, I'd have to go down fighting. I had my finger on the trigger of my rifle all night long. About 5:00 or 6:00 a.m., still pitch-black, I heard the sergeant say, "Get up, we must go now." One of them bumped me and said, "Let's go." I said, "Yes, I'm coming." They left without discovering me.

Describe the most intense battle or firefight you were in.

I don't recall the vicinity, but one night there was a valley below us, and our G2 intelligence told us the Germans were amassing troops and readying to attack that sector. There was snow all over, and the 1st Infantry Division had dug in. We crawled through their lines and told them we were laying booby traps in the valley so the Germans couldn't attack through there. So we laid concertina and placed mines in the valley. The whole time, star shells were being fired and lit the whole area. The star shells had little parachutes and flares. We'd be still until the flare would go out, and then we'd crawl forward until we laid all of our mines and booby traps. We started back up the hill, and the Germans attacked so we jumped in the foxholes with the infantry. Fortunately, the infantry had the area scoped with machine guns. The Germans hit our lines and concertina, which knocked out the tanks. The Germans fired heavily, and the battle went on for about two hours. Finally it was over. It was getting light, and there were Germans stacked like cord wood where they hit the concertina and were raked with machine gun fire. It was intense.

As a combat engineer, what was your most important contribution?

Our job was to keep our forces, tanks, and equipment moving. Plus, we also fought as infantrymen when necessary. But our most important accomplishment was bridging rivers and streams to keep our forces moving. Whenever we got to these streams where the bridges were blown, the Germans always zeroed in with artillery and machine gun fire so we lost a lot of men. One night we were putting a Bailey bridge across a stream, and I was running down the road with angle iron and fittings for the bridge when a German plane flew over and fired a 20 mm gun point-blank. I zigzagged down the road while shells were hitting all around me. As the plane moved away, the rear gunner kept shooting at me from the back of the plane. Fortunately, he didn't hit me. But we were always under attack because the Germans didn't want us to bridge those rivers, so they'd drop their bombs around the bridgehead as we were putting in new egress.

How many men did it take to build the bridges?

In our squad there was a half-track driver and twelve of us. And in our particular group, there were three squads to a platoon and four platoons to a company. So depending on the situation, we would try to get a bridge built with twelve, twenty-four, or thirty-six men working at one time to try to get it across. But you'd hit an area where you didn't have enough equipment or you couldn't get the job done, so they'd call in Corps or

Army. When we hit the Rhine River for instance, this was a huge river to get across, like the Mississippi River, so we had Corps and Army equipment to build our pontoon bridges across. But we would get three pontoons in, and the Germans would blow them up; they had us zeroed in. So after repeated attempts, we finally brought in smudge pots and enveloped the entire bridge area with smoke. Then we moved three hundred yards upstream, got our cable across, and finally got our bridge in. Without that smoke cover, we never would have gotten that bridge across the Rhine. We had eight hundred to nine hundred people working on it, and it took us about a day and a half to get that bridge done.

Were you ever wounded?

I was never wounded, but I did have my clothes torn off several times. I had pieces of shrapnel drop on top of me, but I guess God was with me because I didn't even have any scratches.

I did have hearing loss from one particular time during the Bulge. That day the Germans had discharged almost all of our tanks. We had one live tank and maybe a half-track left. Come nighttime, the snow was very deep. As I went by one of our knocked-out tanks, I thought I heard somebody crying inside so I climbed up on the tank. The hatch door was open, and I peered down into the tank to see if anybody was in there. From the burning equipment off in the distance, this German tanker must have seen my head silhouetted against the burning light, and he fired point-blank at my head. There was a blast that blew me off of the tank into the snow. I crawled, don't know how far—I couldn't see or hear. I laid in the snow stunned for quite some time. Finally, my eyesight came back, but I didn't really hear again until the next day. To this day I still have ringing in my ears.

Donald Green

Don was drafted shortly after graduating from high school and entered service in March of 1943, taking his basic training at Camp Fannin, Texas, with further training at Camp Atterberry, Indiana, prior to going overseas in October of 1944. He was transferred to the battlefield in early December and fought for twenty months with the 106th Infantry Division in France, Belgium, and Germany. As a result of combat in severe weather, Don sustained life-long problems with frozen feet and hands. He was evacuated on New Year's Day 1945 to the First General Hospital in Paris and later to England. After the war was over, he served in Belgium, where he stayed until coming home in May of 1946. During his military service Don was a cryptologist, radio telegrapher, combat infantryman, and gunner in a mortar crew, and he received the Combat Infantry Badge, Bronze Star, European Campaign with two Battle Stars, Occupation, World War II, Victory, and Good Conduct Medals.

Date of Birth:
April 1925

Place of Birth:
St. Louis, MO

Military Assignment:
106th Infantry Division, 424th Infantry Regiment

Military Duties:
Infantryman

Highest Rank Achieved:
Technician Fifth Grade

Postwar Occupation:
U.S. Postal Service

Do you recall your first battlefield engagement during the Bulge?

Yes, I do. Once we started, the first battle was continuous purely because of the situation we were in. We replaced part of the 2nd Division, which was pulled out to move up to the Ruhr pocket to take the dams, and we were assigned to what was thought to be a quiet area. When the Bulge started—it began about 4:30 or 5:00 in the morning with a rolling barrage—we managed to hold our own position for that day and the next. During the early morning hours, we withdrew back over the Our River and put up a roadblock on just the other side west of the Our and had to defend the bridge until we could get the bridge blown. But they never did destroy the bridge, and the German armor was able to get across there. We were there for twenty-four to thirty-six hours, and then we had to withdraw again up the Skyline Drive towards St. Vith. You have to remember that the 106th lost a lot of men, so we were a pretty small group that survived and managed to withdraw. I found out years later that we withdrew because the 28th had sense enough to start pulling their people back and the colonel in charge of our regiment pulled out what men he could to go back and form the defense around St. Vith.

What was that first battlefield experience like, apart from the tactical maneuvers?

I was scared to death, to be honest with you. When the barrage started, the only one in our group who was a little bit older was the sergeant in charge of our mortar crew, and he knew what was going to happen from experience. Even though he told us to be ready and what to expect, it was still pretty terrifying. Here I was, an eighteen-year-old kid just out of high school. How do you adjust to something like that? How we did or what prepared us in civilian life for this, I have no way of knowing. We were never subjected to a rolling barrage for over two hours. The bombardment was such that some of the explosions were so close, men were bleeding from the eyes and ears from the concussions. But we were fortunate that our unit had such a good position over the road that the enemy was using, we managed to hold our own and not give in to that initial assault. If you want an idea of what the Ardennes was like, go down for a drive through the Ozarks on the back roads. It's not a huge mountain range, but all their little roads led to a few meeting points. The key road junctions were Bastogne, St. Vith, and Elsenborn, and unless you walked cross-country, there was no other way out. That's why the Germans were trying to get through there.

What role did the weather play during the Battle of the Bulge?

It was the biggest enemy we had. Our baggage train with our mess train and kitchen truck had all our extra equipment and extra clothing. So what you had on your back was what you survived with, or you picked up along the way the stuff that had been discarded, or you ran through a little supply sergeant's tent and picked up extra stuff. I particularly was fond of socks, and that's another story. I don't know where we picked it up, but we were having trouble keeping our feet dry with that heavy snow and the cold temperatures, and they kept barking about trench foot, trench foot. We finally did discover that if we took our wet socks off, let our feet air-dry, and put on a dry pair of socks, you could kind of cope pretty well. Now, what do you do with wet socks? We unbuttoned our uniforms and put them as close to our skin as we dare put them, and we covered them up, and by the end of the day when you wanted to change again, they were fairly dry. I don't know where we learned it, but it was a generally accepted practice to try to keep your feet dry. But I still ended up with frostbitten hands and feet. The doctor wanted to amputate my left foot at the ankle to stop the gangrene, which wasn't very serious yet. But I said, "No, let's wait and see if it goes any farther. Then you can take it off." And the doctor and the medical staff agreed and pumped me full of penicillin. I think I got so much penicillin there in the hospital that I am allergic to it now, but it did manage to save my foot.

Do you remember where you were on Christmas Eve or Christmas Day of 1944?

We were along the Skyline Drive, and there was something about that daylight when it first cleared enough for all of the American aircraft to get into the air. That's something I'll never forget, in the Ardennes with those beautiful pine trees and the bombers dropping tinfoil to jam the German radar. They were dumping it out by the ton to protect the airplanes coming behind them. When the sun came out, it was the first time we had seen the sun really since two or three days before the battle started. There were so many planes in the air, it seemed you could almost walk on them, there were that many of them. But the tinfoil hanging in those pine trees was really a pretty sight. It sparkled in the sunlight like tinsel and danced on the snow.

Jim Green

Date of Birth:
September 1917

Place of Birth:
Brooklyn, NY

Military Assignment:
75th Infantry Division, 289th Infantry Regiment

Military Duties:
Ammunition Carrier and Machine Gunner

Highest Rank Achieved:
Private First Class

Postwar Occupations:
Sales and Company Management

Jim was drafted in 1943 at the age of twenty-six with a wife and three children (ages three, five, and seven). He was accepted as an Air Corps cadet, but the Army decided they had enough pilots and sent him to Camp Blanding, Florida, for basic training. He went overseas on a British ship and landed in Wales on November 3, 1944. He crossed the Channel on December 12, 1944, and landed at Le Havre, France. Jim served with the 75th Division through France, Belgium, and Germany. He earned the Combat Infantry Badge and was awarded the Bronze Star and three Battle Stars (Ardennes, Rhineland, Central Europe). Jim returned to the United States in November of 1945 and pursued a career in sales and management for Knollmann, Co.

Did you learn battlefield survival techniques as you went along?

Yes. The old story about being on the battlefield and sights and sounds and smells. Well, we didn't have any smells in the Battle of the Bulge. Everything was frozen. But it really doesn't take you very long to understand what the sounds are. But you learn quickly, and if you don't learn quickly you're not going to be there very long. We learned just like an animal would learn. You actually become like an animal. You're anxious. You anticipate. You don't know the next second if you're going to be dead, and you're constantly looking around. You just didn't know what was going to happen next.

Are there any individuals that you want to recognize for something they did?

I guess the biggest battle we had came on Christmas Eve, and the 2nd SS Panzer Division was trying to get through us for a week. They were hitting us in different parts of the line. So that night, they made a division advance and our two machine gunners, the gunner and his assistant, fired and fired and fired. And the next day, when it was light, they took one of the trucks and cleaned up the battlefield. And they almost filled up half of the truck with dead German bodies, as close as a couple of yards in front of our foxholes. They were no more than six feet sometimes, that's how close they were. Of course, we could hear them when they got hit, things like, "Heil Hitler" and "Ach mein Gotten." We stopped them that night. But our machine gunners never got the recognition they deserved because we had no officers there at the time to document it so they could get their medals.

And during that battle, of course, they needed ammunition. And what am I? An ammunition carrier. So I had to go back to where the supply was, and we had foxholes that you would have to go through for maybe a hundred yards. And they were staggered all over and it was dark, so I called to the second ammunition carrier to go get some ammunition and got no response. I called again, and I got no response. So I thought, "Well, he's dead." So I took off my overcoat and my jacket, and I shed whatever equipment I had on me. Now, if you remember, the Germans were in American uniforms. So I thought to myself, "What am I going to do? How am I going to get through this line without getting killed?" They'll think I'm a German in an American uniform. And well, everybody cusses. So I started out and I used every cuss word I knew, and I invented some and I made it back and forth with the ammunition that night. It is unreal what these two machine gunners did. And nobody knew about it but me.

What was the saddest moment or moments that you experienced either during the Bulge or during your military service?

We made our push to the Rhine River on January 15. I was by then the last one left in the machine gun squad. I was carrying the machine gun, the tripod, the spare barrel, and two cans of ammunition. So we had been two or three days below this bluff, and I was dug in with the machine gun. I kept looking at that bluff, and I kept thinking to myself, "I'd hate to be the SB that has to go up that bluff." Well, I was one of the SBs that went up the bluff. Got up to the bluff, and at that time the Germans were firing 88s like rifles. So we got up there, and I got set and then one of the original sergeants who had been in the company since the beginning came up to me in my foxhole. And he said, "Jim, I'm so sorry I haven't been with you. I haven't been able to help you." He said, "But I'm going to stay with you from now on." Well, a shell exploded, and he fell right by my face in my foxhole, dead.

What was your greatest moment of fear?

You know, I didn't really have fear. The anxiety, I can remember that. I can never think of fear except when the phosphorous bombs would explode overhead. You know what a knuckle ball is like; you don't know where it's going. That's the way those phosphorous bombs were. You never knew where they were going to fall, and if they hit you they burned right through you. If you could shut the oxygen off, you could stop the burning. One never hit me, but that was my fear. They were real bright as they were coming down, and you'd be in your foxhole watching them, wondering if one would get you.

Were you wounded at all?

I had one close call on January 15, 1945. The ground was frozen as hard as a concrete floor. By that time you had a sixth sense about you, and I hit the ground just as an 88 hit within a yard of my head and I was knocked out. When I came to, I felt warm liquid coming through my gloves, and of course, I thought, "Well, what am I going to do?" Well, you gotta find out where you're hit. So I opened my eyes and looked at where the stuff had come down on my gloves, and it didn't look like blood. What happened was the heat from the shell melted the ground and covered me with mud and ice. That was dripping down on me and not one part of me got hit by a piece of shrapnel. If it hadn't been for the frozen earth, I wouldn't be here today. But I got a concussion to my left side, which I still feel today. There's a deadness in the left side and a problem with my left eye, and I have headaches. A lot of it's gone away, but it still reminds me of that day.

Leo Feldman

Leo was drafted in 1942 and took his basic training at Ft. Benning, Georgia, and Ft. McClellan, Alabama. He went overseas on the *John Erickson* and landed in Liverpool, England, on Easter morning. Leo fought with the 90th Division in the Northern France, Ardennes, Rhineland, and Central Europe campaigns. He earned the Combat Infantry Badge and was awarded the Good Conduct Medal, the Purple Heart, Bronze Star, and four Battle Stars. After the war, Leo returned to the United States and pursued a career with a propane company.

Date of Birth:
February 1922

Place of Birth:
Edwardsville, IL

Military Assignment:
90th Infantry Division, 358th Infantry Regiment

Military Duties:
Machine Gunner and Jeep Driver

Highest Rank Achieved:
Private First Class

Postwar Occupation:
Service Work for a Propane Company

Do you remember your first battlefield engagement during the Bulge?

Yeah. I was with Patton most of the time following him, and when the Battle of the Bulge started, they pulled us out of the Saar area, and we went straight on through to Bastogne. I was a machine gunner and Jeep driver at the time. Over there in the Battle of the Bulge, you didn't know who was who. Some of the Germans

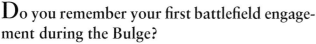

spoke perfect English and had our vehicles. In fact, one night, I was given a password for that day, and that evening they sent me back to get rations and ammunition. On the way back they stopped me, but the password had been changed. They wanted to throw me in the stockade 'cause they thought I was a German. So they had to call on the radio to find out who I was before they would let me through.

Was your first battle during the Bulge similar at all to what you experienced during basic training?

No, it was altogether different. In basic training, we didn't realize what combat would be like—somebody shooting at you all the time; a lot of artillery and a lot of confusion. You didn't know who was who. And the weather was terrible; cold and snow up to your knees, up to your hips sometimes. We had no place to get warm. Sometimes you had rations, sometimes you didn't. If we could, we tried to get in a house or a basement at night. And if you could, you'd make a fire, but you couldn't always do that because the smoke would give you away.

What was the most intense battle or firefight you participated in?

One night during the Battle of the Bulge, they took my Jeep, and they said, "You lead these tanks across this open field." There was snow about one and a half feet deep. And the Germans opened up with all their artillery. I'm sitting here in this Jeep with my assistant driver, and these tanks are all buttoned up. I didn't think we'd get out of there. That was scary. Out in an open field covered with white snow, and the Germans could see us. We were sitting ducks, so we both jumped out and crawled under the Jeep. I said, "Hey, let's just get turned around and get out of here." The tanks were all right. They were buttoned up.

Would you say your most important contribution was either in a battle or helping out another soldier?

Well, right before the war ended, they sent me and three other Jeeps, and we got in this town, and white flags were hanging out. They had surrendered, but all at once they opened up on us, and a bunch of the boys got captured, and we lost three Jeeps out of the four. We were on a narrow blacktop road where you couldn't turn around because there were apple trees all around. But I finally got turned around and picked up all the guys that I could off the other Jeeps. Then I went down the road and got between two big embankments on the road, and I guess I saved all those guys. I got the Bronze Star for that action.

Robert Enkelmann

Bob was drafted in March of 1943 and took his basic training at Wright-Patterson Field, Ohio. He spent some time in the ASTP and was sent to Camp Swift when the ASTP was ended. He arrived in Le Havre, France, in October of 1944 and went on line in November of 1944, when his division relieved the 2nd Armored Division at Immendorf, Germany. After the war, he stayed in Germany in the Occupation Forces, helping to set up city and county governments before free elections were held. At this time, he arrested hundreds of former members of Wehrmacht and Nazi organizations responsible for war crimes. Bob received the Bronze Star, Presidential Citation, European Theatre Service Medal (two Battle Stars), Good Conduct Medal, Army of Occupation, Expert Rifleman, and the Combat Infantry Badge. He returned to the United States in October of 1946 and pursued careers in electrical engineering, in real estate, and as a travel agent.

Date of Birth:
November 1923

Place of Birth:
Breese, IL

Military Assignment:
102nd Infantry Division, 405th Infantry Regiment

Military Duties:
Mortarman; Special Agent, Counter Intelligence Corps

Highest Rank Achieved:
Warrant Officer, Junior Grade

Postwar Occupations:
Electrical Engineer; Real Estate; Travel Agent

Describe your closest encounter with death.

The Bulge had started, and we were getting ready to cross the Ruhr River. Since they expected a big tank attack through our area, we dug division positions, regimental positions, battalion positions, company positions continuously, in case we had to move back. We had big Teller mines which were hooked together with wire, and at night they would spread them across the road and pull the pins out in case the tanks came through, it would blow off their tracks. In the daytime, they would stack them up against the wall and put the pins back in so our Jeeps and everything could move around. Well, I was sleeping in the basement of the house where these Teller mines were located, and my guardian angel told some guy to come in and wake me up. I was supposed to go over to help the cooks set up a kitchen in a bombed-out house nearby. About twenty minutes later, there was a tremendous explosion, and a ball of fire came down the street. I ran back, and the building where I had been sleeping had collapsed, so I would have been buried alive if I had still been there. What had happened was, we had 81 mm mortars, and the Germans had 80 mm mortars, but their shells would fit in our mortars. So we were actually firing captured German ammunition in our mortars, and about every third or fourth one would misfire. Then we'd have to take it out of the mortar and stack it up against the side of the building. We weren't allowed to fire anything except the ones which had been inspected, because some of the slave laborers that made those sabotaged a lot of the shells. So they had a big stack of these German mortars up against the building. So they send up a three-quarter-ton truck to pick it all up, and they were loading that ammunition, and Bed Check Charlie come flying over, and guys were firing at him with pistols and everything else. So the truck driver jumps up on top of the roof. They always had machine guns mounted on the roof of their cab so they could fire if they were strafed by German aircraft. So he jumps up there, and he starts shooting at this Bed Check Charlie. All of a sudden the gun jammed, and one of the guys was standing in this big hole in the wall watching him. He said, "Throw me up a brick." So he threw him up a brick, and he used it to knock the breech open and eject the shell. He threw the brick over his shoulder. It landed right on top of all those Teller mines, and somebody had forgotten to put the pins in that morning. So it set off the whole bunch. Blew the front end off of the truck, blinded the guy that was standing in the doorway, and I don't know what happened to the truck driver. That was on New Year's Day of 1945, the closest I came to being killed in the war.

Clyde Erb

Clyde was a student in the University of Cincinnati ROTC program when he received his induction notice in May of his junior year (1943). After he completed basic training at Camp Wheeler, Georgia, he was sent to Harvard University as part of the ASTP. In March of 1944, the program was ended, and he was sent to Camp Campbell, Kentucky, and Ft. Jackson, South Carolina, for advanced infantry training, before going overseas in August of 1944. He went directly from New York Harbor to Utah Beach and fought with the 26th Infantry Division in the Northern France, Lorraine, Germany, and Ardennes campaigns. He earned the Combat Infantry Badge and was awarded the Bronze Star, European-African-Middle Eastern, and Good Conduct Medals. Clyde returned to the United States in August of 1945 and pursued a career as a civil engineer.

Date of Birth:
August 1924

Place of Birth:
New Athens, IL

Military Assignment:
26th Infantry Division, 328th Infantry Regiment

Military Duties:
Infantry Squad Leader

Highest Rank Achieved:
Staff Sergeant

Postwar Occupation:
Civil Engineer

Do you recall your first combat engagement?

Yeah. Paris had been declared an open city. So we were taken down around Nancy and Metz, and as we got near to the lines you could hear what sounded like thunder. And that was our waking up to the reality of war then, when you started hearing that, you were getting close. You kind of get a lump in your throat wondering what was going to happen. So that was my first impression, was that this was thunder. That night we went in and replaced another outfit. We got in there in the foxholes, on a hill overlooking a valley, and the first night they shelled us, I guess 'cause we were new. And when we went back for some kitchen food, we learned two of our men were killed by a direct hit to their foxhole. Two nice young guys, and I knew them both, Connolly and Foley. That's pretty tough. [Pause] I'm sorry.

Do you recall being ordered to respond to the German offensive on December 16?

We got to the German border around the beginning of December, and I was on the first patrol that went into Germany, across this little creek one night. It was an intelligence and reconnaissance patrol. Just to find out what was there and how many and so forth. And we heard nothing and saw nothing. Seemed very quiet. So we reported back to the company command post there that we had seen nothing. Next morning we took off, and as the company crossed the little creek and started going up a hill, the Germans came up to the very crest of that hill and started firing at us directly with 88s and tanks; we suffered very heavy casualties. We were pinned down; guys would scream for help, and our medic was killed. Pretty tough. I think there were only twenty-three of us who got out of there the next morning. [Pause] I'm sorry. I broke down like that.

We were relieved that night by the 87th Division, and we pulled back. And we were a bunch of sad sacks walking down the road leaving the front lines that time. I remember we were worn out, and we went back to Metz for a rest and to pick up replacements, since we didn't have enough for a company anymore. But we were only there a few days, and then we had reports on December 16 of the breakthrough up in Belgium. We were alerted, and everybody had to get everything packed. I had replacements in my squad (by that time I was a squad leader), and to this day I can't tell you their names. You lost a lot of them without even knowing them. They were green, coming from Air Force ground crews and different motor pools, and we tried to train them as best we could in a couple of days, and then we were put on trucks. I think that was about December 18.

When you consider the logistics, it's remarkable to move a whole division from down around Metz up to Luxembourg, which we did. So we got up there into Luxembourg, pretty close to the Belgian border, and we got out and stayed there for the night. The next morning they got us up, and we walked in columns up the road. We didn't know where the German lines were, so we went walking down the hills, and I mean it's hilly and dense woods and cold. And you could hear machine gun fire up ahead of us. So we knew we had encountered the Germans then, and we all scattered out and dug in for the night.

By then it was very, very cold, and you could hardly dig a hole with a pickax, but we tried the best we could. And then we took a couple of villages the next day, and it was pretty severe fighting. And my feet were hurting, since before Metz. When we were at Metz for this so-called rest, I went on sick leave, and they told me I had a touch of trench foot, but with rest I'd be okay. Well, we got up there, and with this cold, snow, and wet again, I could hardly stand it. I guess it was about December 23, I told Dutch Frye, who was my assistant squad leader, I just can't make it, Dutch. I'm gonna go back to the aid station and take care of my feet. He said okay, so I got to this aid station, which was a tent and some lantern lights, and they said what's the matter with you. I said my feet are killing me. They said take off your shoes, and when I did, my feet started swelling and turning red. A doctor came over and put a tag on me—trench foot. So I was taken by ambulance to Luxembourg City, and the next day they took me to a field hospital outside of Paris and then over to England. I guess I got there around the end of December. The whole time, I never walked; I never set foot in England. All the while I was there, I had to be in bed, or they would take me in a wheelchair if I had to go somewhere. The doctors didn't know what to do. We had whole wards of people with frozen feet. By the way, this is as an aside. Those at the aid station they put trench foot on there. That was one thing. If they put frozen feet on your tag, you got a Purple Heart. Not for trench foot. That doesn't make sense, but that was the Army way. They had just whole wards of people with this foot problem. In March I was taken back on a Swedish luxury liner—still on a stretcher—to Ft. Sam Houston and was discharged on the first of August, which was my twenty-first birthday. Got to be a man, and Uncle Sam didn't want me.

Earl Falast

Date of Birth:
January 1923

Place of Birth:
St. Louis, MO

Military Assignment:
9th Infantry Division, 47th Infantry Regiment

Military Duties:
Cook; Machine Gunner During Bulge

Highest Rank Achieved:
Technician Second Grade

Postwar Occupation:
Cooking

Earl was drafted in January of 1943 and took his basic training at Camp Howze, Texas. He went overseas on the *Aquitania* in August of 1944 and landed in Gurock, Scotland. Shortly thereafter, he crossed the Channel, landing at Le Havre. Earl served with the 9th Infantry Division in France, Belgium, Germany, Luxembourg, and Czechoslovakia. He earned the Combat Infantry Badge and was awarded the Bronze Star and three Battle Stars (Ardennes, Rhineland, Central Europe).

How did your military experience begin?

When I was in Texas, I was sent to Cooks and Bakers School, and that's how I got started in cooking. So I ended up in London and became part of a cadre. A cadre is where they have usually a commanding officer, and he can be anything from a one-star general on down to probably a lieutenant colonel, and a first sergeant, a company clerk, some medics, cooks, and anything else needed to start a new company. So at that time I went to Salisbury, where they were bringing in new recruits from the States. Basically, they were sent to us for further training for the upcoming invasion, and we operated pretty much as a unit. The same thing happened when I finally went to France. I went over there after D-Day, again as a cadre.

So what was your experience in the Battle of the Bulge?

I think pretty much everybody who was not an active soldier at that point, if you were a clerk in Paris or if you were whatever, were then brought into the Bulge. And I was one of them; they simply said, "Okay, you're not a cook anymore, you're gonna be a machine gunner again." And of course, that's the way it stayed until the end of the war.

So what was the terrain and the weather like when you set up your machine gun?

Well, we actually ended up being replacements. In other words, such-and-such company has lost five men, so we send five men to that company. The first night I got to my unit, they said the machine gun is set up in this foxhole outside, so that's your job. Twenty minutes after I got there, I'm sitting in a foxhole by myself. The other guys, maybe eight or ten, were in the house having some wine and relaxing. My job was to see that the enemy didn't attack us while we're resting. And I remember just killing time and digging with my bayonet in the dirt, because this dirt was all piled up, and the machine gun's on top of it. And I came across this sole of a shoe, and it was obviously a German shoe, because we didn't have hobnail. And so I'm meticulously cleaning away the mud off these spikes from the bottom of the shoe. Wasting time, because I knew I've got to sit out there for two hours; and as I'm digging, I uncovered more and more of the shoe, until I found out that there was a leg attached to it. And with that I got the hell out of that foxhole and went in the house. I said, "There's a body out there." They said, "Go on, it's not gonna hurt you." So they evidently piled a dead German up there in the front of the foxhole and just covered dirt over the top of him and put the machine gun on top. Later on we got a good laugh out of that.

Did you stay in that area for a long time?

Probably not more than a day or so, 'cause things moved fairly fast at that time. We ended up in the Black Forest around Easter, and the Black Forest has a lot of hills. What happened was, the Germans had cut some trees down on the top of a hill and dropped them across the road to block our vehicles, and the GIs from getting through. We ran into a couple of those, and the engineers with us went in there with chain saws and cleared them off so we could get through. The next one, they were all climbing up on top, and this whole pile of logs blew up. The Germans had booby-trapped it, and we lost a lot of guys because of that.

Floyd Mann

Date of Birth:
August 1925

Place of Birth:
Platteville, WI

Military Assignment:
26th Infantry Division, 101st Infantry Regiment

Military Duties:
Mortarman

Highest Rank Achieved:
Private First Class

Postwar Occupations:
High School Teacher and Principal

Floyd volunteered on his eighteenth birthday in 1943 and took his basic training at Ft. Bliss, Texas. He received infantry training in 1944 at Camp Caffee, Arkansas, before being sent overseas in August. Floyd spent two days in England before crossing the Channel, landing on Omaha Beach on September 2. He served with the 26th Infantry Division through France, Belgium, Luxembourg, and Germany. He earned the Combat Infantry Badge and was awarded the Bronze Star, Good Conduct Medal, American Campaign, WWII Victory, Army of Occupation, Distinguished Unit Citation, and the European Theatre Service Medal with three Battle Stars (Ardennes, Rhineland, Central Europe). Floyd returned to the United States in November of 1945 and pursued a career in education (thirty-eight years).

Where were you on Christmas Eve or Christmas Day of 1944?

We got into a little town about midnight on Christmas Eve, and the captain was good on public relations. Because he wanted the burgermeister, and so they woke him up, and we wondered what's taking him so long. We're standing out in the streets, and he had put on his suit, tie, and his emblem of office—big chain and a big emblem in the front. So the captain said, well, these men have got to get inside. And the bürgermeister said, well, there's no room in the houses, just like no room at the inn. But he said there's lots of room in the barns, so I ended up in a barn. Some of the guys slept right by the cows, just to get warm. I went up in the hayloft and buried myself in the hay. When I woke up in the morning, I was near the hay chute, where you can see down, and I thought, boy, this is a miracle. I looked down, and the kitchen had moved right into the barn. They were down there, and they had a grill and were frying eggs and all kinds of good things. So I said how many eggs can I have? All you can eat. So I got down there early, and I had bacon and eggs and toast and orange juice. I had a real breakfast. Generally, you're either eating C-rations or K-rations. Then the captain did another nice thing. He told the villagers that we were going to be there until at least noon and to bring all the children, twelve and under. The bürgermeister estimated that there'd probably be a dozen or fifteen. So the children came with their parents, and the parents stood back, and they got Christmas dinner with us, which was really nice in the middle of what was going on all around us. That gave us a little Christmas joy. And we were generally well received by the Luxembourg people. They came outside 'cause we were coming through a town slow. They'd come out and pat us on the backs. The women would give us hot bread, right out of the oven. And they really were supportive.

What was your impression of the lines of communication during the Battle of the Bulge?

I told you this story during the Bulge that I fired 450 rounds, continuous fire, and the captain was trying to get some artillery for some tanks, 'cause he said we couldn't hold them. And we fired everything we had, we were, we didn't run out of ammunition, but we were firing HE light, HE heavy, phosphorous, anything we could get our hands on, and I fired those 450 rounds, and the other mortars were firing too. So it looked like a city dump, 'cause they come in wooden boxes, so all this is scattered around. Well, we had a telephone line lying on the snow back to battalion, and we had field glasses and I looked, and this is hard to believe, but the chaplain's coming. So he came up to me, and he said, "Son, what is this, a supply depot?" And I said, "No sir, this is not a supply depot." And he said, "What is it?" Well I said, "This is the front line." "The front line?" And I said the last time we fired about nine hundred yards, and they pulled back, 'course we don't know how far back. And he didn't say a prayer for us, nothing. He says, "Oh my goodness. There are some things back at battalion that I got to take care of immediately."

What sorts of things did you do with your fellow soldiers when you weren't in combat?

Well, usually writing letters, little letters. We didn't have any card games going or anything like that. And just visit with each other, and that's about it. We never had, if you got in a house you thought you were in heaven. And you could wash your face at least. And you didn't want to, some of those guys, they'd get into a bed, you know, they'd end up with bedbugs and stuff. I slept on kitchen tables, church pews, under pine boughs up there, during the Bulge. Or if you could get inside, anyplace, in a church, in a barn, in a house, anything to get out of the cold. My mother sent me a nice package, and guess what I got? The only thing that was left was the wrapper. Had my address on there; there was a piece of candy left on the wrapping paper. Everything else was gone. Were you happy to get it still? Sure. Just to hear from home.

What was the saddest moment or moments during your time in military service?

Well, I think sad moments would be to go into a house, and both parents were dead, lying on the floor in the kitchen, and then you run downstairs to see if they had a basement. A lot of those houses didn't. To see if there are any Germans there, what was down there, and the rest of the family would be just terrified by you. Afraid. I think the slaughter, I can remember one where there would be so many bodies that were nothing but parts. The slaughter that went on is hard to conceive. You see pictures, but it's not the same. Then some of those guys, I never did, but when it came time to eat you got nothing to sit on sometimes. I've seen guys sit on a corpse and eat. I never did that. Yeah, you don't forget things like that.

Norman Eggemeyer

Norm was drafted in April of 1944 and took his basic training at Camp Hood, Texas. He went overseas on the *Wakefield* to England in October and crossed the Channel in November, landing at Le Havre, France. Norm joined the 87th Infantry Division and served through France, Belgium, and Germany. He earned the Combat Infantry Badge, and he was awarded European-African-Middle Eastern Service Medal with three Battle Stars, Presidential Unit Citation, World War II Victory Medal, American Theatre Medal, Army of Occupation, and the Good Conduct Medal. Norm returned to the United States in April of 1946 and pursued a career with the railroad as a foreman, switchman, brakeman, and conductor.

Date of Birth:
December 1925

Place of Birth:
Chester, IL

Military Assignment:
87th Infantry Division, 347th Infantry Regiment

Military Duties:
BAR Man

Highest Rank Achieved:
Sergeant

Postwar Occupation:
Railroad

What weapon did you use when you joined your unit?

They give me a BAR. They said that the BAR man had been wounded badly, and they needed a BAR man, so that's what they gave me. That's an automatic weapon that has a clip of twenty, and when you pull the trigger three or four shots fly out at a time. It's almost like a machine gun. Oh, I loved it. That's why when they made me assistant squad leader and squad leader. I wouldn't give it up 'cause it saved me a lot of times.

What happened next?

I was assigned to the 87th Division outside of Metz as a replacement, and they put me on a hillside there. The Germans were across the valley, and the very first night they tried to get me. They must have had me spotted, 'cause about midnight I heard something coming. Coming closer and closer, and me being a farm boy, I knew what every sound was. And they kept coming closer, and they got close to me. And they stepped on some twigs, and I could hear that. I had a grenade, so I took that, pulled the pin, and threw it right between them. That way I didn't give my position away, and they did some scrambling to get out of there. I don't know if I wounded any of them or not, but that was my very first night.

Were you alone in the foxhole?

Yes, I was. And then we were in a holding position for three or four days, when the Battle of the Bulge hit. Maybe a week later they loaded us on trucks, and that was about a three-day experience, 'cause it turned real cold. They hauled us around to Saint-Hubert, Belgium. Well, then the 345th and 346th of our division was there before us, and I was in the 347th Regiment. We were setting on top of a hill before we were supposed to relieve one of them, and I looked across that valley and here was one Red Cross truck after the other, bringing back the wounded and the dead. And I thought, "Man, that's where we're going." And before that evening came, there we went. We relieved, it turned out, the 346th, and the very first night they put me on a road crossing in a foxhole, and it started snowing and covered me up inside the foxhole. Luckily, no Germans showed up that night, 'cause I don't know if I could've even pulled the trigger. It was like it was blown shut in that foxhole, it was snowing so bad. After a couple of days, they took us back for a warm meal, and where we were eating in that chow line, and nearby there with a canvas over one of those Army trucks. It had about forty or fifty dead inside. I don't know if they were all Americans or Germans. All froze stiff, all stacked up on top of one another.

Did you have any special methods for dealing with the cold?

Oh, yes. They told us, "Whatever chance you get, you take off your shoes and rub your feet." And I always tried when it was so cold to dig my foxhole real deep, so I could get down in there to kind of get away from the cold. I had trouble with my feet even after I got out of the service, but I never had to have anything amputated.

Please describe crossing the Rhine.

That was supposed to be the last stand, and the Germans really put up a fight. So that night they had us all lined up, and our company was the first one to cross. They had us all lined up, the engineers and then twelve men in a boat. When we went across, the minute we hit the far shore the whole sky lit up. We had orders not to take prisoners. What were you going to do with them? Shoot them, I guess. And the first house we got to, twelve Germans came out and surrendered to us. I had to leave one man behind to guard them while the rest of us worked ourselves up the bluff. Well, the Germans made the mistake of shooting a tracer every fourth round. Our tanks on our side shot point blank into where the bullets were coming from and knocked them out ahead of us. So by daylight, a couple of guys in my squad and I were among the first ones up on top of the hill. When I looked across the field, there was an opening and here they were coming out. I guess they were going to drive us back in the river. The Germans had a habit of burying their potatoes and stuff in mounds and I threw myself behind one of these mounds and started shooting, and the Germans all hit the ground. I don't know what made them cross the open field like that. It wasn't real far—I'd say an eighth of a mile—where they came out of the woods. And they all hit the ground, and we just kept shooting. They got up and tried to get back in the woods. You're taught that in basic training if you ever get pinned down, to run and then hit the ground real fast before your enemy starts shooting again. That day, we advanced. There were quite a few soldiers who died on that field.

John Masterson

Date of Birth:
February 1921

Place of Birth:
St. Louis, MO

Military Assignment:
80th Infantry Division, 318th Infantry Regiment

Military Duties:
Infantryman

Highest Rank Achieved:
Technician Fifth Grade

Postwar Occupations:
Teacher and Coach at Normandy Sr. High School

John was drafted in September of 1942 and took his basic training at Babler State Park, Missouri, and Nanticoke, Pennsylvania. In June of 1943, he and several other soldiers were sent to Tunisia to bring back about seven hundred Italian and German POWs to the United States for internment. After several months of duty in Tunisia, his detail and their prisoners were sent to the United States, arriving on New Year's Eve 1943. After additional duty at Pine Grove Furnace, Pennsylvania, Ft. Eustis, Virginia, Camp Reynolds, Pennsylvania, and Camp Miles Standish, Massachusetts, he was sent overseas in July of 1944 as a replacement. John joined the 80th Infantry Division in September in Alsace-Lorraine and served with them through the Ardennes and Rhineland campaigns. He earned the Combat Infantry Badge and was awarded the Purple Heart, Bronze Star, the Good Conduct Medal, and two Battle Stars. John returned to the United States in December of 1945 and pursued a career in education (thirty-three years years).

Please describe your first battlefield engagement.

My first engagement was something I will never forget. We were told to carry very little extra equipment—only a few hand grenades, our combat uniform, no extra jackets or coats, and two bandoliers of ammunition. We were in Alsace-Lorraine, and they told to us to line up in a skirmish line across the field, and we were going to attack for five miles. It was an early sunrise morning, and we attacked until we reached a stream and crossed it. Then we hit a barbed wire fence, climbed over the fence, and attacked the high ground and dug in there. I was always a pretty good athlete, but when they told me we were attacking for five miles, I didn't know if I could do it. As we started the attack, running forward, I was confronted with the problem of the stream. I never did learn to swim, but luckily it was only chest deep. But this is October, so it was cold, so I waded across and climbed over the barbed wire fence. But then my clothes were starting to freeze on me, but the bad thing was, they always told you to check your equipment; we would always run forward, fall, and fire, and all of a sudden we were running forward and my gun jammed. My clip of ammunition was jammed in the breech and wouldn't let the gun fire. What I failed to do was put the clip in there straight. I finally came to a small garage-like building and took refuge near a wall. After a few minutes, I disengaged the clip and got the rifle working again, so I could go forward with the other guys on the attack. After that, I always checked my equipment before going into battle.

What was your impression of the lines of communication during the Bulge?

I personally thought they were not very good, especially for the men in the infantry. There was a lot of confusion at the time. For example, we were initially sent in the wrong direction when we were moving up to the Bulge area from our location in the Alsace-Lorraine region. Later, we were shelled for a period of time by friendly fire when we were in the forest, and we lost all but fifteen men in the company.

Are there any individuals you would like to pay tribute to?

Yes, Corporal Frank Rivera got me out of enemy fire after I got wounded and probably saved my life. I got shot on Christmas Day and the Germans were trying to finish me off, so I kept down low in the snow until after dark. I knew Corporal Rivera would come looking for me, but since I was 6'4" and he was short and stocky, he would have a hard time carrying me back. He solved that problem by bringing a wheelbarrow and using that to cart me into town to the hospital tent.

John Vinke

Date of Birth:
July 1924

Place of Birth:
Harvey, IL

Military Assignment:
26th Infantry Division, 101st Infantry Regiment

Military Duties:
81 mm Mortar Gunner

Highest Rank Achieved:
Corporal

Postwar Occupation:
Family Lumber and Coal Business

John was drafted in April of 1943 and took his basic training at Camp Grant, Illinois. He was enrolled in the ASTP at Harvard and was subsequently sent to Ft. Jackson, South Carolina, before being shipped overseas from Camp Shanks directly to Cherbourg, France. He landed in Normandy in September of 1944 and served with the 26th Infantry Division through France, Belgium, Luxembourg, Germany, Czechoslovakia, and Austria. John earned the Combat Infantry Badge and was awarded the Silver Star, Bronze Star, Good Conduct Medal, American Campaign Medal, the Distinguished Unit Badge, two overseas service bars, and the European–African–Middle Eastern Theatre Ribbon with four Battle Stars (Northern France, Ardennes, Rhineland, Central Europe). John returned to the United States in January of 1946 and pursued a career in the family lumber and coal business.

What was your moment of greatest fear while you were overseas?

Sometimes in the artillery you had to suffer through. Things were pretty bad; you tried to find a place or foxhole or a place in the ground you could hide, but those shells came in, and they came whistling in, and they were real noisy and exploded close to you. That was a fearsome sort of a thing. But one time we took over a farmhouse, and we were attacked all night long by a German patrol outside. And I know I had to go up into the attic of the barn with a friend of mine, Lloyd Gates, to try to make contact with our troops from the attic 'cause the 300 radio wouldn't always work unless you had elevation. So when we were up in the attic, I was trying to make contact to our other GIs across the river, asking for artillery support. Well, we got artillery support, and the shrapnel was coming right through our tile roof into the area where we were. We were above a hayloft, and it caught fire downstairs, and our guys were able to put that out, but there was firefighting going on all night between us and the German patrol outside. One of the Germans got shot, and I could hear him gurgling in his death throes out in the yard. And I still remember that to this day.

Being in the front line and being exposed to enemy fire, it must have been a relief to know that you had this air support but at the same time see women and children could be casualties of this. How did you feel about the air campaign? Did you feel it was a wise idea and worthwhile?

When we saw the armadas of airplanes flying over, so far in the sky you could hardly see the beginning or end of where they were, we were thrilled. We thought that was really great.

But as far as civilian casualties, I remember one time in Luxembourg we went up a hill, and the infantry was ahead of us. We were in a mortar unit, heavy weapons unit, so infantry was ahead of us. So I went into a farmhouse—a real small farmhouse—and I was shocked to find inside a mother and her child dead on the kitchen floor. And I think they had been killed by our GIs as they attacked up the hill, because you never know who's going to be in a house. They may have thrown a grenade in that house or something but anyhow that was hard to see.

Is there anyone you would like to mention because of their bravery or friendship?

There was one fellow by the name of Lopez. We had been wiped out on Hill 310, Côte St. Jean in France. We walked into a trap, and there were about three companies up on that hill, L Company, K Company, and I Company. And there were wounded guys lying all over the place. I don't know how many times my buddies and I went up there with litters to get people out. And we walked by this Lopez one time, and he had been wounded and lying alongside the trail. And he said, "Don't bother with me. I'm okay. Go get some of the other guys that are hurt worse than I am." So we did leave him behind. We went up the hill to get somebody else, came back, and Lopez was dead. I remember planting his rifle in the ground and putting his helmet on it, but he was the guy who gave up his life for somebody else. And I also remember on Hill 310, we hauled wounded till we couldn't go anymore. There were still guys up on the hill crying for help, some of them were crying for their mothers, but there was a limit to what we could do. There was one fellow up there; he was wounded, lying in a bush, kind of in a bramble. And I went up to him, and he was hard to get at! I said, "Can you drag yourself out here a little bit?" And he gave me a look on his face that I'll never forget. But he did—he dragged himself out so we could get him on the litter, and when we got him on the litter, we found out that his leg was almost off at the thigh. And we had made him drag himself out of that bramble so we could get him on a stretcher.

Roy Lynch

Roy was drafted in 1943 and took his basic training at Ft. Knox, Kentucky. He served with the 2nd Armored Division in Tunisia, Sicily, Holland, France, Belgium, and Germany. He earned the Combat Infantry Badge and was awarded the Good Conduct, WWII Victory, and ETO Medals.

Date of Birth:
February 1918

Place of Birth:
St. Louis, MO

Military Assignment:
2nd Armored Division, HQ

Military Duties:
Jeep Driver to the Company Commander; Tank Driver

Highest Rank Achieved:
Sergeant

Postwar Occupation:
Welder

Did you have an opportunity to talk to any of the German civilians while you were in Germany?

Oh, yes, very much. In battle sometimes we would pull our tank up alongside of somebody. Usually, they would post a tank outside of where we bivouacked. One time I remember we parked a tank alongside of the house, and I asked the lady of the house (she had a store there) if we could have some hot water to make coffee. So she brought us out some hot water, and she said would you care to have some cakes or doughnuts with them? We have some if you want to come in. And so there were three of us there, and only two could come in at a time because we couldn't leave the tank. So we went in there, and oh my gosh, we had a good time there. We were there for a while, and first thing you know the man and the wife was there, and later on there was another man there. And after we talked for a while in German, she brought her son out, who was about twelve years old. She was hiding him from us, but after she found out that we weren't going to hurt them, she brought him out. And then they brought food and set it on the table for us, so we went and got food from the tank and brought it in, and boy, we had a good meal. We must have stayed in that house, one of us in there almost all night with them, because it was warm in there. Otherwise we had to sit out in the tank, and that was cold.

Is there anyone who you think deserves to be mentioned here?

I had a very good friend of mine, Colonel Bailey, and I overheard him say that he'd like to have a German Jeep. Well, I knew we had just passed a couple of German Jeeps on the side of the road back maybe four or five miles, so I told him that I knew where one was. So he sent an officer and me back in a Jeep, and we got one of them started and brought it back, and just as we got back to the area where Colonel Bailey was, it stopped running. So they said hook it on the back of the scout car, and we'll go on. I was one of the mechanics in the company, and while trying to get the Jeep started, I did a fairly foolish thing. I took the air filter off, and when I got it started, it backfired and blew gasoline out everywhere and caught the Jeep on fire. And I was in it, being towed by the scout car. So the guys were hollering at me, "Your Jeep's on fire." So we got out, unhooked it, left it there, and went on about our business, and then the next morning was when Colonel Bailey got killed. We were passing two columns of American soldiers right up at the front, and being Headquarters Company, we were going ahead of them. It was dark, and all at once everything lit up. There were German planes up there, and they were firing on us, and Colonel Bailey got shot right through the mouth and was killed.

Bernard Luebbert

Bernard was drafted in July of 1944 and took his basic training at the Infantry Replacement Training Center at Camp Robinson, Arkansas. He went overseas on the *Thomas R. Barry* and landed in Le Havre, France, in early January 1945. Bernard served with the 1st Infantry Division through Belgium, Germany, and Czechoslovakia. He earned the Combat Infantry Badge and was awarded the Bronze Star, Good Conduct Medal, Army of Occupation Medal, WWII Victory Medal, and three Battle Stars (Ardennes, Rhineland, Central Europe). Bernard returned to the United States in May 1946 and pursued a career at McDonnell-Douglas.

Date of Birth:
July 1922

Place of Birth:
Brinktown, MO

Military Assignment:
1st Infantry Division, 18th Infantry Regiment

Military Duties:
Machine Gunner

Highest Rank Achieved:
Sergeant

Postwar Occupation:
Worked at McDonnell-Douglas Corporation

Describe the biggest battle you were in.

One night we moved out and right away started taking machine gun fire. Then a German plane flies over and strafes us in the moonlight. We start moving, and it took five hours to move about two miles. That German plane would pick up more ammunition, swing back, and strafe us again, turning on his lights to scare us a little more. We finally got close to the road junction, which was our first objective, and we took machine gun fire again. So we called for help, and three Sherman tanks came up with bazookas. They knocked all of those out, just like that. All night long, you just hoped you'd make it. We lost thirty men that night.

Another day, our tankers didn't put out their colored ID, which they usually dropped over the back of the tank. We called for our planes, but they didn't come for a while, so we moved into town anyway, and a tanker setting above us shot over our heads. You could look up and actually see the bullets flying. We took the town and started up the hill. A half hour later, our Air Force came. And since our tanker was unmarked, they thought we were Germans, so they came down and strafed us—two of our own planes. I don't know if anybody was killed, but some were hit with falling rock. I kissed the dirt at the bottom of the ditch; I thought I'm gonna die.

Then we crossed the Weiser River and lost ten men. Not one SS would surrender, so forty-four SS troops were killed along with our ten men in about an hour. I know because I worked in an office later and read the casualties.

Many times snipers would shoot at you; you could hear them. On the very last day of the war, we lost three men right next to me on the sidewalk. This guy with me was looking around, and the next thing I know, he's slumped over, a sniper killed him. I started to move, and the sniper shot at me. He missed me, but that was quite an experience.

What was the greatest lesson you learned from your military experience?

How important one man was in the war. You felt like a grain of sand, each one of us had a job to do. I started out carrying ammunition, and then when the gunner got bumped off, I took his place. You had a job to do. Somebody else could have done it, but they were doing something else. You find out your importance and that you did something worthwhile. You put your life on the line, and now years later I see all this that happened, and I feel proud that I was there to do a little bit. I was in Czechoslovakia in 2003, took the tours, and learned how they suffered during the war. And I'm proud that I took part in helping. Then in 1994, on a D-Day tour in France the hotel had a big sign as you went in, "Thanks to our Liberators." So it made you feel pretty good.

Kay Williamson

Kay enlisted in 1942 and took his basic training at Aberdeen Proving Grounds, Maryland, with additional training at Camp Edwards, Massachusetts, and Camp Stewart, Georgia. He served with the 95th Infantry Division through France, Holland, Belgium, and Germany. He earned the Combat Infantry Badge and was awarded the Bronze Star and four Battle Stars. Kay returned to the United States in February of 1946 and pursued a career in auto parts and service.

Date of Birth:
August 1921

Place of Birth:
Lake County, TN

Military Assignment:
95th Infantry Division, 377th Infantry Regiment

Military Duties:
Repairing Damaged Tanks

Highest Rank Achieved:
Technician Fourth Grade

Postwar Occupation:
Automotive Parts and Service

Talk about the role that the weather played during the Battle of the Bulge.

We didn't have any special uniform, or shoes. But after I nearly froze in the Battle of the Bulge and went through the Reppa Deppa going back to my outfit, which took a long time, well, I saw that these fellows behind the lines had all kinds of beautiful, warm equipment with snow pack shoes. And here we were cleaning out basements with just a candle that we'd taken out of some church or something like that. And these fellows had all kinds of flashlights, and we didn't have a one. We just didn't get supplies, but I guess that's because of communications. When you have too many people, you have less communication.

What was the time you were most afraid during your service overseas?

When the war was about over, we crossed a river on pontoon boats and went over on tanks. The infantry hated riding tanks because they were a target for every kind of weapon that the Germans had. After we got on the other side of the river, we started going through a forest, down one of the old forest roads. And then the tanks ran out of gasoline, and we had to wait overnight for them to get gasoline. And the tankers, they not only shared their food, but they gave us their bedrolls, and of course, we slept on the outside—wasn't room enough to sleep on the inside with the tankers. The next morning the lead Jeep come roaring back, and he says there's an 88 on the far hill over there across the valley. They're centered, and they have destroyed several vehicles when they came out of this forest. So the tank commander says there's only two squads of us left and about twenty men at the most, and he says I want you fellows to go up and see what you can do about that 88. So it took us almost a day to go around and come in from behind, and when we got up there we had some good sharpshooters who picked off the soldiers that were manning this 88. It was an antiaircraft gun, but they could lower it down where they could blast our vehicles across the valley. So we silenced it, and they had a bunker there, and one of the men come up to me and says, "Hey Sarge, you should hear the voices inside of the bunker." When we opened up the bunker, there were about ten or twelve female soldiers in uniform, and they were ones manning the antiaircraft gun. We were so tired, and we knew that we wouldn't be able to march them maybe ten miles back and turn them over to a prisoner of war camp. So we spent the night there and we had heard about how mean some of these female soldiers were, how cunning they were, and so one of the fellows says, "Sarge, shouldn't we search them for weapons?" And I said, "Yeah, I guess so." So we had one fellow that had been married and had children, and he knew more about women than probably anybody else in the outfit. So he gave them a search, and we had them in one room; he would search them in another, and then we'd put them in a different room that we'd cleaned out all the weapons. The next morning bright and shiny, we marched them about five miles down to a road crossing and flagged down an American truck that was going back to the rear. So we got a big laugh every time we told the story about our wonderful capture of the Rhine River Warriors.

Jacob Wright

Jake was drafted in September of 1943 and took his basic training at Camp Fannin, Texas. He went overseas on a converted freight boat and landed in Le Havre, France, in January of 1945. He fought with the 89th Infantry Division through Luxembourg and Germany. Jake earned the Combat Infantry Badge and was awarded the American Theatre Ribbon, European-African-Middle Eastern Ribbon with two Battle Stars, World War II Victory Medal, two Overseas Bars, and the Good Conduct Medal. He returned to the United States in April of 1946 and pursued a career in trucking.

Date of Birth:
June 1925

Place of Birth:
Lusk, WY

Military Assignment:
89th Infantry Division, 353rd Infantry Regiment

Military Duties:
NCO Duties

Highest Rank Achieved:
Staff Sergeant

Postwar Occupations:
Railroad and Thirty-seven Years in Trucking

What was the most intense battlefield engagement in which you fought?

We crossed the Rhine River at two o'clock in the morning, and the engineers were trying to get a pontoon bridge across to get the tanks and the other equipment across. It seemed like about every time they got the bridge halfway across, lo and behold, a mortar would just blow it out, and they'd have to start all over. They found out that there was a forward observer for the Germans up on the bluff; he was giving them the coordinates for their mortar fire. So we took two guys out of each squad as a patrol to paddle across, and they were shooting .50 calibers down there, with tracers that would go down and hit the water and skip off of it and go up the bluff. When we got across to go up the other side, there was nothing but rocks and grape vineyards. And it was steep! As we were going up, we heard a shot, and here comes a helmet rolling down the hill by us. And when we got up there, we found out that one of the lead soldiers did a good job. He had shot the forward observer, dead. When we got up there, everybody dispersed. My buddy and I went to the right, and we were out there about a quarter of a mile from the rest of them, and he said, "Jake, I think there's some Germans over there." I said okay. So he could speak a little German, Deutsch, and he had the Browning automatic, and I said, "Tell them to come out, or we're going to shoot." And he told them to come out, and there were two privates, so to speak, and one non-com, and I said they're looking back. There's got to be another one. And I said tell them to come out or we're going to shoot all three of them right here. So he did, and pretty soon here come an officer out. That was the end. And they were the ones that had the mortar that was dumping on our bridges down there. And we kicked the mortar down and took them as prisoners, and we took everything they had. I mean, they had guns, and I think he got a Luger. I got a P-38. And the officer, he had a saber that the officers carried. We took them all down and turned them in as prisoners of war and went on about our way.

While you were in Germany, did you witness any of the concentration camps?

That's nasty. Yeah, we liberated a concentration camp. My book has got pictures in there of it. Yeah. And these people did not know what was going on, but they were not dead. And there were others that they piled up to burn. But they didn't know what was going on. All they could do was holler. They had them piled up, wood, people, wood, people. It's hard to believe that a guy could do this kind of stuff, but let me tell you, until you see it, it's hard to believe. But I do have pictures in that book. At that time, if you got caught with a camera over there, that was it for you, brother. You were not allowed to have a camera. After the war was over, you got cameras, but during the war you didn't have a camera. I can tell you over and over and over, but until you see it, you don't know what it's like.

James Whitney

Jim was drafted in February of 1943 and took his basic training at Ft. Jackson. He landed in Tidworth, England, in November of 1944 and crossed the Channel to Le Havre in January of 1945. Jim served with the 8th Armored Division through France, Germany, and Holland and participated in the Ardennes and Central Europe campaigns. Jim returned to the United States in February 1946 and pursued a career in advertising, marketing, and public relations.

Date of Birth:
January 1924

Place of Birth:
Ann Arbor, MI

Military Assignment:
8th Armored Division, 7th Armored Infantry Battalion, CCA

Military Duties:
Armor Infantry Unit, Overseeing a Prisoner of War Camp

Highest Rank Achieved:
Master Sergeant

Postwar Occupations:
Advertising, Marketing, and Public Relations

Describe your role at the POW camp.

When I went to Bad Aibling, I helped run PWE-26, an American prisoner of war camp. It was an old German Luftwaffe airfield. I worked for Captain Riley King, who was West Point. "I'm the post's Captain Riley. You got that?" "Yes sir." Every morning we would play a German composer on the loudspeaker, and the German prisoners would come out and shake hands. So I would go out there among them; I made friends.

In the hangar there was a row of tables with typewriters with Germans sitting there. That's where Hans worked. And to the left you'd see all these disheveled characters, maybe a couple thousand of them eating their ersatz cheese. Hans, the guy who ran the place, would yell, "Achtung!" when I came in. I told him, "Cut it out, I'm just a stupid master sergeant." And that was so damned embarrassing because they'd all jump up; made me kind of nervous. Then the captives would be interviewed by the Germans in the office, who'd fill out papers marked discharged or the captives were held.

One day Hans saw my sketchbook and introduced me to Charles Benedict, a prisoner who was a very famous German war artist on the Eastern front. I convinced the colonel and Riley to let Charles have a room down the hall from me, which we made into a studio. Then Captain King and I went to Munich to an art store and bought supplies for the art studio. Charlie did these sketches and painted portraits of them. One day, he said his family didn't know where he was or even if he was alive. They lived in the Alps, and there was no way of communicating with them, so I got permission to take him there. It was a beautiful, rare, warm December day. He directed me, and we pulled up before this very substantial house. His family hadn't heard from him, and they figured he was dead on the Eastern front. They just erupted when they saw him. It was one of the most emotional things I've ever witnessed. You should have seen the food on their table, and they talked and talked. They invited me in, but I felt out of place so I sat outside on a little bench and three hours later, Charlie came out. I lost track of Charlie; I regret not staying in touch.

Was this POW camp for German army Wehrmacht, Luftwaffe, or SS?

Wehrmacht, but we were looking for SS. One day, Riley King threw a letter from the state department at me. It said that a group of repatriated SS prisoners from Fort Custer, Michigan, were going to arrive, treat them differently, and give them immediate transportation home. A few days later, these footlockers arrive, and these SS guys had been processed just like American soldiers! They arrived on a day when it's two above zero, and they're laughing and talking, and Riley just scowled at this. He was behind the lines at St. Lo, and he really saw a lot of action—his men killed and he hated Germans. So he has Hans line them up on the tarmac, and Riley starts inspection. "Tell them to strip down, everything off." So Hans tells them, and they strip down to naked, two above zero. Captain Riley goes down the line one by one and makes them raise their left arm and show him the SS, and then he comes over and talks to me, stretching it out as long as he can. Finally, he tells me, "Okay, get these guys in prisoner uniforms." Boy did they break for the barracks! They came in American uniforms with a little bitty PW on them, and we exchanged that for some old stuff.

A couple days later, I walked into the office, and Riley said, "Whitney, you're going to miss all of the fun. Your orders just came in to go home. But I'm going to bust their ass before they get out of here."

I got that artist, Benedict, discharged early. He went down to the gate, and before he got on the transport truck, he turned and saluted me. I saluted back. The same thing happened to me a month later: POWs going home saluted me as the truck drove off. Two or three times Germans would come to see me at the post, and I would go down to the gate and talk to them. When that B-25 smashed into the Empire State Building, the Germans were amazed there was a building that tall.

What told you that the POW Wehrmacht soldiers were SS?

They had a little tattoo inside their left arm that looked like a piece of lightning. They were the bad guys, and they weren't going to get discharged. The SS would just not give up. They were the ones who organized roadblocks, and you would see a whole line of Shermans. The great thing about the Shermans, we had so many of them, and they were fast. A lot of people don't know, but the King Tiger could traverse mushy ground better than a Sherman 'cause the pounds per square inch on the tread was less than the pounds per square inch on a Sherman. The tread was almost as wide as a Jeep on that King Tiger.

Is there something you'd like to tell future generations?

I walked off from the war—went home, buried my uniform, pretended that it never happened, and tried to start over again. And that's the greatest mistake our generation has made. I just wish I'd kept contact with the people I met over there. What a unique experience God gave me, and I didn't embrace it the way I should have.

Warren Allen

Date of Birth:
January 1924

Place of Birth:
St. Louis, MO

Military Assignment:
87th Infantry Division, 335th Field Artillery

Military Duties:
Artilleryman

Highest Rank Achieved:
Sergeant

Postwar Occupation:
Engineering

Warren went into the service in May of 1943, in the ASTP at North Carolina State. When that program was ended, he took his basic training at Ft. Bragg, North Carolina, and in April of 1944, he joined the 87th Division at Ft. Jackson, South Carolina. The division left the United States in October 1944 for Macclesfield, England. In November of 1944, they crossed the Channel uneventfully on an LST and went up the Seine River, entering the line at the right flank of the 3rd Army down at the Saar Valley. Warren fought with the 87th Division in France, Germany, and Belgium and ended up in Czechoslovakia at war's end, having earned the "standard battle ribbons." He came back to the United States in July because he was on redeployment and slated for Japan and was in St. Louis on V-J Day. He was then sent to Ft. Dix, New Jersey, and processed dischargees until he had enough points himself and was discharged in January of 1946.

What specific challenges did you face as an artilleryman versus a rifleman on the line?

Well, our challenges and experiences were totally different. Those fellows up at the front, they were under those conditions continuously. They really had the tough time, and when you'd see those people pull out of the line and come back, they'd be just slogging along, heads kind of down. Zero expression. Total blank faces on the people coming out of combat from the infantry. Where we were living, we could dig a hole and sleep in it and change our socks and the helmet liner. We had inbound shells and occasional strafing, but nothing like what they had.

When you prepared a position for your artillery pieces, could you expect to stay in that location for a long time?

Not long, no. There was a lot of moving, and moving was a chore because you had all those 94-pound projectiles to move, and I was a machine gunner, so I had a machine gun crew. I had a machine gun and three other fellows. We put out the perimeter security, and by night we were in at the back of our .50 caliber ground mounts. During the day, we had on the antiaircraft aerial mounts. If we were setting up a position, we were the ammo handlers, so we'd be loading and unloading the 94-pound projectiles. So I remember the moves, and they seemed to be very frequent.

Are there any specific instances of engagement or just life in the field that you recall as being a singular experience?

One incident is very clear in my mind. Of course, the Bulge was way north of us when it started. But we had word from our battery commander that the Germans were punching through our lines. They had Germans dressed in American uniforms; they knew the sign and the countersign, and so we put on extra security. They sent me up on a railroad track through an evergreen forest. I was up there all night long, in back of my .50 caliber, and they were kind enough to string a telephone up there so I could call back if something happened. But the only thing happened on the telephone was in the still of the night, when the trees are starting to move and so on, the phone rings. It was the battery commander, "Allen, you okay?" So I remember that phone ringing in the middle of the night when I was trying not to move and be very quiet.

Do you recall where you were on Christmas Eve or Christmas Day of 1944?

Yes, very clearly. On Christmas Day we were making an end-around run. We were at the right flank of the 3rd Army, and we were pulled out. We were told to run overnight with our headlights on, never mind the black-out lights. If we were strafed, we were supposed to keep going and head north to pinch off the Bulge and meet the British. So we were on our way north, and we stopped during the day and had a meal on the side of the road. I don't remember what it was; I just remember stopping, and I think we had mess kits. It must have been something more than rations, but I don't know how they did it.

Did you experience any moments of comfort or happiness during this period?

I remember taking a shower in November, and much later at Easter time I had another shower and a chance to get warm. Unlike the infantry, if they found a building, they were there because that was shelter for them, out of gunfire. But we were not permitted to go in buildings or sleep in a building. I suspect they didn't want any ransacking. They didn't want us just running through buildings. For the infantry, you know, that was a lifesaving opportunity for them.

How do students today respond to your experiences, and do you think there are things these younger generations are having difficulty understanding?

I was surprised on how attentive they were to what I was saying. They were really listening and had some good questions, but the questions were all written out. I think the teachers had briefed them the day before, and many of them were reading the question. So I thought that was a little bit strange. But they did pay close attention, and I like to weave into that talk, on what I think about preparedness, how we got into the war, how we let Hitler have his way, Neville Chamberlain and "peace in our time," pacifism, so I try to weave that into the story. Because I feel strongly that preparedness is vital, and you can't deal with dictators and make deals that stand. So I try to put that in with the high school story. And my thoughts about communism, I think those are important messages, and that's why I feel it's worthwhile giving that talk. And they seem to listen. Another thing I like to talk about when I talk to the high school students is Buchenwald. We did not liberate Buchenwald, but we were there short-ly after it was liberated, and when I hear people say that didn't happen, then I say you should have been there to see how those people were living on shelves, just backed up on bare wooden shelves and see the individuals that are just actually literally skeletons with skin on them. So when you've seen that and have that impression and people say it didn't happen, well, as we all know it did happen.

James Bangert

Jim was drafted in 1943 and went to Camp Callin, California, for basic training, followed by artillery training at Fort Bliss, Texas. After further training in the Sequoia National Forest and Camp Polk, Louisiana, he shipped out from New York to go overseas. He landed in Trowbridge, England, and shortly thereafter crossed the Channel to Le Havre. Jim served in France and Germany and was awarded the European Theatre Service Medal (two Battle Stars) and Good Conduct Medal before leaving service in April of 1946.

Date of Birth:
March 1925

Place of Birth:
Millstadt, IL

Military Assignment:
Attached to 1st & 7th Army, 839th AAA Battalion

Military Duties:
40 mm Antiaircraft Artillery Crew

Highest Rank Achieved:
Staff Sergeant

Postwar Occupation:
Mechanic

What was your role in the 40 mm antiaircraft crew?

I started out as a gunner, so I stood on a platform with a rope around my leg, and we had a director machine that would turn the gun. I was one of the two guys that were turning the guns, and I dropped the 40 mm shells in there. We had a little power plant that gave us the power to run the director, which was a square box. One of the guys could stand way back from the gun with that director and guide the gun by looking in the director. But most of the time we went down each side cranking the gun back and forth. But I had to do the loading and firing no matter what, and I would drop the shells in the gun and fire it with my foot. Somebody would call from the back and pull my foot off the firing mechanism when they wanted me to stop.

How long had you been in France before you received word that you were headed towards the front in the Battle of the Bulge?

We were in a little town in Germany, and so we all hauled infantry up, and we had turned all the trucks around and were coming back out when they started dropping mortars. We were in a town between two mountains, and they were dropping mortars in on us. A guy from Chicago was driving the truck ahead of me, and it got hit. We went underneath the trucks to keep from getting shot. He got wounded in the arm, so we put him in the back of my deuce and a half, and we took off for the aid station. When we got there to unload him, snipers were still in some nearby houses, and they started shooting, trying to get us, but we got him safely inside. Later on, our unit went to the Remagen Bridge and set up there one night. They were supposed to shoot anything that floated or flew, so when a plane came over, it looked like the Fourth of July from all the tracer bullets going up.

Did you have an opportunity to interact with the German or French civilians?

We were in a convoy in Germany on the autobahn, and our luggage trailer broke down; it carried parts for the deuce and a half trucks. So they unhooked the truck and left me with it while they went back for replacement parts. While I was sitting there, here comes a German kid in his teens on his bicycle, and I traded him some chocolate bars. He went home and brought me a bottle of wine, a summer sausage, and some black bread. So it was real good German food. We'd mostly drive at night and would sleep in back of the deuce and a halfs when we stopped. We couldn't have headlights on at night; just those two little cat eyes shining on the reflectors on the truck ahead of you. That's all you had to go by. I would stand on the running board and pull the throttle out so I wouldn't have to look through the windshield, because the fog was so thick. One night when I was driving, we didn't make a curve so I hit one of the rock walls they had everywhere in Germany. I was lucky I didn't go over the wall, 'cause it went straight down after that. The next day they repaired the front axle, and then we went on our way.

Henry Calbreath

Cal was drafted and by March of 1943 was in the Army, completing his basic training and advanced basic training at Ft. Leonard Wood, Missouri. After maneuvers in Louisiana and Texas, he went to Camp Breckenridge, Kentucky. From there the division went to Camp Shanks, New York, before departing in a convoy of eighty-seven ships. He landed at Southampton, England, and proceeded to South Wales before being sent over to Le Havre, France, in early December, just prior to the Battle of the Bulge. Cal fought with the 75th Infantry Division in the Ardennes, Colmar Pocket, Rhone-Rhine Canal, and the Ruhr Pocket. He was awarded the Bronze Star, Combat Infantry Badge, Good Conduct Medal, and medals for the Ardennes, European-African-Middle Eastern, Army of Occupation, and American Campaigns.

Date of Birth:
January 1924

Place of Birth:
East St. Louis, IL

Military Assignment:
75th Infantry Division, 291st Infantry Regiment

Military Duties:
Infantryman

Highest Rank Achieved:
Staff Sergeant

Postwar Occupation:
Union Electric Employee

Describe your first major battle.

My company was part of the company that relieved the 106th Division, which was nearly annihilated at the beginning of the Bulge. Those poor guys, I really felt sorry for them. I asked this lieutenant colonel, who was a regimental commander, "Where's all your men?" He said, "This is us." Him and four guys. That was all that was left out of his regiment of three thousand combat men; the rest had been either killed or captured.

You changed your password every day, and we had to remember that there were guys out there that weren't going to know about that. So we really had to keep on our toes because those guys might give us a password that's nowhere near the password that we would expect to get. So we got to recognize who they were, and you could usually tell by their full beards and ratty-looking clothes.

Our baptism into the Battle of the Bulge was on Christmas Eve night, when we walked into combat. Now, I was in the infantry, so I was on the front line. And I'm not exaggerating, I know the snow was so deep, you could lay down in it, and the Germans couldn't hit you with machine gun or rifle fire. You're lying in the snow, and they couldn't see to hit you. But they'd get you with 88s or their mortars. Mortars were brutal, but you could hear the noise when they dropped one in the tube. You'd pick it up immediately the first time you heard it. They've dropped a mortar. You had no idea who they had shot at until it hit. Mortars were brutal, but their 88s were worse. They used the 88s for artillery, for antiaircraft, and they used it on their tanks: a three-fold purpose. The Germans were so smart, they could take the 81 mm mortars we had and use them in their 80 mm mortars, our shells, but we couldn't take their shells and use them in our 81s. They could take our ammunition from our .30 caliber and use it in theirs, but we couldn't use theirs in ours. Their machine gun fired from 1,100 to 1,500 rounds per minute where our machine gun fired from 350 to 500 rounds per minute. You could hear our machine gun go "doot-doot-doot-doot." Theirs were "burp, burp, burp." That's what it sounded like when they'd shoot them at us. And so you knew immediately whose it was, theirs or ours.

One time we went back on the Rhine River, and the 8th Armored went through us that morning; we were in a holding position. But all day long, B-25 Billy Mitchells and B-26 Martin Marauders bombed the other side of the river. And I thought, well, they've pretty well taken care of the Germans. Well, as soon as it started, when the aircraft left, the artillery started. And you couldn't sleep. It was "boom, boom, boom." That's what it sounded like all night long. The 8th Armored went through us and went across the river on a bridge that the engineers made, and they had nine casualties. Now can you imagine that? We only had nine casualties, and some of them weren't from bullets. There were guys that hurt their legs or turned their ankles and things like that—maybe a broken ankle or whatever. But we really never lost anybody. I mean, the Germans were literally stunned from all that bombing and all the artillery. They were, I guess, like mummies. They didn't know where they were since they were bombed so much.

So a few days later the company commander came up to me and said, "Sergeant, do me a favor." And I said, "Sure." There was a 109 Messerschmitt right across the river. Now, we were on a big levee, a levee like the one on the Mississippi. Well, we had our hole dug right on top of the levee in case they'd decide to come across. We were right there, and if they come up the bank, we'd pop them. But that wasn't their plan. We had the Germans on the run, and they never stopped running, I don't think. And he said, "I saw some activity around that plane over there." And I looked over there, and I said, "Okay." He said, "Pop that plane over there with your mortars." And I said, "Okay." So I lined up and told the guys, gave them a distance. And they asked, "How wide do you think the Rhine River was? It was like the Mississippi about the same distance." So I just figured based on that, and I fired one over. It was about a hundred feet on the other side of the plane. And I told him, "I'll fire some more rounds." So I fired the next one. I had a direct hit on the plane. Pow! I mean right into that plane. And there were four Germans there, and one of them got out. We killed three of them when we fired that. And when we fired it, I said, "Fire three or four more in the same area." And we did, and I see this guy go out. He goes in where a shell had hit, a little crevice, enough where he could go in. And I fired at that guy. Now he had to go probably a mile across a flat terrain before the other levee where we were at. And I don't know if it was like that everywhere, but at that particular area where we were, that's the way it was. We fired at this guy with machine guns, everything that we had, and that evening I saw him go up the levee. And I thought, well that old boy wasn't supposed to die. But I know a couple times I would have swore to the Lord that I put the shell right in the hole he was in, and he come out of it, but I guess I didn't.

Harry Reed

Date of Birth:
February 1924

Place of Birth:
Eldon, MO

Military Assignment:
3rd Armored Division, 83rd Armored Reconnaissance Battalion

Military Duties:
Reconnaissance Squad

Highest Rank Achieved:
Sergeant

Postwar Occupation:
Auto Recycling

Harry was drafted in February of 1943 and took his basic training at Ft. Knox, Kentucky. He went overseas on the *John Errickson* and landed in Liverpool, England, in September of 1944. He crossed the Channel on July 3, landing at Omaha Beach, and fought with the 3rd Armored Division in France, Germany, and Belgium. He earned the Combat Infantry Badge and was awarded the Purple Heart with Cluster; Bronze Star; Good Conduct Medal; Battle of the Bulge Medal; the Belgium, France, Luxembourg, and Normandy Medals; five Overseas Bars; and five Battle Stars (Normandy, Northern France, Ardennes, Rhineland, Central Europe). Harry returned to the United States in October of 1945 and pursued a career in automobile recycling.

Can you describe your first battlefield engagement during the Battle of the Bulge?

As soon as we got in there, we ran into the Germans, and on December 24, I was in a little town. We had set up a roadblock that went from St. Vith and Bastogne. The lieutenant said we're going up to check that out. We heard small-arms fire about a mile up the road. I hesitant, and I asked, "Don't you think we better go on foot?" And he said, "No, we're going in vehicles; we got a lot of firepower." The snow was about half-knee-deep, and it was below zero, and about halfway up there, it turned foggy. The Germans were on both sides of the road lying in the ditches. They started shooting with crossfire and the lieutenant was hit right in his jugular vein, and he fell over my lap. I had a .50 caliber mounted on a Jeep, so I took it and burned it up, and I had a couple Tommy guns, and I emptied them. They'd shot the Jeep up, and it quit running a couple of hundred yards after we got through. I got up there, and I tried the radio, and it wouldn't work. I looked to see if something had come loose on it, and a bullet had come in between my legs and tore the radio up. I was just as bloody as I could be, and they wanted to take me to the first aid station. I said, "I don't think I'm hurt." I said that's blood from the lieutenant. So they decided that was what it was, and we didn't have a Jeep or bedrolls to sleep in. So when we got up to the roadblock, they got me some clean clothes. And the driver and I were without any vehicle, and we didn't know where our outfit was, and the Germans were everywhere. So we hitched a ride and didn't get back to the outfit for about two days, and when we did, we went back to see what happened to the other guys because we didn't hear from them. Turned out the Jeep, the armored car, and the tank were shot up and burnt up, and we never did hear from the twelve other guys, so they either got killed or captured.

What was the saddest moment you experienced in your military service?

Nordhausen concentration camp. I was one of the very first ones in there, and they had three thousand dead lying in a courtyard, and the live prisoners were crawling over the dead. The prisoners that were alive would probably have weighed less than one hundred pounds. They were starved to death. Then they had the furnaces at Dora, where they burned all these bodies and we saw black smoke cloud in the distance and thought the airplanes had been bombing up there. When we got up there, the furnaces were overloaded, the Germans had taken the bodies out in the courtyard. They laid down a layer of wood and a layer of bodies, wood and bodies as high as they could stack, and they set it on fire. And that was the black smoke. Then they had the furnaces at a little place, oh, it was five or six or maybe ten miles from there, where they trucked them in and burned them. Well, we didn't know what it was. The SS had left because they didn't want to be caught there.

Gerald Myers

Date of Birth:
July 1918

Place of Birth:
Oregon, MO

Military Assignment:
80th Infantry Division, 317th Infantry Regiment

Military Duties:
Infantry Mortarman

Highest Rank Achieved:
First Sergeant

Postwar Occupations:
Sales and General Sales Manager With Quaker Oats and Continental Grain

Gerald was drafted in May of 1944 and took his basic training at Ft. Hood, Texas. He landed in Liverpool, England, on October 22, 1944. He crossed the Channel on the same day and landed at Omaha Beach on the 23rd. He was assigned to the 80th Infantry Division and joined his unit at Pont-à-Mousson, France, on October 1. Gerald served with them through France, Luxembourg, Germany, and Austria. He earned the Combat Infantry Badge and was awarded the Purple Heart, the Silver Star, two Bronze Stars, the Good Conduct Medal, and three Battle Stars (Ardennes, Rhineland, Central Europe). Gerald returned to the United States in January of 1946 and pursued a career in sales.

Do you think that the drill work and the discipline that you received in basic training played an important role in your success on the battlefield?

I was an infantry replacement soldier, so you had to learn how to fire the machine gun, the rifle, the sniper's rifle, the carbine, the BAR, the .45 revolver, and you had to learn how to take all these apart, clean them, and put them back together. One day you would be taught how to take this piece of equipment apart, then you would be told how to put it back together, and you would practice that. Then, the next day you would go into a movie theater and see how that weapon was used in combat. And then they would take you out for a half a day on what they called field problems. A field problem was using that piece of equipment as close to combat conditions as you could. Well, by the time that you spent two days on each one of these pieces of equipment that you were going to use, like they taught you how to use the bayonet, how to put it on your rifle, and how to use it. They taught you how to throw a hand grenade and so forth, and so you really only had two days on each piece of equipment. And they would try to tell you about combat and try to make you realize how important it was to listen, and you thought that you did, but when you got into actual combat, things didn't work the way they had in basic training. When I got overseas, they assigned me to a 60 mm mortar squad. In basic training, they taught us to set up our pieces of equipment maybe three hundred yards in back of the combat line so that we would fire over our soldiers' heads. The first time we went into combat, we started setting up the mortar about three hundred yards back of where the rifle line was, and the lieutenant came back, and he said what the hell are you guys doing clear back here. We said we're setting up our mortar like we've been taught to do. He said, "Get up here on the line with me because you have to be close enough so that I can tell you what to fire on."

What was the most important contribution you made during your experiences?

Well, that would be pretty difficult to say, because every day was a different experience. During the Battle of the Bulge, I earned two Bronze Stars and one Purple Heart. And right after the Bulge, in April of 1945, I was given the Silver Star, which is the second-highest honor that an infantry soldier can get. I got that when we crossed the Rhine River. The fighting was not as bad at that time, but it happened that I captured fifty-six Germans in a building along with the map of nineteen artillery emplacements. Our bombers and artillery used that map and knocked all of them out before the Germans could use them on us. But I just happened to be there and did that when an officer was nearby and saw what happened. There were a lot of guys that did things that were braver or the contribution was greater, but there was never an officer around when that happened. I didn't even know that I'd won the Silver Star until June of 1945.

Marvin Korte

Date of Birth:
April 1925

Place of Birth:
St. Louis, MO

Military Assignment:
84th Infantry Division, 334th Infantry Regiment

Military Duties:
Mortarman

Highest Rank Achieved:
Private First Class

Postwar Occupation:
Sales

Marvin was drafted shortly after graduating from high school and entered service around the end of July 1943, taking his basic training at Camp Wallace, Texas, with further training at Camp Claiborne, Louisiana, prior to going overseas in September of 1944. He was transferred to the battlefield a month later and served with the 84th Infantry Division in Holland, Belgium, Luxembourg, and Germany, where he was wounded in March of 1945 and subsequently evacuated to England before being returned to the United States. Marvin earned the Combat Infantry Badge and was awarded the Bronze Star, Purple Heart, Good Conduct Medal, World War II Victory Medal, American Campaign Medal, and the European-African-Middle Eastern Campaign medal with two Battle Stars (Ardennes, Rhineland). Marvin earned a degree from Washington University on the GI Bill and pursued a career in sales.

What was your first battlefield engagement in the Bulge like?

I would say it was similar to what we had been through before, because we had already been in battle by then, so we were not green troops. I remember one engagement we had when I was a forward observer for our mortar squad in this little town, and there were some German soldiers on a hill. There was a big forest behind them, and they were on a barren hill coming down. We were supposed to fire across their line of attack with the mortars, and we kept watching them come down there. Our machine gunners were down at the bottom of this hill, and the Germans were just being killed one right after another. I couldn't believe it. They were right in the line of our machine gunners' fire. We found out afterwards that a lot of them were young kids and older people, and I guess they had no choice but to go forward. I'm sure they had some officers that kept moving them forward. We did what we were supposed to do, but it was very sad to see these people killed needlessly.

As you went on during the Battle of the Bulge, did you gain insights on how to survive?

You learn Number One to stay out of forests or tree areas if you can avoid it, because if they hit a tree burst, you can get killed, even in a trench or a foxhole. And you learn to keep your feet as dry as possible, because when you're in a foxhole, you get down below the freeze line, and you're in a little bit of water and mud down in there. That's why there were so many frozen feet, because once you came out of that trench, you're back into the cold with wet feet. And you learned to try to rest whenever you can, because you don't have time to take a six-hour or eight-hour nap. You take little stretches of sleep, and whenever you had a chance to hit a town, you would get inside somewhere so you could relax. The only trouble was you'd wake up the next morning after sleeping all night, and you'd cough up black phlegm. What we would do was to put gasoline into bottles and put a wick in them and use that for light in the room, but they put out a lot of soot, which we breathed in. But that was the way we lived, in foxholes and cramped quarters.

How were you wounded?

Well, it was March 4, 1945, and our squad was to move in to take over a barn. We were making sure it was clear when the German shells started hitting. And that's when I was wounded. I got hit first in the arm. Shrapnel went through and came out of the other side of the arm. I was next to Dick Edge and Kelly. Dick was slightly wounded, and Kelly was killed. We were trying to get out of that barn, since we figured they had that zeroed in. I started to head for the courtyard, and another shell hit behind me, and I got shrapnel in my back. And I just sat there thinking my arm was gone, because I couldn't feel anything. As I was sitting there, I reached behind with my other arm, and I felt it was wet back there, and when I brought it back and there was blood on my hand. But it didn't seem like too long before the medics came and got us out of there. They took us to a nearby little building and patched us up, and the next thing I knew I was in an ambulance. Then I don't remember anything until I woke up in a hospital, somewhere in France. I looked around this huge room, and we're all lying in beds with white sheets on them. And I thought, "My goodness, where am I? Did I die?" Then I realized I was in the hospital. After a while, I was sent to a hospital in England and was put in traction for several months. They put a pin through my arm, and I lay there in traction. You're trying to keep the bones apart, so they set properly.

We'd have visitors that would come to see us, different groups that would come and visit the troops. The whole time I was in England, I was in bed, so I wasn't able to get up until they took me out of traction. And they had books, but not much entertainment other than people coming to visit with you. And you'd talk with the people around you and the nurses that were there. When I was sent back to the States, we went back on the *Queen Elizabeth*. It had been changed to a hospital ship and went out of Glasgow, Scotland. That was my proudest moment—being carried off that hospital ship on a stretcher, and there were about a thousand people in New York Harbor cheering us as we came off the ship. I was in the hospital in Staten Island, New York, for a while and flew from there to a hospital in Kansas, and that's where I was discharged from, in September of 1945, after a total of seven months in the various hospitals. When I came home, I talked to my uncle who was a doctor, and he said if it weren't for penicillin, I wouldn't be here today. That was about the time they started using penicillin, and that's what saved a lot of lives.

George Kottwitz

George was inducted in October of 1942 and took his basic training at Camp Polk, Louisiana, with additional training at Camp Barkley, Texas, and Camps Ibis and Cooke, California. He went overseas on the *Hermitage* and landed in Southampton, England, in October of 1944. He crossed the Channel and landed at Cherbourg around December 18. George fought with the 11th Armored Division as a machine gunner through France, Belgium, Germany, and Austria. He earned the Combat Infantry Badge and was awarded the Bronze Star and combat medals for the American, ETO, and Ardennes campaigns. George returned to the United States in January of 1946 and pursued a career in railroading and train services.

Date of Birth:
August 1919

Place of Birth:
Bland, MO

Military Assignment:
11th Armored Division, 63rd Battalion

Military Duties:
Machine Gunner

Highest Rank Achieved:
Staff Sergeant

Postwar Occupations:
Railroading, Train Services

Are there any individuals that you would like to pay tribute to for something they did?

No one in particular. It was a group effort, a squad effort, a platoon effort, a company effort. We went through minefields and across the Siegfried Line twice. One night our captain chose me and one other guy, and we made our way through the Siegfried Line and wound up behind the enemy pillboxes. The next morning we took the whole company across there, trying to avoid tripwires and stuff. You can capture a pillbox from a frontal attack, but it's bad business. You can get into a pillbox with hand grenades down the ventilation system or satchel packs next to the door. A satchel pack is a hunk of dynamite; slap it against the door and set it off, it will usually open. But two hand grenades down a smoke pipe don't hurt a thing. We attacked one town, and we made a mounted attack with half-tracks. You're not supposed to do that, but we did it anyhow because we didn't have any tanks. We made it okay to this town, Rieffs, but the half-track behind us hit a mine and blew all over the place. They were supposed to have been cleared the night before by our mine removal detail. Then from there, we worked our way eastward from town to town. Sometimes you could use the road, sometimes you couldn't. If some other outfit had orders to use that road, you couldn't use it.

What was the most intense battle or firefight you participated in during the Bulge?

Well, one time we went up a hill, and a couple of our lieutenants got shot. The first lieutenant got killed. He was a real gung-ho guy. He got right in there. An officer and any NCO would carry a carbine. Not him. He would carry a rifle, which was his business. A rifle was much better than a carbine. A carbine is a small rifle, best used for street fighting—street fighting by the way is the nastiest thing you can get into. So we get into the first house, then what? The enemy is in here, and he's looking at you out of windows and doors, and you have to go from this door over there. That door's locked. How do you get in there? The back door is a little bit easier or through the window, but the door would probably be locked. In the street, you're exposed to everybody out there. One of our guys was shot right in the middle of the street. So somebody had to go get him. I said you give me some fire cover, and I'll get him. I think I wound up with the Bronze Star for that. It didn't take very long. I dragged him by his hair back to our doorway. I think he didn't make it; he had one shot right through the middle, and it probably hit his spine.

What was the saddest moment or moments either during the Bulge or your time in military service?

Well, when your buddies got killed or shot up. There were quite a few of those. Along about the middle of January, we got replacements from the States, and I do mean they were fresh. So during our off time, we did our own little maneuvers around the area, and we were in deep snow at that time. We showed them how you dig a machine gun out there in the snow and do what you're supposed to do in the real thing. These people had never seen a machine gun before, and you have to know a little bit about .30 caliber machine guns before you can do any good with them. We had twelve men in the squad. We had a squad leader, assistant squad leader, a driver, five riflemen, two machine gunners, and two assistant gunners for carrying ammunition. If you set up in a place where you are going to use a lot of ammo, you could get rid of a box of machine gun bullets in a big hurry, so you had to have a large supply, 'cause if you run out, that's not good. So you ration it a little bit, take it a little bit easy.

Was there ever anything that happened that made you more determined to defeat the enemy?

Well, on May 15, we liberated Mauthausen concentration camp. Our outfit, the 11th Armored Division, wound up about forty miles east of Linz on the Danube River, the farthest east of any Allied units. I wasn't there because different units of our division were going different directions. But Mauthausen was a nasty thing. We were not the unit that took it. The 41st, I think, was the one that took it. Well, there's suffering, death all around you, half-dead people, a lot of dead people, corpses, and the rest of them might as well have been dead. They were so close to it. There were several camps; Gusen was one of them, all sub-camps at Mauthausen, which is north of Linz, maybe twenty miles or so northeast. You did what you had to do. The medics took care of those who were still alive. We secured the place and captured who we had to capture.

What were the greatest lessons that you learned from your military experience?

Regimentation. You have to learn to do what you're told, and you have to also expect your men to do what you tell them. Eat when you can. Class A-rations was the food you'd get in the mess hall. Class B-rations was the same thing off the mess truck. Same kind of food but prepared on the truck, and you eat it out of mess kits. Maybe for a week, maybe for a month or two. Out there you had C-rations, you had D-rations. D-rations was a candy bar, a concentrated chocolate bar, and C-rations was a little bit bigger than a Cracker Jack box. The D-rations were strictly for survival purpose. You had one handy all the time.

Walter Mohrmann

Date of Birth:
March 1925

Place of Birth:
St. Louis, MO

Military Assignment:
4th Infantry Division, 12th Infantry Regiment

Military Duties:
Infantryman

Highest Rank Achieved:
Sergeant

Postwar Occupation:
Post Office

Walter was drafted in 1943 and took his basic training at Ft. McClellan, Alabama. He went overseas on the *Ile de France* and landed in Essex, England, in September of 1944. Walter crossed the Channel on D-Day and fought with the 4th Infantry Division through France and into Luxembourg, where he was taken prisoner in Echternach around Christmas of 1944 and was liberated in March of 1945. Walter participated in the following campaigns: Normandy, Northern France, and Ardennes. He earned the Combat Infantry Badge and was awarded the Purple Heart, Good Conduct, World War II Victory Medal, Bronze Star, and the European Service Medal with four Battle Stars (Normandy, Northern France, Ardennes, Rhineland). Walter left the service in December of 1945 and pursued a career with the U.S. Post Office.

Where were you on Christmas Eve or Christmas Day of 1944?

We were in Echternach, Luxemburg, when the Germans overran us and I was knocked out for a day or two. Before they shelled us, I was with Sergeant Smokey, and we had just set up machine guns in the windows upstairs. We came down, and he told somebody to go upstairs and if any German tanks were seen to let him know right away. Then I don't remember a thing at all, I felt no pain, nothing. When I came to, I'm all by myself, and I had a head wound. In battle they say, don't let them capture you, they're gonna kill you. So when I came to I looked out the window, and there was a German soldier going by, and he's got a machine gun. And I thought, what am I going to do, I've got a wound and I need something to eat. I'm dizzy and I called out, "Comrad . . . Yah . . . Where are you? Come out." He didn't know who I was. He thought all the Americans were dead or gone, and I walked out, and I said in German, "Don't shoot me." He said, "I'm not going to shoot you. Come on, can you walk?" I said, "Yeah," so we walked down to another building where they had German engineers in there. When I walked in with this guy, one of their sergeants said, "Hey Henry, where'd you find this guy, the fighting's been over for two days?" And these guys had beer, wine, schnapps, brandy, everything. I thought, I know they're going to kill me. The sergeant said, "Get this American a medic for his head. Do you want a drink? What do you want, beer, wine, schnapps?" "Can I have beer?" So he gave me a beer and I thought, I guess they ain't going to kill me. Then they took me to a German hospital, where they had civilians and military mixed in there. There was a German doctor who looked at me and said he was going to shave my hair to get to the wound with a straight razor. While he was doing all that, he says, "You understand German?" I said, "Yes sir." "Where'd you learn it, high school?" I said, "No, from my mother and father." He got mad and said, "What, you're German?" I said, "No, I was born in America." He said, "That don't make no difference, you're German." So I was in there for a couple of days, and they put us on trucks and sent us to a regular POW camp. Americans, British mixture.

And how long were you there?

A week or so. They just registered us there. Then we marched out, just kept marching across the beautiful German country. Then they put us on a train and sent us up to the Baltic Sea. That was in March, and the Russians were coming from the other way, so they got us out of there. All we did was walk down the highways. They marched us to get us away from the Russians. We slept in barns, didn't get proper food. Guys suffered worse than that, though in other places. Sometime in March, the Germans started throwing down their arms. We were on this march, sitting on the roadside, and we looked up and saw this column of American Jeeps and tanks. We went crazy, and the first thing they said was President Roosevelt died yesterday. That was March 13; but he had died the twelfth. So then they sent us to Le Havre, France, and got us ready and put us on ships back to the States.

John Waidmann

Date of Birth:
February 1925

Place of Birth:
Bourbon, MO

Military Assignment:
99th Infantry Division, 393rd Infantry Regiment

Military Duties:
Reconnaissance Patrol

Highest Rank Achieved:
Corporal

Postwar Occupations:
Radio News Editor; Technical Writer and Editor

John was drafted in June of 1943 and took his basic training at Camp Maxey, Texas. He landed in England in late October of 1944, crossing the Channel in early November and landing at Le Havre. John fought with the 99th Infantry Division through France, Belgium, and Germany. He earned the Combat Infantry Badge and was awarded the Bronze Star. John was captured on December 17, 1944, and was held at several POW camps until April of 1945, when he was liberated and spent time recovering in Le Havre. He returned to the United States in November of 1945 and pursued careers at KXOK radio, Emerson, and McDonnell-Douglas.

Describe the circumstances of your capture.

Our company had been marched to the rear, and we went through a clearing into a wooded area. And right as we were getting into the wooded area, a number of German troops were leading a group of Americans that they had captured previously. They yelled at our lieutenant to surrender, so he surrendered to the Germans. We all laid down our weapons, and the Germans took our steel helmets and our overshoes.

While I was a prisoner of war, we were sent to various small towns and did have contact not only with some of the civilians, but also with German soldiers. In one instance, we were in a town helping the German troops bake bread in a portable oven on wheels. The Germans had used sawdust to knead the bread, and I got sick the first time I tried to eat it. I had enough of a background about electronics and electricity and radio that I bypassed the switch in the building they kept us in. Twenty of us Americans were in this little small town in the middle of a civilian neighborhood, and the German guard would lock us in our room and turn a switch off outside the room. I had somebody keep the guard occupied while I shorted out the electrical switch, so that we could go ahead and have our lights on at night. The power would be on continuously, but someone would unscrew the bulbs inside the sleeping area, and we tried to maintain a quiet position in that way.

So you weren't in a formal POW camp with hundreds or thousands of other prisoners?

After I was captured, I was moved around and then was put into Stalag IV-B, which actually was a British-run camp about one hundred miles south of Berlin. About all that the Germans did was patrol the outside. The British ran everything. They had a store, in which you could buy things for cigarettes, if you were lucky enough to have cigarettes. This camp also had a Russian compound, which we never did get close to. The Stalag IV-B at the time was at Mühlberg, on the Elbe River, and we were there for about three months and then were moved to this small town, where we lived in a building under one German guard. We worked there for both the German civilians and for the Hungarian army. That was an interesting project. The Hungarians would check us out, and we would all go generally to our work position, and we often moved clothing and blocks of wood. I guess they were spindles from thread. We would move the material on horse-drawn wagons, and then we would be walked back to our position. In one instance, another soldier and I encountered a chute where German-made beer was descending, so we swiped beer and put some in our pockets. Each of us had been given a topcoat with a red triangle on the back, which indicated that we were prisoners. So we packed bottles of beer in our pockets and padded them with whatever we had and walked right past the guards and then enjoyed the beer later. In one instance, someone left an empty bottle of beer outside the lager building, and there was all kinds of hell raised about that. We were able to steal potatoes and coal and pieces of wood that we could use in our building, and what we would do is tie the bottoms of our trousers and stuff all this material in our pants and walk out past the guards. That worked reasonably well, and we were virtually never stopped from doing that and had heat and beer and potatoes whenever we had an opportunity.

Walter Gaterman

Date of Birth:
December 1921

Place of Birth:
St. Louis, MO

Military Assignment:
28th Infantry Division, 112th Infantry Regiment

Military Duties:
Infantry Rifleman

Highest Rank Achieved:
Private First Class

Postwar Occupation:
Lithography

Walter was drafted in December of 1942 and took his basic training at Camp Roberts, California. He fought with the 28th Infantry Division through Luxembourg and Belgium, was taken prisoner during the Battle of the Bulge, and was a POW for about five months before being liberated by the Russians in April of 1945. He earned the Combat Infantry Badge and was awarded the Purple Heart, Bronze Star, Good Conduct, Prisoner of War, World War II Victory, Presidential Unit Citation, and the European-African-Middle Eastern Medals. Walter returned to the United States in May of 1945 and pursued a career as a lithographer.

Do you remember your first battlefield engagement in the Battle of the Bulge?

Well, we did a lot of night work. You'd maybe lose one or two people. Little skirmishes, you know, but then my biggest battle was just before I got caught. We had been in this town and were pulling rear guard to get the rest of my unit out. As a matter of fact, my unit—the 112th—got a Presidential Citation for doing an excellent job. But in this town of Rogery, Belgium, we held them off, and then we got surrounded. We couldn't get out, and I was captured. There were five of us, and that was a bad experience because we had done a lot of damage. We were trapped in a barn and finally had no choice but to surrender, since the German tanks were already in the town. Then they marched us for days and days with no food and bad sleeping facilities. As a matter of fact, we finally accumulated about fifty other guys, and they put us in this one particular place. I remember we had a big barrel. This is what we did our job in. It was terrible. We picked up lice, and they finally got us to a transit camp called XII-A in Limburg. It was a filthy place, and they put us on a train, and we were on there for about three days. We had a little bucket in the middle of the train for forty people. I never even had a chance to sit down. I was standing all the time, and you had guys urinating and other stuff in the bucket, and it's all over the floor. You're sliding all over, and you get no food. It was just horrible, horrible. But we finally got to a camp called IV-B in Mühlberg, and that's where I finally ended up, in the British compound. And there's nothing more frightening than when you're interrogated by the Germans, and don't think they're not smart, because they are. And when they interrogate you, their pants have got creases like a razor, and they're sharp as a tack, and they know more about you than you do. I was interrogated three times. I had one guy slap me around a little bit, but that was the only time I had any trouble. Most of them were pretty reasonable.

How long did the interrogations go?

Maybe half hour or an hour. What you were supposed to give, name, rank, and serial number, when I told that to one officer, he rapped me across the head and reached for his gun. Why, I was so demoralized and so weak at the time, I couldn't do anything anyway. He said every soldier knows what outfit he's with. So forget that stuff they tell when you're in New York, he said to me, "You're in our hands now. We run the show," which is what they do. See all this hokeypokey, they can break you anytime they want to. People say, "Well I can hold out." Well, you can't hold out. They can break you, and no human being can hold out forever. And there's nothing you can do. You hold out as long as you can, and that's all you can do.

Did they feed you?

Let me tell you, when I came home out of a prison camp when I was released, I weighed less than 100 pounds, from 165. When the Russians liberated my camp, an Englishman and myself went out on our own, and there were thousands and thousands of people on the highway. People with their babies, all different nationalities. You're looking for food. You're trying to survive. You're worn out. You're demoralized. See all of these John Wayne movies are not like real battle. That was April 23, 1945. All I know was in the morning, there were no more guards, and a British guy named Paul Ginney and I just walked out. Well, I was out on my own for about three weeks. The Englishman left me after about probably a week or so, two weeks maybe, and I was sleeping in different barns and villages and village homes, and eventually I got to the American line.

What was your impression of the lines of communication during the Bulge?

I think it was pretty well chaos. From what I can remember, it seemed like nobody knew what the hell they were doing. What really won the Battle of the Bulge was groups of five, ten, fifteen guys, 'cause they delayed the Germans long enough that we could regroup. In our case, we'd blow up little bridges here and there, and that delayed them enough. Don't let anybody ever tell you the German army didn't have the equipment 'cause they had some of the best. They just didn't have enough of it. The Germans were fighting just about the whole world at that time. For every tank we lost, we could replace. But they couldn't replace their equipment that quickly.

Do you remember where you were on Christmas Eve or Christmas Day of 1944?

I was a prisoner of war then. I got caught on December 23, 1944. That was before I hit the camp, and it was miserable out there, because they weren't feeding us. Miserable. There were over 25,000 in the prison camp. But it was a multinational camp. There were Poles, Russians, French, English, Indians. There were Danes, but the Danes had it good because they were trying to make them a model, so they were getting fed. We would strive to get even potato peelings. And the only bath I had was when I first came in. They'd clean us up a little bit, and they'd make you sit there and they'd swab you down with disinfectant and you're full of lice by then. You never got rid of the lice all the time you're in the prison camp. And the best break I ever got was, I got a half of a Red Cross parcel, and another time I think I got a quarter or an eighth, which didn't amount to much.

Walter Dayhuff

Walter was drafted in November of 1943 and took his basic training at Camp Fannin, Texas. He went overseas to Scotland on August 25, 1944. Walter earned the Combat Infantry Badge and was awarded the Bronze Star, Battle of the Bulge Medal, Good Conduct Medal, World War II Victory Medal, Army of Occupation (Germany) Medal, and the European–African–Middle Eastern Campaign Medal. Walter returned to the United States in 1945 and pursued a career at Pevely Dairy.

Date of Birth:
August 1910

Place of Birth:
Beecher City, IL

Military Assignment:
28th Infantry Division, 110th Infantry Regiment

Military Duties:
Infantryman

Highest Rank Achieved:
Sergeant

Postwar Occupation:
Pevely Dairy Route Foreman

Describe how your troops stopped the German counterattack at the front lines.

In Clervaux, Luxembourg, we received orders to advance till we met the enemy. We went up a hill, but there were too few of us. It was early morning, and we could see the Germans coming down the other side; then it all broke loose. The field was full of heavy clay that sucked at my shoes; I fell down. When I finally stood up, there was a German soldier coming at me. Fortunately, he surrendered, so I turned him in and went back to fighting. That night we pulled back, and I and another guy were on lookout. After dark, we heard tanks going down the road behind us.

I told the commander so they cut all communications to us. All of the houses in the nearby town were burning. A female from one of the houses said she wanted protection, but our commander wouldn't let her stay.

We tried to infiltrate the enemy's line during the night. We slid down hills, waded streams, and crossed a ravine. Everyone was quiet. After the enemy went by, we crossed the road to some trees where we stayed until morning. We ventured out but were surrounded by Germans. It was rough staying "friendly" with them and not getting captured. We managed the first day, but in the evening we topped a hill—plop into a German company. They fired some shots. We surrendered.

Describe your imprisonment.

The Germans took us nearby and told us in English to sit. That night they took us to a barn with a hole in the roof. I tunneled in the hay for warmth but that didn't work. The next morning we ate, which was my last food for some time. We were put on a train that went to a place by the Baltic Sea. It was cold, but we were not mistreated.

We survived. Eventually, we took a train to a camp in Clervaux. They asked for a volunteer for a *Schneider* (tailor). I volunteered, so I stayed in the barracks while the others went on detail. The rations were a handful of potatoes for breakfast and flour boiled with water. It tasted pretty good. Some fellows wanted to escape. We tried to dissuade them, but they didn't listen, and the next morning they were lying in the rain, dead. We decided we were safer together in the camp. We were there for five months; then we were loaded on trucks. We rode into the evening. Suddenly the trucks stopped; the guards disappeared. We were on our own. It was raining so we found some trees and slept there overnight.

The nearby village had surrendered to the Germans, and we were shot at by a drunken reveler. Next, we crossed a bombed bridge. We finally hopped a train and rode all day to unknown destinations. We saw German tanks and armor, but they didn't stop us. We finally got into Luxembourg; they were still fighting. We saw a guy sitting, his hands behind him being shot. We just kept going.

We met a guy who took us to his apartment. He fed us; the first food we'd had for some time. He wanted to come to America, but we didn't know how to do that. During that night in his apartment, we heard people next door captured. Finally, we got to Camp Lucky Strike and were there a few days. We heard we could go to Paris, so four of us went. Paris was not very good until we found a refugee camp. It was heaven in the midst of hell: There were tablecloths, bands playing, everyone having fun. To get out of Paris, two of us hopped a freight car. We rode back to Camp Lucky Strike and stayed there until transportation home.

Karl Das

Karl enlisted in 1942 and took his basic training at Camp Crowder, Missouri. He went overseas in June of 1944 and landed in Liverpool, England. He crossed the Channel in December, landing in Le Havre, and went up the Seine to Rouen, where he was assigned to the XIX Corps and 2nd Battalion (9th Army under Montgomery). He served with the 3257th Signal Service Corps through France, Holland, and Germany. Karl was awarded three Overseas Bars, the World War II Victory Ribbon, American Theatre Medal, and three Battle Stars (Ardennes, Rhineland, Central Europe). He returned to the United States in March of 1946 and pursued a career as a brewer at Anheuser-Busch.

Date of Birth:
April 1918

Place of Birth:
St. Louis, MO

Military Assignment:
9th Infantry Division, 3257th Signal Service Company

Military Duties:
Radio Intelligence

Highest Rank Achieved:
Technical Sergeant

Postwar Occupation:
Brewer at Anheuser-Busch

What would you do for radio intelligence on an average day in France?

As radio intelligence, we were always on a five- or ten-hour notice that we had to move, as the front changed. We stayed back so that we could not get hit. We had our radios, and we had two antennas in little outhouses, bona fide outhouses on wheels. Inside each outhouse we had an antenna coming down through the roof like a protractor, and we had a map underneath there. We had three locations, two of these outhouses, plus the main group that we had back wherever

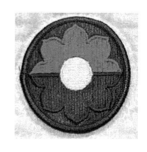

we were bivouacked. So we had triangulation from all three, and it would come over here and point where that guy was operating.

Radio detection.

That's what we were. And they, in turn, would copy down these messages, and someone was in there breaking these codes down as much as they could. We only could hold them for so many hours, and then they had to be forwarded back to the battalion; the battalion forwarded it back to headquarters or whatever we were, the 5th Army or 9th Army, whatever it was. They would always look for us to try to get us, because we were the ears of the Army. There was never a dull moment.

What was one of the more unusual conversations that you listened to?

Well, they were just giving numbers to their German divisions and that, whether it was asking about coffee or food or something like that. But we would circle them all. And one day one of these radio operators came up and said, "I think I've got something." And he said, "I've got this Kraut who is getting quite interested in talking to me." So we followed his code, and while he was talking he was practicing how to get that decoded. And he finally got this guy to open up. Well, this German Panzer outfit was going to push right up to the Rhine, right where we were moving up to. And this kid got a Silver Star out of that.

Did you ever run across any German radio equipment?

In some of the towns, the Germans would put their telephone equipment in the basement, sometimes three stories down, so they were shielded from the bombs. Or it might be in a farmhouse, right out in the middle of a field. And if you went into a barn and went downstairs about three floors, they had it hidden down there.

Did you get along well with your fellow soldiers?

See, we were in the back. We weren't the front line; we were the ears for the support troops. We worked as a group, and everybody helped one another, so if you got in a bind somebody would help out. Like I would come in and try to help them out on breaking the code. We weren't as regimented like you were being a riflemen and that, because we were a service organization. But I gave them a free hand, and they did the best that way. They weren't just clamping down—you can't do this and that. And they'd always work with you. If they got through early, they would ask, can we help you out; we always wanted to work together.

Richard Lindsey

Richard was drafted in June of 1944 and went to Ft. Bragg, North Carolina, for basic training. He went overseas on the *Aquatania*, the sister ship of the *Lusitania*, landing in Scotland. After going by train to Southampton, he went across the Channel to Le Havre and joined the 99th Infantry Division as a replacement just after Christmas.

Military Assignment:
99th Infantry Division, 924th Field Artillery

Military Duties:
Wireman; Lineman

What did the veterans of the 99th Division think about having a novice replacement join their unit?

Well, I was treated all right, but you were the low guy on the stick. If guard duty came up from two to four in the morning or four to six in the morning, you were the one that got it, not the older fellows. You're going to get broke in one way or the other. I was a lineman, a wireman in Headquarters Battery, and we had a three-quarter-ton pickup truck, which had a wire reel on it. When they needed a line laid from A to B, we'd go out and lay that line. Whether it's climbing the poles or running through the fields or whatever had to be done, that's what we did. I never really had what you'd call battlefield engagements like the infantry did.

Did the wire get severed during combat very often?

Oh, yeah. One night it happened about six times, and it was our tanks that cut the wire. We laid it through the field into a town and the tanks came up and cut across the field. So we moved the line further into the field, and they went further into the field. They kept cutting us all off, all the way off until the corporal had said, "Let's lay it down the railroad tracks, ain't nobody there, no trains, no nothing." So we took that three-quarter-ton truck and ran down the railroad tracks and laid the wire in between the tracks, and it stayed in all night.

What were the moments where you felt you might have been in the greatest danger?

One time we were laying wire in some town, and they started shelling the town, so we bailed out and went into a basement. When we came out, the tires on the three-quarter-ton truck were all flat. The spare tire on the side of the driver's side had a piece of shrapnel that was about a foot long and about six inches wide stuck right in the top of the tire. Then another time, when the war was almost over, I was up on the pole, and I had a bullet go through my belt. I was hanging on the back of the pole tying a line in, and a bullet went through the belt, and that was one of the closest ones I had in.

Did the weather make the poles too icy or anything?

No, no. Well, you had the spurs on, and you make sure you embed them into that pole when you go up there, or your tree, whatever you're climbing. We did a lot of tree-climbing, too. You'd just grab ahold of that pole and go up the pole. Just like they do out there at Bell Telephone; you'll see them guys walking up the pole, doing the same thing. That's exactly what I did.

How did you cope with the cold weather?

Shivered like the rest of them. Well, I was with the artillery in B Battery. The Number 2 gun crew. They kind of took me in because they had a big hole dug up, and they had a little five-gallon gas can they cut up. They turned it into a little stove they put some coal in. It warmed us up a little, but it wasn't that bad there. I mean, we were not stuck out in the cold like the Infantry were.

What do you think was the greatest lesson you learned from your military experience?

Follow orders. Do the right thing. That's right. If you have to do something, you do it. If you think it's wrong, say so, but you do the job.

William Pilger

Bill was drafted in 1943 and took his basic training at Camp Maxey, Texas. He went overseas on the *Queen Elizabeth* and landed in England. Bill crossed the Channel in September of 1944 and landed at Omaha Beach. He served with the 9th Army through France, Belgium, and Germany in a variety of capacities involving communications. Bill was awarded the Good Conduct Medal, World War II Victory, Battle of the Bulge Medal, American Defense Medal, and the European Theatre Ribbon with three Battle Stars (Northern France, Ardennes, Rhineland). He returned to the United States in 1946 and pursued a career as a carnival roustabout.

Date of Birth:
August 1925

Place of Birth:
St. Louis, MO

Military Assignment:
9th Army, 758th Field Artillery Battalion

Military Duties:
Field Lineman, Telephone Operator/Switchboard for Field Artillery

Highest Rank Achieved:
Private

Postwar Occupation:
Carnival Roustabout

Did the training you had in basic training prepare you for the battlefield conditions?

Before I went into the service, I didn't know how to run a telephone line. That was my main job. I was a field lineman, telephone operator, switchboard. They taught me how to tear one up and down and put it back together. But nobody's ever prepared to get shot at. During basic training, everything was just kind of routine. Didn't know I was in a war until I got over

there and somebody started shooting back. Our closest experience was in Aachen. I was hanging on a telephone pole, putting in some wire, and the pole chipped out in front of me like that. You never saw a monkey get off of a telephone pole as quick as I got off of that one. So when I got down to the bottom, my buddy said he almost died laughing. He said, "You ran for fifteen minutes before you finally realized that you were still attached to that pole." But I guess that's about as close I ever come to getting shot. And I've often wondered if that sniper setting up there in that window, if he died laughing or one of my friends shot him.

What role did the weather play in the Battle of the Bulge?

It slowed things down; that was about all. I think if it hadn't have been for the ice and the snow, if it had been pretty weather, they might have overrun us and never slowed down. But they couldn't move any faster than we could, and we had these guys up on the front line that wouldn't give up. We lost a sister battalion—a 155 Howitzer Battalion. Most of them were either captured or killed, and they were right next to us. So we learned to appreciate one another pretty much after that. I put a fireplace in our bunkhouse. I had a fireplace, a regular fireplace—made out of a five-gallon can. The inside of it was cut out, had a chimney that went up through all the dirt. It was just like home. As a matter of fact, sometimes it was better than the home I left to go over there. I could walk around that thing anywhere and never see a glow from a fire. And trying to stay warm, I just kept digging a bigger hole. Then we went out and chopped down some trees. One thing I learned about chopping down a tree, hit it with something first, cause soon as you hit it with an ax, all that snow and stuff up there will knock you over when it comes down. It knocked me down a couple of times before I realized I was making a mistake.

How were the lines of communication during the Bulge?

It was helter-skelter. We had one bad situation at the Hurtgen Forest, when an 88 knocked out the lines. I traced my line down to where the lines were knocked out, and there must have been seven or eight other lines crossing there. So I met guys from other units I had never seen before, because they were in the same situation. The problem was, I had my wire in my hand, but which one of them other wires out there went to my forward observer? So we had a good chat, and each one of us got a telephone line and we identified ourselves, and we finally got communications back in.

Leo Rufkahr

Leo was drafted in early December of 1941 and took his basic training at Camp Roberts, California. He went overseas on the *Alexander* and landed in England in April of 1944. Leo crossed the Channel on July 7 and served with the 35th Infantry Division in the Normandy, Northern Europe, Ardennes, Rhineland, and Central Europe campaigns. He was awarded the Good Conduct Medal, Bronze Star, and the European Theatre Service Medal with five Battle Stars. Leo returned to the United States in October of 1945 and pursued a career as an electrician.

Date of Birth:
October 1919

Place of Birth:
Wellston, MO

Military Assignment:
35th Infantry Division, 216th Field Artillery HQ

Military Duties:
Communications Chief

Highest Rank Achieved:
First Sergeant

Postwar Occupation:
Electrician

After training, what was your assigned task?

Because I was an electrician, I was put in the wire section. We ran all the telephone wires and such, and I got a lot of that training in California. We had to run wires to each battalion and then the forward observers up in the front lines, all that stuff. They made me a staff sergeant, or a wire sergeant. And I was a wire sergeant through most of the war, and then right before I went across the pond, the communications chief says, he got on a bender, and I had a bottle of whiskey in my locker, and he told me to keep it locked up. Never give it to him. But he kept raising Cain with me about pulling rank and everything, so I finally gave it to him. Next day, he was yelling, and they really rode me about that, getting him drunk and then taking his job. But he did it himself; he kept after me so I just gave it to him. So the next day I was communications chief. And I was communications chief all the way through the war, until the end of the war, and the first sergeant, then he went home on points, so I took his job as first sergeant.

Would your task be more repairing damaged phone lines, or were you laying new cable as your unit advanced?

We were doing both. If the wire got knocked out, we'd have to repair it, but we were moving up, so we had to keep going. We were supposed to pick up a lot of the wire, but we didn't have time for that. The wire came in half-mile spools and one-mile spools, and we had to get that laid to each battalion and then up to the 320th Infantry. And we had to run forward observer lines for the forward observers. That was a rough job. When you got up real close to the enemy lines, they didn't like that too much, and they let you know it. By shooting at you or shelling you or anything to keep you down. See, the forward observer was way up front with the infantry and right up there at the front lines. They had a lot of firepower and this, that, and the other. The Germans tried to keep you down as much as they could, because they knew if you got your communications in, you'd knock them out. So we had to keep communications going, and we did the best we could with what we had.

It seems that you would be at a more dangerous exposed position than many of the riflemen, because you had to move out in the open.

Yeah, that's right. We laid wire with chains on four-wheel Jeeps and go right across the field laying wire. 'Cause it was shorter if you get away from the roads. But our wire wasn't as good as the German wire. The German wire, they had plastic, and we had rubber. That plastic they had on their wire was really hard, but a tank could run over ours and ruin it, but run over theirs, it wouldn't. So they had better wire than we did.

Winston Pendleton

Rusty was inducted in August of 1943 and took his basic training at Ft. Bliss, Texas. He went overseas on the *Seawolf* and landed in Liverpool in October of 1944. He crossed the Channel on December 17 and landed at Cherbourg. Rusty fought with the 11th Armored Division in France, Belgium, Luxembourg, and the spearhead across Germany to Mauthausen, Austria. He was awarded the World War II Victory Ribbon, American Theatre Ribbon, and the European-African-Middle Eastern Theatre Ribbon, European Theatre Service Medal with three Battle Stars (Ardennes, Rhineland, Central Europe). He also received the Good Conduct Medal and SMG Ex-Rifle MM. After spending a year in the Army of Occupation, Rusty returned to the United States in March of 1946 and pursued careers as a route salesman, hospital maintenance, and carpenter.

Date of Birth:
July 1924

Place of Birth:
Maries County, MO

Military Assignment:
11th Armored Division, 575th AAA Battalion

Military Duties:
Cannoneer on a Half-Track

Highest Rank Achieved:
Sergeant

Postwar Occupations:
Route Salesman; Hospital Maintenance; Carpenter

Do you recall what your first battlefield engagement was in the Battle of the Bulge?

They set us up in position to guard against airplanes, and then the whole company took off and over two hundred guns—rifles—firing all at the same time. I'd been on the firing range many times, but I'd never heard a noise that big. They started across the field, and the enemy was only fifty yards away. I saw guys getting hit, and I didn't understand what was going on. After all that training, watching movies, watching everything, and I didn't understand; still didn't soak in what was happening. Then a whole convoy of ambulances pulled up by us. And I thought, gee, why do they need all of them? Well, before the day was over, I found out. The fighting moved down the hill, and there was a lot of stray bullets coming our way from the enemy, and so the fighting moved down, farther down the hill. Then they began hauling the wounded up on Jeeps, laying a couple of stretchers across the back of a Jeep and bringing them up. That was an unbelievable experience. I saw many, many wounded that day, and my division book says there were 100 killed and 117 wounded at that time. We didn't win that battle that day, because there's 220 men in a company usually, and the only ones left were the guys in the tanks and us sitting back on the half-tracks and the in-between people. That battle lasted for a day and a half.

Describe your experiences in liberating the concentration camp and how that happened.

In March of 1945, we approached the city of Linz, Austria, and our division was recorded as going the deepest into enemy territory. This was Mauthausen, which was eight miles south of Linz; there was a wall across the valley, it seemed like. It had the big German eagle up on it, and I had no idea of what it was, but when it was opened, it was this small city, a concentration camp. We found out later that most every European nationality was in there, except Germans. It was chaotic and the Holocaust for sure. I was back that afternoon with people that I didn't even know. They just picked me up in a Jeep, and we went there. They hadn't started doing anything with it as yet; no way that they could, and the bodies were stacked like cordwood in the streets of that complex. There were cabins on either side of the streets, and there also was a rock quarry there that they were being worked in. I don't know what they needed with stone during the war, but they were starving to death or dying at a rate of more than two hundred a day. They had ten ovens going to burn the bodies. What I saw at that time was a glimpse of the number of bodies that were lying in the street in stacks. So I had no desire to research any deeper than that. But I do know that Patton had the people from the towns of Mauthausen and Linz come out and see this, because as I understand it, the civilians didn't want to admit that they knew anything about this. But ultimately, it took thirty-five days for a division of people to clean this up. And they found more than 31,000 dead bodies. Being a rock quarry, they had the quarry stacked full; they had mass graves outside of the camp, and the town fathers were forced to come out and look at this. They came out in their white shirts and suits for some reason. These were older men who were too old to be in the war, and they were handed a shovel and made to open up some of those graves to prove to them what was there.

Did you actually enter this city, as you call it?

I'd walk through the entrance of that wall and to see these stacks of bodies, and there were gallows and a firing squad wall and things of that nature, and people just looked like skeletons walking around. I totally lost compassion. It was so horrible that I could not have human compassion to what I saw. I just wanted to get away from there. It wasn't an emotional thing, it was just a nightmare of a dream from which you could not awaken. You just wanted to get away from it.

So then you went in, and then you left and didn't have to go back?

Yeah. I don't know if it was the military government forces, but anyway there was a division of people who moved in. I don't know for sure, but I don't think the American soldier cleaned it up. I think that they guarded German prisoners to do that chore. We were the first to find it. And I mean liberate it because we did. It was astounding that the guards that they had there were German women. This large woman was managing the place as I remember it.

They were all dressed alike, and they were taken into custody, I'm sure. We were at Gallneukirchen, which was nine miles east of there, where we stopped our fighting. I saw more than I would have liked to have seen there, and I'm not an authority on any part of it, but the pictures that I have shown you this morning were taken that morning by a friend of mine who is in this organization (Gateway Chapter, VBOB) now. Fifty-some years later he gave me a set of those pictures. Some of them that you will see are the actual operation of the ovens. It shows men standing in front of the oven with a body lying on a steel stretcher. It's just a big gas pit closed in, and they simply put them on this steel stretcher and pushed them into the oven.

Joseph Trimberger

Date of Birth:
December 1924

Place of Birth:
St. Louis, MO

Military Assignment:
75th Infantry Division, 730th Field Artillery

Military Duties:
Artilleryman

Highest Rank Achieved:
Corporal

Postwar Occupation:
Warehouse Worker

Joe was drafted in March of 1943 and took his basic training at Ft. Leonard Wood, Missouri. He went overseas on the *Queen Mary* and landed in England in October of 1944. Joe crossed the Channel shortly thereafter and fought with the 75th Infantry Division through France, Belgium, Holland, and Germany. He earned the World War II Victory Medal, Good Conduct Medal, two Overseas Bars, and the European-African-Middle Eastern Service Medal with three Battle Stars (Ardennes, Rhineland, Central Europe). Joe returned to the United States in January of 1946 and pursued a career as a warehouse worker.

Do you recall your first battlefield engagement during the Bulge?

Well, being in the artillery, your job was to fire. When they called for support, you have to be on the team, go. And we did pretty well. We were in one position, and they wanted rapid fire, so we fired three rounds, and the observer called back, said we only want one gun firing. Well, we put three shells in the air. The time the first one hit, the second was going, we were loading the third, and it was on its way. And that was one of our better times.

Describe the snowfall and things like that?

Well, it came down in big flakes, and it was quick, and it snowed that evening into the night. We got up the next morning, and there must have been two feet of snow, and out in the field you could see it looked like somebody had pie-plates, and they threw them out in the snow, and those were your land mines. We didn't get a chance to bury them because we were pushing, and we knew where they were, so we didn't have to worry about them.

Are there any individuals, either fallen or otherwise, that you wanted to pay tribute to for a role that they played during the Bulge or during a given combat scenario?

We only lost five guys, and they were messing with the land mines, which were booby-trapped. They were our ammunition carriers, and the booby trap got tripped, and it was on an Italian box mine. Those were our casualties right there. We didn't get strafed or bombed; I guess we were lucky.

What were they trying to do with the land mines, just disable them?

Well, we were in the position, and the first lieutenant comes along. They put the old buzzer out, and they found one, so they were going to disconnect it instead of doing what they're supposed to do, call in and tell them we got mines. They didn't do it. They didn't bother putting tape around it or anything, and it was booby-trapped. And it wasn't in a road; it was up in a farm. You drove in, and it was off in a section where you were taking a chance of getting blown up. But we never had any problems. We didn't have artillery coming in, nothing. We were sending it out, but we weren't receiving any.

Was there ever a time when you heard news from headquarters or something happened that made you more determined to defeat the enemy?

Not really. My attitude was, get rid of them, I had no problems with that. The only time I think that really got us mad, we went into a Displaced Persons Camp, and you can't imagine the sight. We opened the gates, and the people would peek out, then we would open the doors, they would run all over you and grab you and hug you and kiss you and all that, 'cause you saved them. And then, they smelled bad. We'd smell bad, but they did too, only worse. All I know is that we opened the furnace doors, and some of the bodies were cremated, hidden somewhere, and everybody in charge was gone.

Carl Light

Date of Birth:
April 1924

Place of Birth:
Bunker, MO

Military Assignment:
10th Armored Division, 61st Armored Infantry Battalion

Military Duties:
Antitank Platoon

Highest Rank Achieved:
Sergeant

Postwar Occupation:
Auto Mechanic

Carl joined the service in March of 1943, took his basic training at Camp Polk, Louisiana, and spent some time in the ASTP before receiving further training at Camp Gordon, Georgia. He went overseas on the *General Black* and landed in Cherbourg, France, on September 23, 1944. Carl fought with the 10th Armored Division through France, Luxembourg, Belgium, Germany, and Austria. He earned the Combat Infantry Badge and was awarded the Bronze Star, Good Conduct Medal, World War II Victory Medal, American Campaign Medal, European-African-Middle Eastern Ribbon with three Battle Stars (Ardennes, Rhineland, Central Europe). Carl returned to the United States in January of 1946 and pursued a career as an auto mechanic.

Can you describe the conditions in the Battle of the Bulge?

Well, I thought I was going to freeze to death. It was cold, cold, cold. And for some reason we were dismounted and walking; we usually went in the half-track. We had on those old GI overcoats, and they stopped us and said everybody throw their overcoat in the Jeep, and you could pick it up later. Well, something happened to that Jeep, and we never did find it again. I guess the Germans found it before we did. So that was the end of the overcoats. I think they may have gotten us some later on, but we didn't have weather equipment at all. We had the regular leather GI boots, and you know this is very cold weather. Well, you huddled down, and at night you put your blanket over your head, no matter where you were, sitting in your half-track or in a foxhole, you put your blanket over your head because you can't sleep if you are breathing cold air. So you get that cover over your head, and pretty soon you would doze off.

How were you received by the German civilian population?

Just the way we were received in France. The German people, for them the war was over when we came, which made it good. But it was bad for the people because I suppose everybody had lost some members of their family, and many of them had their houses knocked down. They're pretty much the way we are, you know. We used to take prisoners, and in the latter part of the war you take a lot of prisoners. And some days they'd leave you to guard the prisoners. So you got your pack of cigarettes, and you'd pass them around, and most of them were happy because for them the war was over. And they were going to eat better as POWs than they ever ate in their army.

What about Dachau?

Dachau? Oh yeah, we didn't take it, but we were close by, and they needed volunteers, and they said we've taken a POW camp. We want volunteers to go in and help take them out. I thought it was GIs, but when we got up there, it was Dachau, and it was terrible. They kept telling us, don't give them anything, you'll kill them if you give them a piece of candy or something to eat, they were in such bad shape. And they didn't have enough ambulances, so they had to put them in GI trucks, and me and another guy stood there and lifted, you would load a whole truck and never even breathe hard. I don't think a one of them weighed over a hundred pounds. We were there less than a day. Sooner we got out of there, the better.

Was it pretty bad seeing all those malnourished?

It was, it was. Because, and everything was rush-rush, see they were afraid the Germans would bomb or shell it to set it on fire, to burn the evidence. It was bad news. 'Course all over Europe we run into these displaced persons, people from all over Europe were there. Some of them was farm workers or factory workers, several of them were farm workers, and you'd move through that area, well right, here they'd come, and we'd feed them, sometimes one would hang around for four or five days. It was bad.

Ralph Forys

Date of Birth:
December 1925

Place of Birth:
Madison, IL

Military Assignment:
26th Infantry Division, 104th Infantry Regiment

Military Duties:
Antitank Gun Crewman

Highest Rank Achieved:
Sergeant

Postwar Occupation:
Packaging Specialist

Ralph was eighteen years old when he was drafted right after he graduated from high school in 1944, and he was shipped to Camp Hood, Texas, for basic training. He took approximately six weeks of infantry basic, and the remainder of the seventeen weeks was spent in antitank training. Ralph went over as a replacement on the *Queen Mary,* landed in Glasgow, Scotland, and went down to Southampton, England, before crossing the Channel and landing at Le Havre, France. He fought with the 26th Infantry Division through Luxembourg, Belgium, Germany, Austria, and Czechoslovakia. Ralph earned the Combat Infantry Badge and was awarded the Bronze Star, World War II Victory Medal, European-African-Middle Eastern Campaign Ribbon with three Battle Stars, Good Conduct Medal, and the Army of Occupation Medal. Ralph was discharged from service in June of 1946 and pursued a career as a packaging specialist at the Defense Contract Administration Services Region in St. Louis.

Describe your first battlefield experience.

We loaded in trucks with our antitank in tow, and our mine layers went through there first and cleared a path in this woods, through the snow. The trees were cut down man-height from all the shrapnel that went through the woods. As we were going through the woods, our truck stopped. It felt like we were running over logs from the trees, and then I looked over the side and saw that we were running over frozen, dead German soldiers; their heads were sticking out from the wheels. And then we went into Wiltz, which had been cleared out by a unit before us.

We were to take this town the next day, and they said that we were going to stay in some German trenches. And I remember going over the German line. Right before I got there, I heard shots, and there was a GI killed right before I got there. And he was lying directly outside, and basically I examined my conscience that night. The stars were out, the moon was real bright, and I said to myself, "Am I going to be like him the next morning? What am I doing here?" So the only thing I could remember was I was there because of my sister, my mother, and dad back home. That was the only reason I could give myself. The next morning we loaded on a Sherman tank, the lead tank, with a lieutenant in charge. Sergeant came to me, and he loaded me down with bandoliers of ammunition, and my nickname was Pollock. And I'll never forget him saying, "Pollock, take care of yourself."

There were another two guys from my squad: one on the machine over the turret and another one on the other side. So we're going down this road, and the lieutenant had his hatch open just a little bit, and he told his driver to cut off to the right through this woods. And I thought, "What's wrong with this guy?" You run over them like kindling wood. And all of a sudden a branch came out and hit me across the nose and because it was down below zero, and I thought my nose was broke. I was bleeding. Finally, it stopped, and all of a sudden I see a huge fence in front of us. Off to my right was a barn, and off to the left was a house. And we went through the fence, and as we're going by the barn, I noticed the door was open approximately two or three feet. I didn't pay attention, and we got down just before, and the third tank behind us stopped, locked his tracks, turned around, and faced the tank to the barn. And they shot up the whole side of the barn with the .30 caliber machine guns on the tank. Out fell three Germans with a machine gun. Then we went down just a little bit farther, and there was a road out there, and off to the right we started down this road. All of a sudden I look way up ahead, and there was a German pillbox. When we got within a certain distance of the pillbox, the lieutenant opened his hatch just a little bit and he says, "Soldiers, take that pillbox." Well, I had my idea of what I thought of him, take that pillbox. He said, "We'll give you protection from the rear." Well, yeah, protection was .30 caliber machine guns from our back.

So we got off the tank, and the three of us said, what are we going to do? One of us could speak a little German. He got off to the right. My deal was to get over the opening of the pillbox and the other one to the left of the pillbox. So we made it around to the back and over, I got over the pillbox door, and with that he told them to come out in German, this buddy of mine. And the first one came out, and he looked up, and he saw me with hand grenades in my hands. And his eyes got big as half dollars, I guess. Then my buddy hollered, bring the rest of them out. Bring the rest of them out. And they hesitated, and they hesitated. And I did pull the pin on the grenade, and he hollered to them to come on out. And they came on out. Now, I don't remember exactly, we got eighteen or nineteen prisoners out of this pillbox. And just as soon as we got the prisoners out of the pillbox, here comes the lieutenant in the leading tank. He got out, and he says, "We'll take care of these prisoners right." Now I never got any of my medals or nothing from World War II, until 1983, when I got a box from Philadelphia, when they brought my records up to date, and they sent me all my medals. So in there was enclosed a Bronze Star, so basically I don't know what the Bronze Star was for, I understand that somebody says something about us putting in, taking all these prisoners in that pillbox. On that, or whether it was based on the Battle of the Bulge. But all I know is they sent me my Bronze Star with my name engraved on the back of it.

Leonard Schneider

Leonard was drafted in June of 1942 and took his basic training at Camp Pickett, Virginia. He went overseas on the *Strathmore* (a British steamer) and landed in England in April of 1944. Leonard crossed the Channel on D+8 and served with the 79th Infantry Division in the Normandy, Northern France, Rhineland, and Central Europe campaigns. He earned the Combat Infantry Badge and was awarded the Bronze Star, the Good Conduct Medal, World War II Victory Medal, and the European-African-Middle Eastern Campaign Ribbon with four Battle Stars. Leonard returned to the United States in March of 1946 and pursued a career in automobile sales (forty-five years). In addition, he was first vice commander of the Catholic War Veterans in Belleville, Illinois, for twenty-two years.

Date of Birth:
June 1919

Place of Birth:
Pinckneyville, IL

Military Assignment:
79th Infantry Division, 313th Infantry Regiment

Military Duties:
Infantry Squad Leader and Maintenance of Vehicles

Highest Rank Achieved:
Technical Sergeant

Postwar Occupation:
Automobile Salesman

Describe your first battlefield engagement.

I was a squad leader at the time, and an officer came by and told me, "Pick out who you feel are your best men and come with me." So we got the squad together, and there was a pillbox, which was dug in so that it blended in with the terrain and the ground. They're firing mortars out of the corner of this pillbox, and those shells were hitting right in the middle of the road. And we're lying in these ditches, and the officer said, "When I give the command jump up and start running and don't stop." So we did that, and we went up this bank, and the first thing I saw was a dead soldier lying there, and it really affected me, but I kept running and we all got behind the pillbox. The officer saw a couple of tanks on our flank, so he called one over, and there was about six-foot double metal doors that entered the pillbox. So he asked them to fire in there and they put in about three rounds, and you know the tanks fired a 75 mm gun, so it just kicked that door open. We had two homemade pole charges; we took about twelve pounds of TNT blocks, taped them together, put a fuse in them, had a stick down to there with a fuse lined up here that you would light, and it would go down and set that off. We took two of them and threw them in on the open door of that pillbox. The officer give the command, and I was in charge so I had my rifle ready and I went up to that door, so help me there were three live Germans who came out of that pillbox, and they hollered, "Comrade, don't shoot!" So I backed up and let them out, and an officer was over to our flank, and he said, "Don't shoot those guys. I want them over here." So they didn't stop running until they got over to him, and that was the end of the siege.

Were those the first enemy soldiers that you saw?

Yes. And maybe I shouldn't say this, but I thank God that I never had to shoot anybody. I'd still be worried about it if I had. My duty was to keep the battalion vehicles going. I had to see that they were maintained and that they were fueled. Most of the time I would take a Jeep and one of those little trailers and go back to Service Company to get gasoline in these five-gallon cans. Usually, I'd go by myself at night, and I wasn't afraid. I always felt like the good Lord was watching over me. Usually, they'd say, "Service Company's back here. Stay on that road until you find it." And then one time they moved the Command Post before I got back, and I didn't know where they were located exactly. This was in France, where the farms have got big wooden fences along the roads, and so I stopped my Jeep, and I went behind the doors, and all I could see back there was the moon shining beautifully. And I looked up, I was standing right beside a German soldier. I saw the silhouette of his helmet, so I thought, "This ain't no place for me." I got out of there, and I moved on up the street a ways and finally found my way back to headquarters.

At Camp Lucky Strike, France – homeward bound

Courtesy Rusty Pendleton

SERVICE TEAM
QUARTERMASTER

Courtesy Charles Pratt (first row, second from right)

Courtesy George Kottwitz

Courtesy James Kyle

Courtesy George Kottwitz

Courtesy Wilbur Cruse

Courtesy James Kyle

Courtesy James Kyle

Devastation at Aachen. Courtesy Elmer Potzmann

Flushing out snipers. Courtesy Robert Gravlin

Courtesy Ralph Forys, second from right

Germans caught in crossfire. Courtesy Robert Gravlin

Courtesy Robert Gravlin

Dragon's Teeth Siegfried Line. Courtesy Robert Gravlin

Dragon's Teeth Siegfried Line. Courtesy Charles Ryan

Courtesy Speed Barton, at left

Courtesy Glenn Hillgartner

Courtesy Paul Neuhoff

Courtesy Les Korsmeyer

Courtesy Oscar Covarrubias

Belgium, 1944. Courtesy Joseph Keough

Combat patrol, Lammesdorf-Imse, Germany, C Company, 2nd Ranger Battalion, November 1944. Courtesy Charles Ryan

Lasey, France, C Company, 2nd Ranger Battalion, August 1944. Courtesy Charles Ryan

Charles Ryan

Charlie enlisted in December of 1942 and took his basic training at Camp Wallace, Texas, and his ranger training in Plymouth, England. He went overseas on the *Queen Elizabeth* and landed in Southhampton, England, in February 1944. He crossed the Channel on D-Day and landed at Omaha Beach (landed at Dog Green Sector and scaled Point et Raz de la Percee). Charlie fought with the 2nd Rangers through France, Holland, Belgium, and Germany. He earned the Combat Infantry Badge and was awarded two Purple Hearts, Silver Star, Bronze Star, the Good Conduct Medal, and the European Theatre Service Medal with five Battle Stars. Charlie returned to the United States and founded an Aerospace Hydraulic Company.

Date of Birth:
March 1924

Place of Birth:
St. Louis, MO

Military Assignment:
2nd Ranger Infantry Battalion

Military Duties:
Infantry Ranger

Highest Rank Achieved:
Second Lieutenant

Postwar Occupation:
Founded an Aerospace Hydraulic Company

Describe your landing on Omaha Beach.

Well, first off I was terribly seasick. Everybody was sick on the landing craft going in. We got on the craft at twelve at night. The sea was rough, and then we swirled around for several hours and finally made our run into the beach. And everybody was decimated. We lost probably 40 to 50 percent of our men on the beach. We only had a sixty-four-man company, and we landed all by ourselves next to the 116th Regiment of the 29th Infantry Division. This was at the western edge of Omaha Beach adjacent to the Dog Green Sector. We landed all by ourselves. We got up to the beach wall, to the cliffs just west of the Vierville-sur-Mer draw. Our job was to get on top of the cliffs, which we did, but by the first day, of the sixty-four men, we had thirteen men left. After scaling the cliffs, we proceeded west to our designated position at Point et Raz de la Percee to knock out the radar facilities. Once we confirmed that the radar facilities were destroyed by the pre-invasion shelling, we proceeded east, took out sixty to seventy German soldiers who defended a fortified house and then attacked and destroyed the pillboxes and fortifications on the west side of the Vierville draw, which then allowed the 5th Ranger Battalion to overrun this draw. Prior to this, all the companies of the 116th Regiment had taken heavy losses.

What was your first battlefield engagement in the Bulge?

You have to understand what was happening where we were. They were trying to capture the Roer River dams from September until December, and they had lost three divisions going in there. The dams really controlled the whole northern flank of the front of the invasion, and they were afraid the Germans would blow the dams, flood the plain, and catch our army out in the middle of the plain. And that would be disastrous. So we were trying to capture these dams. These dams were in a very hilly section of Germany, which was on the northern flank of the Bulge, and it was heavily defended. There were a bunch of these hilltop fortifications or hilltop towns that were actually forts, if you want to call them that. Well, a regiment of the 28th Division got almost completely wiped out in the process. They lost about six hundred men. They had to pull them off the line and regroup, and it took them a couple of months, and they were thrown down south of us in one of the holding divisions that went to the Battle of the Bulge. They then brought in, I think, the 106th Division. And they had them strung out real narrow. We were a heavy force, a heavy combat force. We had what they used to call the Varsity, which is the 1st Division, the 9th Division, and all those old good divisions, and they were making these attacks on these hilltop towns. And like I said, they were just hard to capture. We captured two or three of them two or three times and then got kicked out. So the Germans swung in south of us, and we had just attacked the towns of, I think, Schmidt, Kesternich, and a few other towns like that, and we were in a holding position, and all of a sudden we heard the Germans were twenty miles behind us. So then we swung around south back to the west and formed a perimeter of defense holding the northern flank.

What was the weather like, and what role did it play in the Battle?

I remember on December 7, we made the attack on Castle Hill and Kesternich. This was a wide division attack. There were two full divisions involved in it. And the weather was getting cold, with intermittent rain and snow. Then all of a sudden it turned real cold, and it got down to 3, 4, 5, 10 below zero. One night, it got down to minus 17, and it was bitter, bitter cold. For us, it probably wasn't as bad as it was for the guys that were fighting, trying to hold off the German offensive. We were in a defensive position, so we could dig in, and we did have the opportunity every once in awhile to get warm, but we lost a lot of guys. I had my fingers frostbitten, and we lost a lot of guys with frozen toes and frozen fingers.

Are there any individuals who impacted your company?

Our company commander, Ralph Gorenson, and our battalion commander until the Bulge, Colonel Rudder. Both were great guys. We weren't like a regular Army unit; we were a close and small unit, so we knew each other pretty well.

What was your most intense battle or firefight in the Bulge?

We attacked Castle Hill, December 7, 1944. It had a four hundred–foot elevation and was just southeast of the Hurtgen Forest. It was a hill town with artillery spotters and was heavily defended. From their position, the Germans could command the whole countryside. Every one of our companies that previously attempted possession lost 70 to 90 percent of their men. We took Castle Hill with less than 125 men. Our success was linked to our artillery barrage while our battalion charged the hill. The Germans had to keep their heads down, but the downside was that some of our GIs were killed from friendly fire with this assault. Although we were victorious, the number of casualties was staggering.

For the 2nd Ranger Battalion, our attack on the town of Schmidt (just south of Bergstein) was one of our most intense firefights in the war.

Johnson Perez

Date of Birth:
February 1925

Place of Birth:
Kirkwood, MO

Military Assignment:
87th Infantry Division, 549th AAA Automatic Weapons

Military Duties:
Artilleryman

Highest Rank Achieved:
Private First Class

Postwar Occupation:
Famous-Barr (Thirty-One Years)

Johnson was drafted in April of 1943 and took his basic training at Camp Edwards, Massachusetts. He landed in Littlecoat Castle, England, in October of 1944, crossed the Channel in December, and served with the 87th Infantry Division in France, Belgium, Luxembourg, Germany, and Czechoslovakia. He was awarded the Good Conduct Medal, two Overseas Service Stripes, and three Battle Stars (Ardennes, Rhineland, Central Europe). Johnson returned to the United States in February of 1946 and pursued a career at Famous-Barr.

What was your training like at Camp Edwards?

It was primarily basic training, and we were attached, at that time they called it the Coast Artillery. But eventually they called it the triple-A, the automatic weapons, antiaircraft automatic weapons. We learned to fire a 40 mm gun, and we used to go out to the ocean and fire our guns out there. We had a seat on each side of the barrel of the gun, and I was on the right side for a while, to sight the target. But shortly after that we got radar, which was a unit by itself, and we had to plug that into the gun. And we would track the target by radar so we didn't have to have two guys sitting on the platform of the gun on the boat, exposed. There were two of us on the radar: There was a loader on the gun and another guy to fire it, and a sergeant telling us what to do. We had to move the dials on the radar thing, but it locked onto the target much better than the visual sighting.

Did you have much combat with German aircraft?

No, not at all, really. When we were in the Saar valley, we didn't do any firing, and we didn't see any airplanes at that time. But when we got into the Battle of the Bulge, the German air force was almost depleted, so they were using us as antitank weapons. We couldn't do much against a Tiger tank, but against a half-track or a weapons carrier, we could do some pretty good damage. And with one of the larger tanks, if you were lucky enough to hit the tracks of the tank a couple of times, then you might be able to stop it. But that generally gave your position away, and the guns they had on those tanks, they could swing them around and fire at you. And another thing, we got bombed by our own airplanes. The weather was so bad during the Bulge and clouds were terrible, and they couldn't see where they were dropping the bombs half the time. But one night we got bombed by our own airplanes. We knew the Germans didn't have the planes, for one thing. And we hadn't seen a German plane for weeks and weeks. Because as I understand it, they didn't even use air power in their offensive in the Ardennes. And finally, we were attached to the 87th Division, the Golden Acorn Division, and we were in Patton's Army, and the 87th Division was one of the divisions that relieved the 101st Airborne at Bastogne.

How did your group of men and your weapon—your 40 mm weapon— move during all this?

By truck and by train. And man, it was so cold. At one point, I had every stitch of clothing I owned on. My fatigue jacket, my overcoat, my raincoat, long johns, everything. After Bastogne we traveled pretty fast through Belgium, down into Germany. We crossed the Moselle, and then we crossed the Rhine, and after we crossed the Rhine, we were attached to the 346th Infantry Regiment, as part of the military government. They were moving so fast, and actually that was some of the toughest fighting we encountered, because we were traveling right with the infantry. But each town that we took, we would set up the government. At headquarters, we knew what people you could trust in the town, so once we took the town over, we would set up the government and stay there for a couple of days and then join the regiment and go to the next town.

Adrian Mead

Date of Birth:
June 1924

Place of Birth:
Ellington, MO

Military Assignment:
87th Infantry Division, 334th Field Artillery Battalion

Military Duties:
Gunner on a 105 mm Howitzer

Highest Rank Achieved:
Corporal

Postwar Occupation:
Printing

Adrian was drafted in 1943 and took his basic training at Camp McCain, Mississippi. He landed in England in November 1944. He crossed the Channel a couple of weeks later and fought with the 87th Infantry Division through France, Belgium, and Germany up to the border of Czechoslovakia. He was awarded three Battle Stars (Ardennes, Rhineland, Central Europe). Adrian returned to the United States in 1945 and worked in printing.

Describe your unit's involvement in the Battle of the Bulge.

We were in the Saar Valley. Our infantry was getting hit pretty hard. We went overseas in November and got into combat the first part of December. And by the time we got into the Saar, the Bulge had broken out. General Patton told Eisenhower he could get him three divisions there in forty-eight hours; we were one of his divisions. So they pulled us off the line, and we loaded on trucks for a cold, long trip, probably four hundred miles or more. And when moving a division, you don't move too fast: little old roads, no superhighways. So by the time we got to Belgium we lost more guys to frozen feet than anything else.

How did you deal with the cold?

For my feet, I took my shoes off and my old pair of four-buckle overshoes, which wouldn't bend in extreme cold anyway. Then I put on all the socks I had. I had an old turtleneck and one of the GI-issue wool turtleneck sweaters. I put half of those around each foot, and then I filled those old four-buckle boots with straw. I wore my boots like that for quite a while.

I even used my shoes as my pillow in my mummy bag. That mummy bag had an outside covering made of wool, and inside you had your blanket. So you zipped the outside up first, and then you zipped the inside. I think we had two blankets when we got over, but I've always thought they took one blanket away. Before you slept, you had to dig a hole.

By the time we got to Belgium, it was really cold and snowing. We pulled into a wooded area that was part of the Ardennes in Saint-Hubert, southwest of Bastogne, way out on the Bulge. And then they ordered us to get our gas masks, which was a waste of time because those old gas masks were frozen and wouldn't fit our faces. Then we had our dinner for the night; I had a delicious frozen can of hash. We stayed overnight. In the morning we headed south and moved into position.

We followed the 345th because we were a combat team, and wherever the infantry went, we went too. Things moved quickly once we got there. Sometimes you wouldn't stay in a position long at all. We were finally positioned a couple of hills from Koblenz. The 345 and the 334th took that town, so we stayed there for a while. We manned the guns 24/7, so we had to break up the section—the chief took half the guys; I had the other half. We had to dig a hole—six-foot-wide by six-foot-square—and then we dug a shelf-like bench where we could sit down. We'd put a pole in the center and throw an old tarp over it. In the hole we even had an old pot-bellied stove where we could build a fire.

Later on, we moved to Soffeld, Germany, where we parked all the guns and trucks and set up a bivouac area. The war had practically ended, so we weren't doing hardly anything. And then for some unknown reason, we had to pack up and move to Plauen, which had been bombed extensively. We would sit there for a while, fire a few rounds, then sit there. We stayed there for a while until the orders came that the war was over, and it was time to move the division out. We packed up and went back to Camp Lucky Strike in France, where we stayed for a few days waiting for a boat. Many men slept in a fifteen-man tent, but after sleeping on or in the ground for a while, sleeping on old cots was difficult. It was so cold at night that I slept on the ground as close to my cot as I could get.

Phillip McKnight

Date of Birth:
June 1921

Place of Birth:
Puxico, MO

Military Assignment:
82nd Airborne, 325th and 505th Infantry Regiments

Military Duties:
Paratrooper

Highest Rank Achieved:
Private First Class

Postwar Occupation:
Meat Cutter

Phil was inducted in November of 1942 and took his basic training at Camp Robertson, Arkansas. He volunteered for Jump School at Ft. Benning, Georgia, which he finished and subsequently served as an instructor. Phil was a paratrooper with the 82nd Airborne starting in Casablanca and jumped on the Sicilian D-Day (July 9, 1943), into Italy near Salerno (September 14, 1943), and into Normandy on D-Day (June 6, 1944). Later, he took a glider into Holland during Operation Market Garden in September of 1944. Phil was briefly a prisoner of war before managing to escape with a buddy during the Battle of the Bulge, and he continued on past the end of the war, when he remained in Germany to help in the rebuilding of Berlin. He earned the Combat Infantry Badge and was awarded two Purple Hearts, one Bronze Star Citation, two Presidential Unit Citations, and the European Theatre Service Medal with six Battle Stars. Phil returned to the United States in December of 1945 and pursued a career in the meat-cutting industry.

Describe your jump during the Invasion of Italy.

The invasion of Sicily occurred on July 9, 1943. We left Oujda, French Morocco, in C-47s, arriving at the southern part of Sicily in front of the beach landing of the ground forces. Our priority was to cut off and block the advancing German and Italian forces, preventing them from attacking the Allied beach assault. Part of the beach assault was lead by Patton's armored division. The invasion was Patton's first exposure to the 82nd Airborne, and he was very impressed that we could keep up with his aggressive armored forces. After constant and very difficult skirmishes, the entire island of Sicily was overtaken within about two weeks.

Later, the 82nd Airborne jumped into Italy on September 14, 1943. We entered somewhere around Salerno, under the direction of Colonel Gavin. I remember when my unit was positioned atop a large hill overlooking Hitler's troops, who were in the valley below. The Allied artillery was in place in the valley behind us. The artillery attempted to fire over us on the hill and onto the troops in the valley, but stray shells occasionally hit our hill and took the lives of a few of our own soldiers. One of the shells landed very close to me, and I was affected by the concussion. I wasn't physically hurt, but did become extremely disoriented and was sent back to a field hospital, where it took me a few days to recover. On my return I was reassigned to the 325th Glider Regiment, with whom I stayed until the end of the war.

The airborne divisions proved to be an integral part of the success of the D-Day invasion. Because of our training and recent combat experience in Sicily and Italy, the 82nd was the core airborne division. Our preparation training for D-Day began in Ireland. We stayed there for approximately two months, then transferred to Leicester, England, in early 1944 for additional preparation.

Although no one knew the exact date or time of the invasion, as time passed it became more evident to all of us the time was near. Contact with anyone outside the airbase was not permitted. Special clothing and gas masks were distributed to the troops. The clothing had been treated with a chemical, which was supposed to protect us in the event the Germans used poisonous gas. When Eisenhower announced the time for the invasion had arrived, our regiment was assembled on the runway of the airfield in Southern England. Ike actually came and spoke to small groups of troopers. I remember his words were inspiring, but very somber. He warned us many soldiers would not survive this assault.

The 325th Glider Regiment began our assault in the early hours of June 6. Our particular glider had just begun to ascend when we noticed that the nose of the glider was not fastened properly. This was a single plane and glider holding twelve troopers, two pilots, and a lot of equipment. Several of the men tried to refasten the nose while in flight. It could not be done, so we circled and landed back on the airfield while all of the other planes and gliders went on to France without us. After the nose of the glider was refastened and hooked back to our plane, we went to join the other gliders. As our tow plane took us over the shores of Normandy, we began to draw fire from enemy troops, who by this time were well aware the invasion had begun. Instead of taking us to our designated landing zone, our tow plane continued to pull us inland up the coast to escape the firing. Our landing was to be to the right towards St. Mere-Eglise, but our tow plane veered to the north. The pilot eventually told us to release approximately eighty miles from our original landing zone, near Caen, France. We landed in a perfectly flat pasture and rolled to a stop near a wooded area and overtook a lone German soldier.

Once we got our bearings, we determined we were far away from our designated landing area and decided to work our way back to the coast. As we neared the coast, we discovered that the Allied forces had not landed and were still a half-mile offshore. Because we were so far from our original destination, the approaching troops did not know we were friendly. They began to fire on us. Accordingly, we retreated back inland where we waited until the next day.

As the troops came ashore, they began to fire at the pillboxes on the beach. Since we were further inland behind the pillboxes, we also began firing on the boxes from our location. Our combined efforts cleared the enemy in a hurry. The landing troops were perplexed as to why someone would be firing from behind the pillboxes. After the firing calmed down, we sent two individuals waving white flags out to make contact with the Allies, and shortly afterward we joined the Canadian infantry troops until we were able to continue our original mission.

Fighting continued along the beachfronts for several days, preventing us from going out on our own. We stayed with the Canadian troops and helped connect the beachheads. It took us eight days until we rejoined the rest of our company near St. Mere-Eglise. Once back together with our regiment, we carried out our objective, which was to clear out a path across the Cherbourg peninsula. This prevented the Germans from retreating or sending new troops into Cherbourg, which was crucial to the invasion, since it established a secure harbor and docks for fresh supplies and troops to enter.

During September 1944, I went into Holland in a glider landing in Groesbeek, near Nijmegen. The weather turned bad throughout Holland,

and eventually the entire Operation Market Garden Campaign failed. Cornelius Ryan has memorialized this in his book and film, *A Bridge Too Far*. In my opinion, had Patton been in charge instead of Montgomery, we might have been successful. It took the ground troops too long to arrive, and we collectively could not hold the positions. In spite of the mission's failure, my division was able to hold our position for a time over the Waal River. As we held our position over the Waal River, in a real fluke one Luftwaffe plane, so high we could barely see it, was able to score a direct hit of the bridge by dropping a single bomb. The bridge was completely demolished. History is filled with incidents like this where one individual is able to overshadow the efforts of many men.

At the start of the Bulge, the Allies had only two divisions in reserve at this time, the 101st Airborne and the 82nd Airborne. Both divisions were immediately called back to duty and sent to Belgium and Luxembourg. We loaded up in trucks and were told to move out until we found the enemy. By the next day, we encountered German troops, so we set up a line and began to engage in combat. Our position was held until the Allies could send more troops to assist.

On Christmas Eve 1944, we had pushed too far into enemy territory, and we were ordered to pull back. After much debate, instead of retreating, we were ordered to "fall back to a more secured position in order to prepare for future advance." For us the phrasing at least sounded better.

Late Christmas Eve, we were very tired from our "repositioning." The group decided to set up a defense in order to rest. My buddy and I drew the first outpost duty, which would be in two-hour shifts. After our time we went back to wake the next two to relieve us. Still weary from the journey, our replacements fell back asleep during their shift. A German patrol came in quietly and began to take us as prisoners one at a time. They had taken five or six by the time they got to me. After my capture I awoke my buddy. The Germans took us about fifty yards into a wooded area. We were wearing our heavy, cold-weather goulashes. Believing the weight of these boots would hamper our mobility, our captors left us with only one guard while the others went back to capture more of our group. The guard could not understand English, so my buddy and I exchanged a verbal plan to jump him. At the appropriate time, I tackled the guard at the feet, while my buddy went for the upper body. He placed his hand over the guard's mouth to keep him quiet. We overtook the guard and began to run. The other Germans spotted us and opened fire. My buddy and I were running awkwardly with unbuckled goulashes but managed to rejoin our unit and fought back until our defensive position was secured. Later Christmas Day, we withdrew back to a better defensive position where things eventually began to quiet down.

Richard Maskell

Date of Birth:
June 1922

Place of Birth:
Chicago, IL

Military Assignment:
2nd Infantry Division, 23rd Infantry Regiment

Military Duties:
Infantryman

Highest Rank Achieved:
Staff Sergeant

Postwar Occupation:
Worked for Warner-Jenkinson, Frigidare, and Hostess Cake

Rich was inducted in July of 1943 and took his basic training at Camp Walters, Texas. He went overseas on the *Queen Elizabeth* and landed in Southampton, England, on July 15, 1944. He crossed the Channel on July 22 and landed at Omaha Beach. Rich fought with the 2nd Division through France, Belgium, and Germany. He earned the Combat Infantry Badge and was awarded the Bronze Star, Good Conduct, American Campaign, European Theatre Service Medal with four Battle Stars (Northern France, Ardennes, Rhineland, Central Europe), World War II Victory Medal, Army of Occupation (Germany) Medal, and a Sharpshooter's Badge. Rich returned to the United States in January of 1946 and pursued a career with Warner-Jenkinson.

Did the training help give you a good idea of what to expect as far as the battlefield conditions?

No, the training helps you to a certain extent, but what we experienced was entirely different than what we were trained for. In the hedgerow country in Normandy, there were mounds of dirt used as fences by the French. And they had weapons on either corner, automatic weapons, and in the middle. And you'd get out in that pen, and they'd fire at you, and you had a terrible time from one hedgerow to the other. Finally, somebody in a tank division decided to put a knife or a bulldozer underneath the tank to push through the hedges, and then we could disperse and get them. But you had to crawl over the hedge otherwise. The tank would have like fingers, and they would weld them on the tank, and they would hit the hedgerow and push it through, and we could run through there. It was very difficult. After you attacked hedgerows all day long, you were very tired. They were maybe five to six, ten feet wide, and then they tapered up to the top. The French didn't have a lot of lumber, so they put those hedges up, and they kept their cattle fenced in that way.

Describe your first battlefield engagement in the Battle of the Bulge.

Well, Elsenborn Ridge was the most important. The Germans were planning the Battle of the Bulge, and we deflected some of their soldiers because we were attacking, which helped us in the Bulge. But then we had to retreat and come back to Elsenborn Ridge, so we dug in and diverted the Panzer Divisions down into a funnel, more or less. We really had to fight hard to keep that. We didn't have an abundance of ammunition, so we were lucky that we could hold it that long. Well, you have to try to do the best you can, and when one of the German officers came at us and said, "Surrender, lay down your arms," well, my BAR man put about ten rounds in him.

What role did the weather play during the Bulge?

The weather was a terrible thing. The fighting wasn't as bad as the weather, because you tried not to freeze to death, and walking in waist-deep snow is no fun. When you are an infantryman, you don't stay warm and dry. You're out in the weather at all times, and you dig a foxhole to keep yourself from being killed with shrapnel and bullets. And then we would get wood or whatever and put that over our foxhole to keep the snow out. But the snow would melt, and your feet would be in water at the bottom of the foxhole. I got frozen feet in January as the Bulge was coming to a close. What we had first was rubber gulashes, and they were cold. Rubber's cold on your feet. Then at the end of the Bulge, they gave us snow packs. Snow packs were leather on top with rubber in the bottom, and there was a pad in each one.

Then the weather changed, went up in temperature, and rained. Water always went through the leather and got into the boots. You were walking in water, and you couldn't light a fire, or you'd be killed. During the Bulge there was no rest period, you had to keep going. Well, I was sent to England with frozen feet in January of 1945, and in the hospital instead of you having the blanket over you, your feet were exposed. Some men's feet were black, and they had to amputate them. They were real bad, 'cause if they become too frozen, the flesh dies, and gangrene sets in.

Was there ever any news you received that made you more determined to defeat the enemy?

Well, the Germans made a mistake by killing the POWs at Malmedy. Oh, I think it was around two hundred. They took them into a field, and they opened up with machine guns and killed most of them. Some of them got away. When the news about Malmedy spread by word of mouth all over the group, we knew that if you were captured, you were going to be killed. So you fought harder, and that helped us win. Malmedy was the thing that helped us stick together more. I don't think the Germans understood that when they killed those men, that the rest of us would fight harder.

What would you say was the most important contribution made by your unit?

At Elsenborn Ridge. We held the line and prevented them from going to Liege and Antwerp. You see, if they had gone to Antwerp, they would have cut off our supplies and split the army, the British and Americans, in two. I was glad that I was in the Regular Army 2nd Division, because they were a very well-run outfit. Well, Regular Army knows all the tricks to get the supplies, and they do a good job. They would get hot food to you when no other ones would. Some cooks would not want to go up to the front. In the 2nd Division, the cooks went to the front. Gave you things once in a while; not all the time, but once in a while.

What were the greatest lessons that you learned from your military experience?

Well, the lesson is, you might say, freedom is not free, and you have to fight for it. That's one of the things I'd say. People don't realize how wonderful the United States of America is. And they take things for granted, and a lot of people made sacrifices to keep it that way. No terrible thing in civilian life is worse than combat. Anyone who thinks that they have it tough, they should go in combat, and they'll realize how wonderful things are.

George Kegler

George was drafted in 1943 and took his basic training at Ft. Leonard Wood, Missouri. He landed in England in July 1944 and crossed the Channel two weeks later. George served with the 97th Infantry Division in France, Germany, and Belgium, earning the Combat Infantry Badge.

Did you feel your training adequately prepared you for combat?

We had good instructions on how to throw a grenade and use different firearms.

How did you learn things to survive on the battlefield?

Our division trainers would take us green recruits and make us understand what was necessary and what we should anticipate will happen.

Where were you stationed?

I was sent to Ft. Leonard Wood, attached to an infantry division. We went overseas together.

After Europe, we anchored at Hawaii, picked up some supplies before going to Japan. We landed, and then the Japanese government surrendered. General MacArthur saw that the men could be reassigned. We were sent back to the States and discharged from Ft. Leonard Wood.

How was the weather?

Europe was cold. We had big, heavy, bulky

Date of Birth:
February 1923

Place of Birth:
St. Louis, MO

Military Assignment:
97th Infantry Division, 303rd Infantry Regiment

Highest Rank Achieved:
Staff Sergeant

Postwar Occupation:
Construction

overcoats. Our feet were wet all the time, and we only had two pairs of wool socks. The veterans taught us how to tie them around our waist to dry and warm them.

Tell us about Christmas 1944.

It was sad, but we did spend some time in houses we borrowed. Somehow they came up with some beer, and food was sent up from the rear, and it was as good as could be expected.

Anything during the war that really saddened you?

The children would come up and beg for something to eat, especially when they saw the chocolate bars that came with our rations. The children were kicked around the most.

Tell us about your most intense battle.

We had one bad one when we took a lot of losses. But our aircraft inflicted a lot of damage on the enemy and saved lives.

Any news from headquarters that helped in defeating the enemy?

You learned to be leery, because by the time you heard the message the information had changed. But towards the end news was coming through great.

Do you recall any moments of comfort?

Somebody would get a letter from home, and he'd pass it around. You didn't know the people, but we'd read the mail. Thinking about home kept you on your toes.

What would you tell future generations?

Work out problems so you don't have to battle somebody overseas.

Were you on one of the beaches in the Battle of the Bulge?

Our ship anchored, and we went over the side. The water was up to here, and you had your rifle. It scared the hell out of me, because the Germans were on a higher plain firing down at you. After that, we were in trucks, then out you ran, getting down, and you'd dig a foxhole like hell because you were pinned down.

Do you mind talking about your war experiences?

It took me a long time to get it out of my system.

Paul Keilholz

Paul was drafted in October 1941 and took his basic training at Camp Roberts, California. He went overseas and landed in Salisbury, England, in October 1942. He fought with the 1st Division and was awarded the European Theatre Service Medal with five Battle Stars (Normandy, Northern France, Ardennes, Central Europe, Rhineland). Paul returned to the United States in October 1945 and worked in auto body repair.

Date of Birth:
March 1920

Place of Birth:
Chamois, MO

Military Assignment:
1st Infantry Division, 183rd Field Artillery Battalion

Military Duties:
Field Artillery Truck Driver

Highest Rank Achieved:
Technician Fifth Grade

Postwar Occupation:
Auto Body Repair

Describe your first battlefield engagement in the Battle of the Bulge.

I was in the artillery, on a 155 mm gun. The sergeant told us that German tanks were about two miles away, and we needed to stop them or they'd capture us. And we had enough firepower to stop them. Headquarters also told us to dig foxholes and be prepared.

Were there any lessons that you learned in that first battle that helped you in future battles?

Yeah, I guess be on the alert and be careful. Our part went smoothly. It was the infantry and the armored tanks that probably had the worst part of it.

Where was your combat division during the Battle of the Bulge?

We were going towards Cologne, but they pulled us out, made us drive all night. The next day, we circled and regrouped close to Bastogne.

What role did weather play during the Battle of the Bulge?

Pretty bad. Cold, icy, snow, and I'd say our outfit was pretty well equipped for it, so we made it okay. The feet were a little problem. You had to watch your feet. It got pretty cold. We just kept walking around stomping, trying to get warm. And the weather was so cloudy for a week before Christmas; the planes couldn't come over, so we didn't have any air support. It was more or less a standstill until after Christmas or Christmas Day. Some of the sky cleared off, and the air support came in, and that really did save us.

Anyone you'd like to pay a tribute to?

Well, I would say all the thousands of men that lost their lives and those guys taken prisoners. That's probably one of the worst things, they were taking prisoners at that time, and then they killed a lot of them before we even got there.

What was the greatest lesson you learned from your military experience?

Work hard and know how to take care of yourself. Join the service. The training is handy if you ever have to use it.

What was your unit's major contribution during the Battle of the Bulge?

We had these white phosphorous shells, which was what we used over the tanks, 'cause they'd have the hatch open, and the shells would burst above them and knock out the tanks.

When were you most afraid?

We were in Salisbury stationed in a hotel, and the Germans were shelling us. One night, the air raid sirens went off; you could hear the bombs hitting the water. They made us get out of the hotel. I got as far as the curb when a shell knocked a hole in a dam forty feet deep by seventy-five feet in diameter but missed the hotel by only forty feet. I tried to crawl under the curb, but a bunch of blocks and bricks hit me in the back. After that I never slept well again. That was just before D-Day.

Glenn Hillgartner

Glenn was drafted in 1943 and took his basic training at Ft. Bragg, North Carolina. He went overseas on the *Louis Pasteur* and landed in Liverpool, England, on November 12, 1944. He crossed the Channel in an LST to Le Havre on November 27 and was among the first group of ships to go up the Seine, landing in Rouen on December 1, 1944. Glenn served with the 87th Division through France, Belgium, Luxembourg, Germany, and Czechoslovakia. He was awarded the Good Conduct, American Campaign, European Theatre Service Medal with four Battle Stars (Northern France, Ardennes, Central Europe, Rhineland), World War II Victory Medal, and German Occupation Medal. Glenn returned to the United States in January of 1946 and pursued careers as a dental technician and illustrator, retiring after forty years of government service.

Date of Birth:
December 1923

Place of Birth:
St. Louis, MO

Military Assignment:
87th Infantry Division, 334th Field Artillery Battalion

Military Duties:
Artilleryman

Highest Rank Achieved:
Private First Class

Postwar Occupations:
Dental Technician; Illustrator

Your experience in the Battle of the Bulge, was it similar at all to what you expected during basic training?

You're not really ready for anything like that. I think the biggest shock is seeing the dead. In civilian life they're always in a funeral parlor and nicely displayed. And it's not like that when you see them on the battlefield. That's a big shock to everybody, but you get over that pretty quick. So you live and learn. Like they said, if you survive two days, you're already a veteran. Mostly, you had to watch out for German artillery. The 88s were pretty efficient, and there were also mortars, booby traps, and land mines. We were far enough in the back that we didn't have to deal with enemy ground troops. We knew what the infantry was going through, and we were very glad to be where we were. But we tried to support them.

We got advice from some men from the 26th Infantry Division, who we relieved on the line. Things like not to be stupid, standing up, or marching across an open field. You don't do that. You keep a low profile, and you dig in. You have to have some place safe to fall when the shells come in. And you hope you don't get any tree bursts. That's when the shell hits a tree above you, and the metal and wood fragments would come straight down. You can't hide from that.

Can you talk a little bit about the role that the weather played during the battle?

When we first hit the Bulge, that's when we hit the snow. We didn't have that further south in the Saar, and it was cold. Anyone who was in that battle, the first thing they mention is the cold. They remember the frozen feet, and it was just plain miserable. And I found this out just a few years ago, that the temperature was 30 and 35 degrees below zero at night. Of course, they never told us, or we would have complained even more, so they kept that quiet. You just knew it was cold. If you took your shoes off you had to sleep on them or they would freeze, and you'd never get your feet in them again. And we had guard duty; you'd get four hours off, but you'd be out there two hours when you're not working. You might be working those four hours and then go on guard duty on top of it. I think I had six months of that straight before the war ended.

I had about two pairs of underwear on, plus my olive drabs and everything else and a coat, sweater, and a raincoat over that. And we had these overshoes—galoshes, they called them. Without that, your feet really got cold since those Army shoes weren't insulated, and so those really helped. But we lived through it. But if a man got wounded, he could freeze to death. So the medics tried to get them back as soon as possible, and they did a good job. But the Germans had the same trouble. Those soldiers remember the same bad weather that we were in.

Is there anything else that you wanted to share about your experiences?

Yeah, one time after we met the British, we went to Hautbellain, a little town in Luxembourg. It was situated on a road, and on one side were about twenty stone houses of the village. They were just on the one side of the road, and up on the hill further was a bigger house. The cows and everything were in the basement to conserve heat in the winter, and the people lived upstairs. We had our trucks spaced apart and full of ammunition, and a couple planes around noon came over our markings, and we waved to them, and then they came back and bombed us. They were planes that the Germans captured in the Bulge, and they were German pilots. One of the bombs hit between two of our trucks, and thank God it was a dud. The other one hit one of the houses in the village. It was the only house not occupied, so that was pretty lucky.

Then another time, we were sent up with A Battery with ammunition, and we had to stay with them for three days. That's when I got in front of the guns and got my ears almost pierced. We stayed with them, but going up there they had shell holes, detours, and everything. When we came back, the detours were gone, and all the roads were fixed up. At nighttime, we're trying to see and get to our battery, and we went up and down this road and couldn't find it, so finally when it got dark Corporal Blackie ran inside to one of the places. It was the 4th Division, and we asked if we could stay overnight with them. And they said, "Oh, yeah, come on in." So we walked in and had our bedrolls, and the first thing they said, "Did you guys eat?" We said, "No." They were all cooks, and boy did they give us a meal. I always have good feelings about the 4th Division since then. Later on, we found out we missed one turn. It was about five hundred yards off this one road, and we forgot about that, and when we pulled in we found out they weren't worried about us. They were worried about losing that truck because they could get replacements for the men, but they couldn't replace that truck. We got back safe and that was the main thing.

Eugene Ganz

Date of Birth:
April 1923

Place of Birth:
Ballwin, MO

Military Assignment:
1st Infantry Division, 18th Infantry Regiment

Military Duties:
Rifleman and Ammunition Carrier

Highest Rank Achieved:
Staff Sergeant

Postwar Occupation:
Sales

Gene entered the military at Jefferson Barracks on August 1, 1944, and trained at Camp Walters near Mineral Wells, Texas. He was sent to Europe in December 1944 and assigned to the 1st Infantry Division as an assistant gunner in an 81 mm mortar crew and fought in Belgium and Germany. Gene sustained shrapnel injuries to his hand and legs, which required hospitalization. He was released from the hospital in England in early May of 1945. He was then selected to form a company to guard German SS troopers in Neustadt der Aisch, Germany. He earned the Combat Infantry Badge and was awarded the Purple Heart, two Battle Stars, the Good Conduct Medal, and the European Victory Ribbon. Gene was discharged in December of 1945 and pursued a career in sales.

What role did the weather play during the Bulge?

They said that the temperatures dropped as low as 41 below zero. The snow and, of course, the bitter cold were big factors in the battle there. We had two pairs of socks, and I put on both of them and the boots—I was fortunate enough to get ahold of a pair of four-buckle overshoes. I wore everything I had. We had good, heavy overcoats. Those were very good, but that didn't protect the hands and feet. The feet were the big problem there. I was also fortunate enough to get ahold of a snowsuit, which was exactly like a rain suit, only it was white. When you put that on over the top of the rest of your clothes, it did protect you a bit more from the wind and held in your body heat.

What was the saddest moment or moments during this battle or during your whole time in the Army?

My father passed away in January 1945, and I was hit a few days later. The German 88 mm shells were exploding in the pine trees overhead, and I was hit twice. I also had two frozen feet and two frozen legs. I realized that I had been hit in the hand and in the heavy part of the leg and heard the shrapnel hit my helmet as the shells exploded in the pine trees above me. At least I was alive. Then on March 21, 1945, I received my first mail, and that told of my father's death.

Were there any moments of comfort or happiness during this battle or during your time in the Army?

In November or December of 1944 and then again in January of 1945, the ladies at home prepared boxes of cookies, and we started to receive those in August of 1945. They were, of course, completely smashed, and in the evening before bedtime we would simply get out a big bowl and dump them in and scoop out a cupful as you would your breakfast cereal and blow out the plastic that some of the cookies were encased in. And then we had something brand-new that reached us in Neustadt der Aisch guarding the SS troopers; we received something called powdered milk. Very delicious. It was the first milk we had tasted in a year's time, and we would put that on these cookies that had been pretty well hardened. Some had some nuts in them and so forth. They had a little fuzz around the edges, but that was all right.

What was the most important contribution made by you or your squad or company during the battle?

It was a constant firefight, and we were always moving forward. We didn't get bogged down in too many places. If we got in a place where we couldn't move forward, we called for a tank to come up and spray it with .50 caliber machine gun fire to help us get through some difficult forest areas.

Vince Freeman

Date of Birth:
June 1923

Place of Birth:
St. Louis, MO

Military Assignment:
83rd Infantry Division, 329th Infantry Regiment

Military Duties:
Intelligence Section (S-2)

Highest Rank Achieved:
Private First Class

Postwar Occupations:
Real Estate, Accounting, Healthcare, Administration

Vin was drafted and entered service in January of 1943, completing his basic training at Camp Roberts, California. He spent time at Camp Carson and Ft. Meade before going overseas in July of 1944 and spent some time in Southampton, England, before crossing the Channel to Le Havre. He joined the 83rd Division just south of St. Malo as a replacement in July of 1944 and fought with them in Normandy, Southern France, Belgium, Holland, Luxembourg, and Germany. Vin earned the Combat Infantry Badge and was awarded the Purple Heart, Bronze Star with cluster, Good Conduct Medal, Presidential Unit Citation with cluster, Army of Occupation, World War II Victory Medal, and Battle Stars for the Normandy, Ardennes, Rhineland, and Central Europe campaigns. Vin was discharged in December of 1945 and worked in real estate, accounting, healthcare, and administration.

When did you first make contact with the enemy, and what were the circumstances?

Being in a Headquarters Company, I was a bit sheltered from direct contact with the enemy. I was not in a line company. So it was not until we got way over into Germany before we were in a situation where we could actually visualize the enemy. At that time, I was in the S-2, which does the scouting and observation. One time, we set up an outpost that we were very proud of, because we were up on a hill where we could observe enemy troop movements inside Germany. We had dug a hole about six feet deep, eight feet long, and two feet wide, and we covered this very discreetly with branches and leaves. The only contact we had with headquarters was a telephone line, which we buried under the leaves, and we had our telescope. So we stayed there to observe movements and send information for our artillery to direct their fire. And we did such a good job of hiding the place, they sent scouts out to find us, and they couldn't find us.

When did your unit become involved in the Battle of the Bulge?

Well, when we moved up to the northern part of Germany into Duren. We moved in there, and that's one of the most disappointing experiences that I had. The city was barren; there wasn't anything or anybody around, since the troops had already moved through there. We had to come in and check the place out; make sure nothing was left and no one was still remaining in the town. And first thing I saw—and this is practically in the city square— was two dead German soldiers lying there. When we checked them out, we found an engagement ring on one of them. And that never got to where it was supposed to go. In the basement of one of the houses there, we found one of our dead lieutenants that they left behind. This was in December of 1944, and we were in Duren up to December 25. Next morning, we're off for the Battle of the Bulge, because they needed more troops, and they pulled us to the northern area back across Belgium, and we came in past Liege. We were fortunate, because when we got there the main force was stopped, so then it was a matter of pushing them back and cutting them off. And for the next twenty days, we just kept moving in the trucks behind the troops.

Are there any instances of combat that your unit was involved in that you'd like to mention specifically?

Well, there was one place, I'm not even sure exactly where it was. It was in the German area, and we were trying to determine exactly the location of the German firepower. The S-2 was the pioneer section, so we were directed to lay a smokescreen. The idea was to make the Germans think we were trying to cover up something and draw fire from the enemy. Well, we laid the smokescreen, and we drew fire. And that was quite a smokescreen. We did a good job, and the enemy was located. And fortunately, we had no casualties in our particular area, except that many of us were nearly asphyxiated by the smoke. We had to go to the hospital, and because of that several of us were awarded the Purple Heart.

Dick Eggleston

Date of Birth:
September 1924

Place of Birth:
St. Louis, MO

Military Assignment:
78th Infantry Division, 303rd Engineer Battalion

Military Duties:
Combat Engineer

Highest Rank Achieved:
First Sergeant

Postwar Occupations:
Sales and Home Improvement

Dick was drafted in March of 1943, took his basic training at Camp Butner, North Carolina, and received additional training at Camp Pickett, Virginia, before going overseas in September of 1944. He fought in the Rhineland, Ardennes-Alsace, and Central Europe campaigns. He was awarded the European Theatre Service Medal with three battle stars (Ardennes, Central Europe and Rhineland), Good Conduct Medal and State of Missouri Citation. After the end of the war, Dick served eleven months as part of the Army of Occupation in Berlin, before returning to the United States in June of 1946. Dick pursued a career in sales and home improvement.

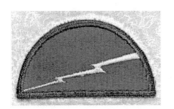

Describe the functions of a combat engineer.

Many individuals envision us building bridges and structures, and although we did that from time to time, combat engineers were at the front line and had several functions. We were frequently assigned to destroy fixed fortifications like pill boxes using either hand grenades, TNT, or flame throwers. In the field, we learned to initially crawl up to the pillboxes on our bellies until we reached a certain distance to avoid being shot. Due to the thick concrete walls on the pill boxes, the Germans could not see us through the slits once when we reached a critical distance of about thirty to thirty-five feet away, and at this distance we were be able to move closer on all fours. We were also responsible for disarming land mines, which were frequently booby-trapped, like placing two mines together, one buried below the other. As infantry units were retreating, we would frequently be in the rear of the retreat, laying land mines to slow down the enemy advance.

Would you like to pay tribute to a fallen comrade?

There are many of my buddies that never made it back and gave their lives for our country. However, I would like to mention Richard Quick, a fellow St. Louisan who I had persuaded to enlist in the Army. Richard died along with another soldier when a land mine detonated when they were trying to disarm it in the Ardennes Campaign. I buried him at the base of a nearby tree. Ironically, his dog tag and his remains were found by a boy named Ron von Reef several decades later. He was then moved to MarGraten Cemetery, where, every year, the Belgium townspeople place flowers on nearly eight thousand GI graves.

Did the training you received give you a good idea of what to expect as far as the battlefield conditions?

Well, it gave you somewhat of an idea, but it didn't give you the extremes. Nobody can. Forty-three days at 8 to 20 below zero in the north end of the Hurtgen Forest; eighty-three-mile run, and we were in the Hurtgen Forest at 8 to 20 below; and eighteen to twenty to forty-eight inches of snow in the same clothes for forty-three days. Not many people have ever experienced anything like that. Over here, they say, "Boy, it's cold." I say, "You've got no idea what cold is.' My two fingers and thumb were frozen to an M1, and it took six and a half hours holding them under my armpit to thaw out, and I still have very little use of these two fingers because of that. We would take canteens, ours as well as those from our departed buddies, and fill them with snow, and we'd put them under our armpits, so they would thaw by our own body heat.

Do you remember the details of one of your first battlefield engagements?

Uh, I wiped a lot out, and I have a hard time remembering incidents. However, I do remember some, like the time with the sharpshooter. Yes, we had one fellow from New York that won all the sharpshooter medals here in the States and he had killed fifty or one hundred Germans. But, when we got over there, we came through a ravine, and there were nine Germans coming up with a tank. There were only six of us, and that was very difficult because you didn't know what was going to happen. And I said, "Now, when I give the command to shoot we are all going to straighten up and shoot." And I had a man with a flame thrower, and he was going to burn the tank . . . in the opening. I then commanded the sharpshooter to open fire, and this guy got up and he couldn't pull the trigger. Now what do you do? He couldn't pull the trigger. He froze and I cracked him with my fist, and the rest of us succeeded in annihilating the group, and we made it. I drug him back and said, "Get rid of this jerk" because he didn't fit. He was always a little outside of the group, and I was glad to get rid of him. He later thanked me and said, "I'm going back to the States." And I said, "That's fine, get out of here." Because I didn't want any part of him. But we were bonded in that one fellow could guarantee that the guy next to him was allright and would be there to cover for him. People ask why, and I say, "Well, because that's the way we were raised. That's the way we came through."

What sorts of things did you do to try to stay warm and dry?

Well, we took the blankets from those that had died. We took the overcoats, and we wrapped our feet in them. Those of us at the north end were embedded in it, and to this day, my feet from here on down are all still discolored, numb and painful from being frozen. We wrapped our feet with any kind of a towel. We cut overcoats up. We cut blankets up. We had blankets around our head. Because at 8 to 20 below zero you'd better get some protection. Thirty-eight men from our company froze to death. I have a battlefield picture that shows how they found a guy that was wounded. He had crawled under a wrecked Jeep, and when they went back for him, he was frozen to death.

What was your impression of the lines of communication during the Battle of the Bulge?

We didn't have any communication. We were in as much as forty-eight inches of snow. We couldn't even dig into the ground. We had to embed in the snow. We had a rubber raincoat we had to put in and line the hole with the raincoat and then an overcoat and a second one if we could get it, and we had one blanket in our pack and one overcoat and one rubber raincoat. That was in our pack that we carried, and that was all we had.

Do you remember what you did around Christmas Day of 1944?

Well, in 1944 we cut branches on December 13 and made Christmas ornaments. We took the packs out of our K-rations, and there were four cigarettes in foil. I was a cigar smoker, so I gave the cigarettes away. But I took the foil, and we made Christmas ornaments out of it. Then at 5:30 on the morning of December 16, Hitler sent twenty-one divisions across, and that was the start of the Ardennes Campaign.

Are there any individuals either fallen or otherwise that you wanted to pay tribute to for a role they played?

Well, Charles Sirak was one. He was a very good friend of mine. I was his best man at his wedding. We were shipping out, and he said, "I want to know when," and I said, "Well, I've got a basic idea, but I can't relinquish it." So he said, "My girl and I want to get married," and I said, "I'll get you a pass this weekend." And he said, "Well, would you come up with me and be my best man?" I said, "Yeh." He was another one that we lost, a staff sergeant in my unit. We were behind our tank, and as we were moving forward, the tank driver got chicken and instead of moving forward when he saw another tank coming up, he backed up and ran over him. And that's another one I carry in my mind, but I have a hard time remembering the whole situation, because he was my best friend at the time and it's difficult.

Ed Bronenkamp

Date of Birth:
April 1924

Place of Birth:
St. Louis, MO

Military Assignment:
8th Armored Division, 148th Armored Signal Company

Military Duties:
Radio Operator for Division Chief of Staff

Highest Rank Achieved:
Technical Sergeant

Postwar Occupation:
Painting Contractor

Ed received his draft notice in March 1943 and took his basic training at Camp Polk, Louisiana. From there, he went to Camp Kilmer, New Jersey, and then overseas to Tidworth, England, before crossing the Channel and landing in Le Havre, France. Ed served as a radio operator with the 8th Armored Division in the Ardennes, Rhineland, and Central Europe campaigns. He received the European–African–Middle Eastern Ribbon, European Theatre Service Medal with three Battle Stars, the American Theatre Ribbon, Victory Ribbon, Occupation of Germany Ribbon, Good Conduct Medal, and a Unit Citation from the 9th Army Commander, Lieutenant General William Simpson. Ed also served in the Korean War before returning to civilian life, working as a painting contractor.

Did you feel prepared for your first combat experience?

Prepared? No way. You see dead bodies all over, shells flying over your head, trees splitting, animals dead, people dead. You're nineteen years old. You've never seen anything in your life like that. Boy, it's quite a deal. We relieved the British 7th Armored Division at Pont au Mouson, France. I was operating the radio in a half-track around 3 a.m. when all hell broke loose. There was a huge artillery barrage the rest of the night. We were green, but we kept our cool. When daylight came, we started to move out the convoy, and I saw German 88 gun emplacements blown to bits and arms, legs, bodies all over the place. Even in trees. This was hard to get used to, but after a while it became reality, and you think, this could happen to me.

What was your task during the Battle of the Bulge?

I was a radio operator on the SCR 399, which was a radio station mounted in a two-and-a-half-ton truck. I had gone to radio school before I got drafted, and it helped me later on. I got in the Signal Corps as a radio operator and then became the radio operator for the chief of staff and later on operated the SCR 399 in the half-tracks for a colonel—sending messages back and forth, recording them, and stuff like that. Our radio equipment was excellent and was superior to the Germans', but a lot of their weapons were superior to ours. Their Tiger tank had an 88 mounted on it that could take out any tank in our outfit. Their machine guns could drop out a barrel for replacement in seconds; ours had to be unscrewed.

What was the weather like during the Battle of the Bulge?

We weren't equipped for that. Twenty inches of snow, ice, and it was cold. We'd get by the tailpipe on a half-track or something like that. We punched each other to keep warm. You couldn't build a fire, 'cause somebody would see it. I don't think the equipment and clothing that we had at the time was adequate, since they didn't figure that we'd get weather like that. We didn't have really good heavy equipment clothing.

What were the greatest lessons you learned from your military experience?

Friendship. A lot of friends and the fellows just now, and you look at the world in a different perspective. It's a different world nowadays. Back then it was different. Everybody was really close and stuff like that, but now they're not that close.

What emotions do you feel when you reflect back on your past military experiences?

Oh, a lot of them. Every time you see a flag go by, you get tears in your eyes. A lot of times, you call up guys, and we talk all night long on the damn phone about things. It's like when we meet here at the VBOB meetings, the whole bunch of guys, we go through a lot of the old stuff here.

William Weindell

Date of Birth:
May 1924

Place of Birth:
St. Louis, MO

Military Assignment:
26th Infantry Division, 104th Infantry Regiment

Military Duties:
Infantryman

Highest Rank Achieved:
Private First Class

Postwar Occupation:
Physical Therapist

Bill was drafted in February of 1943, took his basic training at Cheyenne, Wyoming, and was part of the ASTP at Cincinnati U. when that program was ended. He went overseas in March of 1944 on the *George Washington*, landing in Liverpool. Bill later crossed the Channel, landed at Utah Beach, and served with the 26th Infantry Division through France, Germany, Luxembourg, Belgium, Czechoslovakia, and Austria. He earned the Combat Infantry Badge and was awarded two Bronze Stars, ETO Medal, Croix de Guerre with Palm and Fourragere, Sharpshooter Medal, Good Conduct Medal, and the European–African–Middle Eastern Service Ribbon with three Battle Stars (Rhineland, Ardennes, Central Europe) and refused the Silver Star and two field promotions. Bill returned to the United States in January of 1946 and pursued a career in physical therapy and chiropractic.

Do you recall your first firefight with the Germans?

Oh, yeah. Well, it's strange to say, but a nineteen year old doesn't have any sense, and we actually thought that we were bulletproof. We didn't think that we could be killed. That's why they like eighteen, nineteen year olds. We lost half of our platoon. One of the first firefights we had was in the hedgerows. When we came out of the hedgerows, it was into an open field. It was very difficult for me to try and shoot somebody. I had a hard time with that. And there were several occasions where we were going into small towns. In this one small town, I was a point man, and the point man is the first man out there. I found out, and we weren't stupid, that the point man never got shot, because the Germans would let one or two platoons go through and then start firing at the middle of the second and third platoons, and try to separate us. So the guy that's the point man out there very seldom ever drew the first fire. But as I was approaching this one town, I was going down a hill, one of my friends alongside of me caught an antiaircraft shell. They were using their antiaircraft guns on the ground level, and this one hit the ground and hit my buddy in the stomach and didn't explode. I couldn't help him, because there was another little kid, maybe eight, nine years old carrying a bazooka. This is hard. Nine years old, and I'm the only guy out there in front that could have dropped him. Our tank was coming around the side to enter this town on the side, and I did not shoot him. I couldn't kill a kid. So the kid with the bazooka hit the tank, and all the guys coming out of the tank were on fire. Well, the fellows didn't talk to me for about two weeks, 'cause I let that happen. So, you can bet from then on, anybody carrying a weapon, I would take down. But at that time I couldn't shoot a kid. After that, I shoot anybody carrying a weapon. Woman, man, kid, didn't make any difference.

Were you injured during your service?

I froze my hands and feet in January. They wanted to cut off my fingers, and they wanted to cut off my toes. And again, like a twenty year old, I said you'll do it over my dead body. I meant what I said, and I had my M1 on my lap and said I can still pull the trigger, guys, just let me alone. We'll see what they look like in the morning. But they were ready to take off my fingers and my toes. And since I'm a musician and I play a saxophone and clarinet, I wasn't going to give up my fingers. So the next day the captain came in and he looked at my hands, and he says, "Well, by golly, they're a little better." He says, "I didn't think that would come back, they were black." I said, "Can we wait another day?" He says, "Oh, yeah, we have to wait another day." So after about four days in that medical group, my fingers were almost back to normal, and my toes didn't hurt anymore. And what do you think they did? Sent me right back up to the front. So I joined some of the guys who were still alive, and we went on from there.

Yeah, there are a lot of memories I really can't talk about. One time we were in an area where the tree bursts were coming down before we had the foxholes dug. And there was, I guess, eight or ten guys that had been hit. One of them had been hit right through the nose, and the nose bone was knocked out of there, and his eyes had fallen out on his face. And I wanted to help him, so I helped him. I didn't have any water, and if I touched his eyes, my fingers would stick to the eye, so I spit on my hands, and then I put his eyes back in. Well, I find out later there are twenty-seven different pathological bacteria in your mouth, but I found out from the medical personnel that the man regained his sight. Now, that's unbelievable; they put his eyes back in.

So thanks to you, he could still see.

Well, I did what anybody would do if they could. That's why I was wounded, a Screaming Mimi got me in the leg and the butt, a piece about as big as my hand, because they blew up in big pieces. It hit me on the rump and knocked me about eight or ten feet, and all I had was a bruise. But the shrapnel in my leg, I dug it out with my knife, or bayonet. Put sulfa powder on it, wrapped it up with a bandage, and never did report it. So after the war they wanted to write me up for a Purple Heart, and I said I don't deserve a Purple Heart for that. The guys that need the Purple Hearts are the guys that lost arms or legs and had you know chest wounds and all that. I said a piece of shrapnel in the leg? No, I couldn't take it. So like I said after the war, they also wrote me up for a Silver Star for what I did there in that area with the guys, there were two or three of them, that I stopped the bleeding and wrapped them up. It seems like I had a natural inclination for that, and I didn't know that I was going to become a professional man later on in life. But it was natural for me to help them.

Would you like to mention a friend or a fellow soldier that you think deserves to be honored and mentioned right now?

Yeah, Sergeant Clarence Wilding. He saved my life on two or three occasions, and Clarence was from St. Louis, and he and I came back together. Clarence saved about ten of us. We were captured by a squad of Germans who had a machine gun on us. And we were smart enough again not to do anything. So they had us put all of our weapons in a little ravine, and they started walking us toward the German line. Well, after about five-and-a-half, six hours of that, Clarence Wilding, who could speak fluent German, had convinced the Germans that the war was almost over. That it'd be better for them to come back with us than it would be for us to go back with them. And you know what? The Germans took us back to the ravine where we put our weapons in there. We picked our weapons back out, put our belts on, our bandoliers with our grenades, put their weapons in the hole, and took all eight of them back. So I was a prisoner of war for about eight hours. But does that classify me to be a prisoner of war? Not in my mind. No.

Did seeing Dachau change your attitude towards the German people at all?

Oh, yeah, sure, sure it did. We had heard about Auschwitz, but we plowed into Dachau, there was no prisoners taken after that. We had a hard time to restrain ourselves from taking any prisoners. Of course, we were constantly being reprimanded by the officers and the sergeants not to do any unnecessary shooting, and well, we knew what they meant. But it was very hard after Dachau to take any prisoners. There was an incident in Luxembourg, when the Germans in the Bulge had overrun one of our hospitals. And when we got there, the guys that were patients in those hospital beds, I still see it, their legs broken, and up in slings and hanging out the side of the bed with a bullet in their head. The SS troops had come in, now these are the SS troops. It wasn't the regular army, or the Wehrmacht, it was the SS soldiers. We found out that for a fact that they came in and shot every one of the guys in their beds, before they left. So it is easy to understand why it was awfully hard for young guys to take any prisoners. Again, for another month, we didn't take prisoners. Just like after we saw Dachau, we didn't want to take any prisoners. Fortunately, you're young, and you can recuperate from that someway. I guess some of the guys didn't.

There are so many stories. I had the Williamses. They were not brothers, but they had the same name. Sam, Jack Williams. Jack was out on a patrol. Sam was standing guard. And when Sam said to him, "Halt, who goes there?" No answer. I was there right alongside of Sam. I said, "What do you think?" He says, "Halt, who goes there?" No answer. So Sam's an old country boy, a squirrel hunter. He just put his weapon up there, and he waited until he heard the noise, any noise, and he shot. He fired. The next morning we went out, and we found Jack. Shot right through the head. Sam went crazy. I shouldn't talk about this stuff. We had to tie him up to keep him from killing himself, 'cause he and Jack were buddies from the ASTP program way back. So when he realized that he shot his buddy, when we did turn him loose, there was snow on the ground, and he was picking up handfuls of snow and rubbing it in his face. And then he was taking and punching trees with his fists until they were bloody. So we had to send him back. I never did know what happened to him. But I doubt that he would have survived.

James McElroy

Date of Birth:
September 1922

Place of Birth:
Chicago, IL

Military Assignment:
29th Infantry Division, 175th Infantry Regiment

Military Duties:
Infantryman, Sniper

Highest Rank Achieved:
Private First Class

Postwar Occupation:
Sheet Metal Worker

Jim was drafted in June of 1943, and after basic training in artillery at Camp Callan, California, he was sent to Camp Chaffee, Arkansas, Ft. Bliss, Texas, and Camp Mead, Maryland, for infantry training. He went overseas on the *Aquitania* and landed in England in July of 1944. Jim crossed the Channel the same month, landed at Omaha Beach, and joined the 29th Infantry Division in St. Lo shortly thereafter. He fought with the 29th throughout France, Belgium, Holland, and Germany. He was awarded the Combat Infantry Badge, Purple Heart, Bronze Star, Expert Marksman, and Presidential Citation for his service in the ETO. Jim returned to the United States in March 1946 and worked as a sheet metal worker.

Please describe the fighting in the hedgerows.

I joined the 29th Division in St. Lo, and it stunk. Bodies lying around in the sun, rotting away, and oh, what an aroma. You could smell it just going through there. And we started to make our pushes, so we pulled out of St. Lo, and we got into hedgerows. The company I joined had lost 80 percent of the men from what happened on the beach; they got slaughtered on the beach. It was so bad that the 100 men that came up with me to replace those killed only brought us up to 120 men. And within two weeks, we lost over 100 men again, in the hedgerow country.

Two of us were talking to this scout who told us he just got married and had a baby. He was pretty scared and worried about his family back home. We started to move. A shot was fired. That scout was hit and killed, which scared the hell out of me. We started pushing through the hedgerow. I was alone when I got to the next hedgerow, and I thought they'd come and get me. But they didn't come because just then the Jerrys zeroed in on my company, and shells started flying over my head. And they landed on my company, who had dug in. I was "safe," up in the German hedgerows with the Germans! I was waiting for them to relieve me, help me, but I was caught up there. And I looked back, and I saw the sniper who killed my scout. I got down in the grass up against the German hedgerow. I was hoping they didn't hear me fire, and I shot him.

So now I'm stuck there. What am I going to do? The Germans are on one side of the hedgerows; I'm on the other side. I got rid of my pack and gun belt and kept my two bandoliers and my rifle. I thumbed the safety off and then looked for a place to hide. I saw a little opening in the hedgerow; that's where I was going to hide. I crawled up there, very quietly, looked around; I didn't hear anybody. So I got up real fast and walked in there. I looked up and saw this Jerry looking right at me. He was guarding that little opening in the hedgerow, kneeling port rifle. My rifle was on the side. He looked at me and started to pull up his rifle. But my rifle was already pointing at him, and I pulled the trigger and shot him through the chest. The Jerrys were all lined up back there! So I ran like hell, zigzagging. I jumped and dived back through the hedgerows where I came through and landed on top of another GI. But someone had a slit trench already built, and I just crawled into it. And I looked down the line, along the hedgerow, and it was a bloody mess; the shells had blown up everything, and everybody was bleeding.

We just got out of there; and we tried another spot which was in the lower section, an area that at one time was all full of water, but it had just dried up in the summer heat. There were cracks in the dirt, and we crawled in those big cracks. And there was a German machine gun that had that covered there, so they slaughtered us there too. I was just lucky. I just crawled in one of the cracks in the dirt there and just prayed that they didn't hit me. The guys around me got hit, and finally I backed out of there. We tried another way to get back in, and we crawled around along-side of another hedgerow, and there was another guy in front of me. I was on my belly crawling; he was standing getting through, but the Jerry had that little opening zeroed in. And this guy was right in front of me, and he got it through the head—he just went like a chicken with his head cut off. He just rolled around and cried, and blood was spurting out of his head. And bang again, right in front of that opening, hit in the head a second time, and blood was just spurting out of his head there until he just gradu-ally went down. That particular time they killed two company command-ers right there, two of them. They had just come up on the front line.

Was your time in the military a positive experience in your life?

Oh yeah, it was an education. To see what I saw, what I went through, people suffering, blown up, blown apart, people killed, people hollering for help, and you can't do anything about it.

I remember moving toward a town, and the bazooka man got hit. He's lying in the field, hollering and crying, by himself. It was rainy and muddy. I turned to the guy next to me in the shell holes and said let's go get him. So we both laid our guns down and ran to him. We dragged him to safety, along the railroad tracks. But he died anyway. That kind of thing does something to your mind.

If you're in the infantry, you got three chances: 1. You're going to get killed. You aren't going to get off the line until this happens to you. 2. You're going to be totally disabled. 3. You're going to be lucky like me. You get a million-dollar wound: You get hit, but you're alive, you have all your limbs, and you're not disfigured. They say "million-dollar wound" because anybody would give a million bucks in the army just to be wounded like that to get out. 'Cause otherwise you're not going to get out until you get killed, wounded, disabled, or blow your leg off; these are the only ways to get off the line. If you're in the infantry, you're there to stay until the end of the war.

I did eight months of combat. It was very rare to make it through eight months in combat. The guys who landed on the beach on D-Day didn't even see one day of combat, and they got slaughtered. My own division got slaughtered on the beach on D-Day, June 6. Only twenty remained. I wasn't with them; I was lucky. I was a replacement.

Rudy Reitz

Can you talk about what you think was your most important contribution to a given battle?

Well, it was a big thing for me, maybe no one else. I was captured, and I didn't like the idea of being captured because it was my stupidity. The captain came up from this hill. There was a draw down there, and we kind of reconnoitered the situation, and I knew that the Germans could wind around and come up that draw and be from here to that door [ten feet] away from us. So I went down and set up two machine guns and crossfired them with two light machine guns and two BARs. So he comes to me, and he said, "Rudy, would you go out and check those guns?" He said, "You know that draw winds around pretty good back there behind you over there." I said, "I'll go down and check it out." I went down there. It was a big slab of rock, and I saw that and my machine gun—one machine gun was right next to it. When I got down there and didn't see the machine gun, I knew that something was wrong. I had two men there, plus two of L Company's men, and all of a sudden I heard something. It was a German soldier, and he had a little rock in his hand and his rifle, and he went, against the stock of the rifle, made a noise. And when I turned around, it was this German pointing a rifle right at me, and then he went like this, move, move forward. And I moved forward, and I could see the machine gun was turned over and the ammo box, all the ammo was out of it and so forth. Then I heard another one, knock, knock, knock, another

Military Assignment:
78th Infantry Division, 309th Infantry Regiment

Military Duties:
Machine Gunner

German came out over there. And the same thing. And then another one came out.

There were three of them against me, and I didn't see the two other men from L Company or the two men that were manning the machines guns. Didn't see anybody, so this German officer came up and called me over there. He spoke perfect English. He lived in St. Louis for several years. He graduated from the University of Detroit. Perfect English, and he started asking me questions. I'd give him Sergeant Rudy Reitz, 37603465. He'd say, "Aw, cut out that crap." He said I can talk English, and where are you from, and I wouldn't give him any information, and all of a sudden he said something about St. Louis, and he says, "You know St. Louis," and I made a mistake, but it turned out to be great. I said I live there, he said, "I lived there." He said, "You know this place, you know place?" And he and I got in conversations about his folks moving back to Germany when the war ended, and he stayed at the University of Detroit and so forth. And we became very friendly, but anyhow, they took me back, and when I got back there, there were these two guys from L Company, and there was a dugout. He made us go in there and tried to interview us, but I said I didn't want to be interviewed. He said, "Okay, you know, like, no big deal." But they were lost. We could tell by the way they were acting, they were lost, too. They weren't tied to their organization, and so I said something to him, I said I have to relieve myself. He said, "That's okay, go out with the guard." And so I went out twice to relieve myself, of which I didn't, I was too scared, and since they let us talk, I said to these other two guys, "I'm going to try to escape, you guys want to go?" And they both said, "No, if they catch us, they'll kill us." I said, "How do you know you won't be killed anyway?" So I took off. The Germans took my wool cap, what the guy on *MASH* wears, we had those. They took my helmet, and they took my gloves, and I very easily could have frozen to death. So the third time I told him I had to be relieved again, and he says okay, go ahead you're on your own.

When I got to this big tree and turned around, I took that little branch that I saw, and that was the one that was growing out towards the west. And I felt that branch, and I took off and got back somehow. I didn't know for sure where I was, and I heard somebody say something, and I couldn't understand it. And then the voices came closer then, and it was English, and I knew it was our English and not this German officer. And I was trying to talk, and they didn't see me and I went, "Rrrrrr," and of course, they went to the rifles real quick. And finally they got to me, and one of them said, "He's got GI clothes on," and I did, except that little cap and my gloves. He said, "Who are you?" and I said, "Who are you?"

I got enough energy to talk. He said I'm somebody with this regiment, the 99th Division, and I said I couldn't talk. He asked, "Are you hurt?" I said, "I don't know," and I didn't. So they took me back then and got me all fixed up, and I figured I'm going to get a leave to Paris, or they're going to do something with me 'cause I'm not 100 percent physically fit. Well, they got me a new cap and a pair of boots and all this stuff on me. They came to me, "Rudy Reitz, report to someplace. Get ready to start going back to the front." So, they took me right back to the front. And when I got back there, the most shameful thing was, the guys that I left back there hadn't seen much action. There wasn't much activity, and when I walked up, nobody knew I was gone. It kind of hurt, but I had to laugh.

Don Borcherding

Date of Birth:
September 1924

Place of Birth:
St. Louis, MO

Military Assignment:
Third Army, 468th AAA AWSP, XXth Corps

Military Duties:
Gunner on First Section Half-Track

Highest Rank Achieved:
Technician Fifth Grade

Postwar Occupation:
Coin Machine Mechanic

Don was inducted at Jefferson Barracks in July of 1943 after being drafted. He took his basic training at Camp Callan, California, and then went to Camp Davis, North Carolina, and Camp Hahn, California, for further training. At Camp Hahn, he was assigned to the 468th Antiaircraft Automatic Weapons Battalion, Self-Propelled. His battalion of around nine hundred men was sent overseas on an Australian refrigerator boat, which hauled beef from Australia to England, landing in Scotland. After landing on Omaha Beach in August of 1944, Don fought in the Normandy, Northern France, Central Europe, Ardennes, and Rhineland campaigns, earning the European Theatre Service Medal (five Battle Stars), the Presidential Unit Citation, and Good Conduct Medal. Don left the service in January of 1946 and worked for forty years as a coin machine mechanic.

What kind of antiaircraft weapons were you using?

The first section had quad .50 caliber machine guns, and the second section had two .50 caliber machine guns on each side, one on each side of a .37 caliber cannon. The turret on the second section's bucket was hand-manipulated. You had one person up in the bucket that raised the cannon and gave it elevation, and the other went left to right. Then the fellow that stood in the back would give orders—more lead, more lead—and he would be telling the two people who were manipulating the bucket to move it one way or the other. They did very well. I was on a quad .50, and we had ammunition canisters that were supposed to hold 250 rounds. We generally loaded them up to around 300 rounds. The turret we had was battery-powered, and it had a sight on it similar to what they used in airplanes for dropping bombs.

Was this .50 caliber arrangement on the half-track, or was this towed behind?

It was on the half-track, and there was a place about three inches wide, a railing around the top of the half-track. We also had armor plating sheet that would raise up, and it was hinged. But we never did put that up, because if you had a misfire that armor would cause problems when we tried to get the misfired shell out of the weapon. The turret had a Briggs and Stratton four-cycle engine that had a generator that charged the batteries, and every time you fired a mission you had to run that for a half hour to recharge the batteries. And when we were done firing, all the spent brass would fill up the bottom of the half-track We would have to use a shovel to get all the shell casings off of there. We carried some of our spare ammunition in a trailer we got issued somewhere along the line. And underneath and around the turret were storage wells that we took the ammunition out of the wood box and the metal containers and then placed it in these storage wells. They were perfect except when it rained, and when we were in France and got a lot of mud in and around the turret and on the ammunition. So there were times we had to take it and wash it off with gasoline and oil and use a wire brush to take the rust off the links that held the shells together.

What was the moment of greatest sadness that you experienced during the war?

I think at the Battle of the Bulge. We normally had to do duty along a road or not too far off of the road, and we had a pair of binoculars, and I used them for things besides looking for aircraft. And that's when I would see those bodies come back in the back end of a Jeep, and they'd have new boots. That was the killer because they were all replacements. They had just got off the boat, and here they were, gone now. And that was the worst.

John Critzas

Date of Birth:
April 1925

Place of Birth:
Yonkers, NY

Military Assignment:
12th Armored Division, 714th Tank Battalion

Military Duties:
Gunner in a M4A3 EZ8 Sherman Tank

Highest Rank Achieved:
Staff Sergeant

Postwar Occupation:
Founded Hand Cleaner Company ("Goop")

John was drafted in May of 1943 and took his basic training at Ft. Bliss, Texas. After arriving in England on the *Marine Raven*, he spent time at Tidworth Barracks, England, before crossing the Channel in September of 1944. John served with the 12th Armored Division through France, Belgium, and Germany. He was awarded the French Croix de Guerre Medal and four Battle Stars (Northern France, Ardennes, Rhineland, and Central Europe). John was discharged from service in November of 1945 and pursued a career in the hand cleaner industry.

Describe the organizational structure of an Armored Division.

Now, just by way of explanation, an Armored Division consists of three battalions of artillery, three battalions of infantry, and three battalions of tanks, plus the peripheral services like the medics and the Signal Corps. Well, the combat outfits are in reality the artillery, the tanks, and the infantry, with the tanks and the infantry being the up-front guys and the artillery coming up in support. And this entire division of 10,500 men is mobile. The infantry rides in half-tracks. The minute there's any engagement with the enemy, the infantry dismounts. The tanks keep going.

What was your job as a member of the tank crew?

My job was the gunner, so I was in the turret. The M4 Sherman tank had a crew of five men: a driver and an assistant driver down in front, and then a loader and a gunner, and a tank commander in the turret. All of us knew everybody's job. The driver could be a gunner. I mean, he knew enough about it to fire the gun. Everybody knew how to fire a machine gun. You just pulled the trigger and kept the thing full of ammunition. When you have all the hatches closed, you can't see anything as a driver. You're looking through a periscope, which is about one inch high by six inches wide, and all you see is what you see through that little periscope in front of you. So you rely on the tank commander to yell at you through your intercom system right or left. And if he says right, you pull on the right handle, and the tank goes to the right, and you don't care what's in front of you as long as it isn't a cliff. If it's a building, you just run through it. A building like the one we're sitting in—a tank will just drive through one end and out the other. No injuries. No problems. They're pretty indestructible. You're looking at forty tons, which is eighty thousand pounds of steel, and not too many things are going to stop it.

I was told which way to point the gun. I was told to point it at two o'clock or twelve o'clock or ten o'clock and sight on a target out there. Then as soon as I put it in the direction that the tank commander said, I could see what he was aiming at, provided we weren't moving. If we were moving, it was another story. We were supposed to have equipment to stabilize the cannon to be able to fire it while you were moving, but our equipment didn't work very well. Today, they lock on to a target, and the tank can move in any direction, and it's all computerized, and the gun will fire whenever the gunner hits the solenoid. But back then, it was all manual. You sighted on the target, and you fired. It was difficult to hit a target when you were moving. But when you were stationary, you could hit a target one thousand yards away. You could hit a slit in a pillbox, which was no more than ten inches wide by two or three inches high.

We had a bow gun in the front that the assistant driver handled, and that was a .30 caliber machine gun. We had a .30 caliber co-actual gun. We call it co-actual because it was lined up with the 76 mm cannon, the big gun, and that was antipersonnel. We also had a .50 caliber machine gun, but you had to get out of the turret and climb outside the tank in order to fire it. You couldn't fire it from inside the vehicle. We carried 30,000 rounds of .30 caliber ammunition, 10,000 rounds of .50 caliber ammunition, and 110 rounds of 76 mm (three inch) ammunition. The loader pulled up a quarter-inch steel trap door in the floor, and it exposed all of the ammunition underneath his feet. He'd grab the rounds from there with a handheld device and load them into the breach of the cannon.

You could lie down inside if you didn't have the floor open and all that, and we used to occasionally lie down and sleep on there when you needed to. I slept in my chair. I sat in the gunner's chair in one position and just rode for hours, and when you were tired enough, you slept in any position. You just slept sitting up. When you're nineteen or twenty years old, it doesn't bother you too much.

Describe your first battlefield experience.

We went up the Seine River to a little city called Rouen, which was maybe five miles from the front lines at the time. My first experience was in the evening so it was dark, maybe ten or eleven at night. We could see what looked like thunder and lightning, but actually it was guns firing both ways, from the Germans and from us. We slept outside that night. It was September, and it was still relatively warm, so we had our regular sacks, and we could listen to the sounds of the war. There was no actual contact, no combat or anything like that, but there we were, and we could hear what we were about to get into. The next day, we mounted up and started driving down the road. Usually, the tanks led the way, and the first tank was always a very scary position to be in, because you're going down the road, and you don't know what's in front of you. More than likely, a German 88 or another tank, and everything happens in a hurry, so it's over very quickly. Our division sustained one thousand killed in action, so we were constantly getting replacements from the rear to make up our tank crews. I personally was involved in three tanks that were hit. In one incident, three of the men were killed, and the tank commander and myself were the only two survivors. At the actual front, which we didn't know was the front at the time, we were perched on top of a hill looking down at a village, and out of nowhere an 88 hit the vehicle and killed three men instantly. So I got in the driver's seat of the tank and backed it up and got it out of sight of wherever the gun was. Meanwhile the medics came up with another light tank as a medic tank and removed the wounded and killed. I guess that was our first combat experience.

You mentioned an engagement in January in which your unit suffered heavy casualties. Where was that?

In a city called Herrlisheim, which is in France, just on the west side of the Rhine River. As a corporal gunner in a tank, I knew nothing about where we were going. Nobody told us anything. We were lucky if our tank commanders knew where we were going. They were taking orders from higher-ups. But we were told that we would have to go into the city and capture it. Our battalion in that particular instance was in reserve, and we were lined up in a field outside of the city of Herrlisheim in plain view, while the 23rd Tank Battalion went down the main road and went in. Well, in a battalion that consisted of about thirty-five or forty tanks, they lost about thirty of them, and they had a pretty high number of casualties. The infantry also had quite a few casualties. Out of the more or less one thousand men that were killed, I would say better than 50 percent of them were killed in that engagement. But our orders were to capture the city, which we didn't do. The Germans beat us back out of it. But that was just one or two days, and then we were in the woods and in the forests and in the fields on both sides of it. I was in the 3rd platoon of A Company in the 714th Tank Battalion. Our tank was hit and disabled, and fortunately none of us were injured in that engagement, but we got out and waited for dark. The artillery laid down smoke mortars in front of us, so that we could get out without being seen, and we crawled back to a creek and sat in the creek until about two in the morning. We had a tank retriever, a vehicle that is able to hook a cable onto an existing tank and pull it back, so that our tank was pulled back. We had to hook the cable onto it and everything else, and another fellow and myself at about two in the morning hooked the cable onto the tank, and he got a decoration for doing that, but I didn't get anything. I didn't ask for it, and they didn't give it to me, but we both did the same job. We equipped the tank to be withdrawn from that particular area so that when the smoke cleared and daylight came, the Germans couldn't just destroy the equipment completely, and we salvaged that particular tank. They took it back, put another track on it, fixed it up, and we were back in it again.

James Darmstatter

Date of Birth:
January 1924

Place of Birth:
Freeburg, IL

Military Assignment:
101st Airborne, 595th Ambulance Company

Military Duties:
Ambulance Driver

Highest Rank Achieved:
Private First Class

Postwar Occupation:
Telephone Lineman

Jim enlisted in the Army in 1943 and took his basic training at Ft. Ord, California. He went overseas and landed in Hankelow Court on February 22, 1944. He crossed the Channel on July 12, 1944, and served as an ambulance driver with the 101st Airborne through France, Luxembourg, Belgium, and Germany. He was awarded the Silver Star, three Overseas Service Bars, World War II Victory Medal, the Unit Meritorious Service Award (101st Airborne), Good Conduct Medal, and five Battle Stars (Normandy, Northern France, Central Europe, Ardennes, Rhineland). Jim returned to the United States in December of 1945 and worked as a telephone lineman.

What was it like being in the ambulance?

We were close to the fighting, and we would go from a collecting station or first aid station and then to a field hospital. We traveled many miles to get there. I'd say an average of fifty and one hundred miles wasn't uncommon, and in France we went to Brest with the 6th Armored. They traveled so fast up towards the Brest Peninsula that the infantry couldn't keep up with them, and we went two hundred miles back to a hospital in Reims, France. A lot of that's night driving, and we couldn't use headlights. All you had was cat's eyes, which was a small light by your headlight, and it doesn't do much unless you're right on top of something. We all drove like that. Some cases I know some guys put their lights on, but very few. They had to be foolish to do something like that. So you drive on those unfamiliar roads with hardly any lights. And map reading was a big, big thing. You know where you gotta go, and you have to find it on the map. You're out on the roads at night, and when you'd read that map, you'd hold it on your lap and use a flashlight to read by. And you'd tell the driver, "You got about two miles to go. We're going to see a road, a bridge, a creek, or something up here, or we gotta turn left or do something." Things like that. The artillery fire was there, but you didn't pay any attention to that. You just get going and do what you're supposed to do.

Could you describe the role of the weather during the battle?

During the winter, the roads were terrible, with all the vehicles churning up mud. It was nothing like we have today. Vehicles would be almost up to the hubcaps in mud; a Jeep would be halfway up the wheels. A lot of little Jeeps would get stuck because you couldn't see the holes. The mud looked like eight or ten inches deep, maybe deeper. And they'd get stuck because they'd drop in a hole and couldn't get out. Normally, the holes wouldn't have been there, but there were a lot of them from the artillery fire and all the traveling on them. A lot of times we couldn't take the regular roads and had to use field roads. Not all the time, but during this winter we're talking about a lot of snow.

Did the ambulance handle pretty well?

Yeah, you're not going really fast. They don't have a siren, and you're not traveling down the road. You're trying to survive and still get there, and you don't want to put it in a ditch. So you use a lot of caution and common sense. You had patients in the back, so you tried not to make sudden stops, or you'd have them coming off the litters. We didn't have anything between us and them. Because of the distances involved, you'd have to attend them every now and then. So you'd just get up from your seat and walk back to take care of them. All the ambulances held four litter patients. There were two like halfway up the side. You hooked them in straps and then two down on the floor. If you just had walking patients, which we didn't have many of, you might put two in the litters, and the other side had a bench that folded down, so you could handle maybe eight or ten walking patients. We didn't have seat belts, so you had to drive with a little sense.

How did you find out where you needed to go next?

Well, let's say you left the collecting station. That's where they brought them right from the battlefield, maybe the first aid station, so they got there first, the doctors looked at them first there. Well, we'd take them from there, or we'd bring them to a place like that, where they had a surgeon. It would vary. Well, you know you had to get back 'cause you know how many were there when you left, and they were expecting you. Somebody was there to tell you. And how he got his information I don't exactly know, but he'd say, "Well, we got so many casualties here, but up at Houffalize or some other town, they're getting a rough time so you're going to go up there tonight." Things like that. Word of mouth. I don't know how they really got it, but we didn't see our officers. We used to see our sergeant, who told us what to do and what not to do and where to go, but we did not see other officers.

How many patients would you say you picked up a day?

I think the highest our platoon had was around 115, and the next day there might be 50. The day after that, there might be 90. That doesn't sound like a lot, but it is a lot because we had to go so far to get back and then return and pick up some more. And I'm only talking about ten ambulances in our platoon. I'm not talking about a whole lot of people. There were two other platoons, three to a company, and the other two platoons. You know, I never saw other ambulance companies, but I know there had to be some there. But we couldn't have handled it all. In France, traveling a hundred miles wasn't uncommon.

Was there any time you were under fire?

Well, during the Bulge was the worst by far. One in particular was on the road outside Bastogne. One of the ambulance drivers had been killed a few days before by a mortar that came right through his windshield. So one night this buck sergeant came over and says, "Jim, they've got a GI in Bastogne that they can't take care of." They didn't have the facilities for surgery or whatever he needed, and he had to go to Bouillon, and that's about forty or fifty miles. The corridor wasn't really open at that time. It was, but it wasn't. You just didn't open it and say okay, it's open. He said it's volunteers, and my buddy, we looked at each other, Eddie and I, and said let's go because we were in a cellar with civilians.

"Let's get out of here." Anyway, we picked him up and just him. They wouldn't send anybody else in that ambulance, 'cause they didn't want to put the other ones in jeopardy, not knowing if the road was open. And that particular trip was kind of bad, but we had to get him through, regardless. And we got through fine, so we felt real good about that. I'm glad we did it.

Was that the time you were most afraid during your whole service?
We did a lot of night driving, and at night you can't see anything except the flash of the shells. The sound is intense and so loud, that alone is scary, but you just get over it. You just go, and if it's going to happen, it's going to happen. You just can't be worried about it, or you'll never get there. We were scared several times like that. I know I was. You didn't know where that next shell was coming from. But it was really bad the first week or two in January of 1945. We went continuously for two nights and three days. No sleep, just K-rations to eat, and there again I'm not complaining about this. I think it's a wonderful thing just the way it happened, and by the second day and second night, your eyes are pasty from the strain and from driving. Then you kind of get a headache and start to hallucinate from lack of sleep. I saw vehicles that weren't there and things like that. But the soldiers, the GIs, they went four or five days. They could sleep standing up, they were so tired. But we still had to drive, and you don't want to wreck the ambulance. You had patients in the back.

Did you ever sleep in the ambulance when you weren't working?
Once in a while, when we had no place else to go. I think there were about ten or twelve blankets in that ambulance. One or two on the bottom of the litter and two for the person on top. That depended what time of the year it was, whether it was cold. But it was always warm in the ambulance. And I never had to sleep outside. If we weren't in the ambulance, we were in a house, and we'd start some kind of a fire. And we didn't have that long to sleep, not a full eight hours. You might be awakened in the middle of the night. All that time I never had that ambulance break down and never gave that a thought at night, and that's from Normandy on. You would think at night, you'd be worried about what am I going to do here if the thing breaks down? But that never happened.

James Lewis

Date of Birth: *February 1917*

Place of Birth:

Mountain Grove, MO

Military Assignment:
U.S. Medical Corp/24th Evacuation Hospital (Semi-Mobile), Camp Tyson, TN

Military Duties:
Physician/Surgeon in Field and Evacuation Hospitals

Highest Rank Achieved: *Captain*

Postwar Occupations:
Pediatric Cardiothoracic Surgeon

After Dr. Lewis enlisted in the Army, he took his basic training at Carlyle Barracks and later completed Medical Field Service School. Dr. Lewis then assisted with plastic surgery for casualties from Africa for three months. He then joined the 24th Evacuation Hospital Semi mobile in Camp Tyson, Tennessee. He departed on the *Queen Mary* on Thursday, January 20, 1944, and arrive on January 29, 1944, at Greenock, Scotland. He stayed at Cheddar in Somerset and pursued additional training at the Hammersmith Hospital regarding the management of shock and trauma learned as a result of the Desert Campaign. He then crossed the Channel on June 10, 1944, to arrive at Omaha Beach and was assigned to the 51st Field Hospital behind Easy Red Sector. He served with the 51st Field and 24th Evacuation Hospitals in France, Holland, Belgium, and Germany and was involved in the Medical Corp throughout most major European campaigns. He returned to U.S. in December 1945 and was awarded the Bronze Star for his role in the postoperative management of wounded soldiers. He was assigned as one of President Truman's physicians and completed his residency and fellowship training in thoracic surgery and practiced for many years as a pediatric cardiothoracic surgeon.

Describe your experiences during the summer of 1944

The smells of the sea and land became a distinctive odor, I often recall. On June 12, we've pulled into the area known as Easy Red on Omaha Beach. The beach had debris of ships, guns, shells, a few partially buried bodies, and white tapes marking de-mined areas. I grabbed the side of a truck and rode up the hill into Normandy. The 51st Field Hospital was in a small clearing about one hundred yards behind a large German concrete bunker covering the beach below. We were about a half-mile inland. We reached the hospital in darkness. The rumble of guns and gun flashes were prominent. However, I was assigned to the shock tent and promptly went into the tent. It was ablaze in light with casualties receiving blood, plasma, and IV fluids. I never really saw all the casualties there because I began to work preparing soldiers for the OR. My first casualty was a big 82nd Airborne with a large sucking wound in his chest. He was otherwise okay. I got some plasma into him, dressed his wound with a pressure dressing, and reassured him. He went on to surgery. The next two hours were more of the same. I recall the loud rumble of guns and the vibration of the ground. However, I was inside the tent and felt quite secure!

About 3 a.m., I was sent to check on new casualties in the receiving tent. I took a flashlight and left the shock tent. I stepped from the lighted area into the pitch-dark area, and all hell seemed to break loose. The artillery fire was intense and steady; one could feel the percussion waves striking the chest; my pant legs actually flapped! The sky was ablaze with fire. German planes were trying to hit the ships and American airstrips. They were followed by antiaircraft fire, which was unrelenting. One plane crashed as I walked to the receiving area. The plane exploded probably four hundred yards away, lighting up the sky. It was a memorable moment. Was I scared? No, not really. I had the strange feeling of being suspended in space watching all these terrible things. I was not really a part of it—just an observer! When I went inside the receiving tent, all was dark. The noise was still severe. But I was okay—I was inside the tent!

On June 14, 1944, the 24th Evacuation Hospital Semi-Mobile officially began operation. We drove through badly damaged areas of Normandy to our unit—the first time I had seen it in action. Our unit was mobile but without our own transportation. We had a three- hundred–bed capacity that could be increased. We had approximately three hundred enlisted men covering laboratory and pharmacy, X-ray, receiving, supply, ward service, headquarters, surgery, mess, motor, litter bearers, and miscellaneous sections. We had MAC officers covering administrative duties. Medical officers carried out medical duties. There were forty nurses and forty doctors. We had a receiving area, shock tent, pre-op tent, medical tents, surgical post-op tents, OR tents, and field lab and X-ray. In Normandy, our operating tents were two in number, fifty-by-sixteen-foot ward tents. Each tent had three operating tables and a master table. We had five to seven very efficient OR nurses. We had one anesthesiologist and five anesthetists; there were five to seven technicians. Pentothal and ether were the anesthesics used.

As the weather cleared, we awaited a move. Colonel Rylander sat down with me one day and was very complimentary of my work. I was pleased and encouraged to express my ideas of a post-op center. I pointed out that I was not experienced enough to carry my weight in the OR, but I knew a lot about postoperative care, fluid balance, and management of wounds. I had found it very inefficient and tiring to keep running back and forth from the OR to the post-op tents. I wondered if I could set up and run a postoperative center for all the chests, bellies, heads, and amputees—all those who could not be promptly evacuated. The colonel liked the idea, and I set out to establish the first ICU in a tent hospital in the European Theater of Operations.

On July 7, 1944, our unit moved to a large field near La Folie and L'Epinay-Tesson on the road to St. Lo. We were moving up to support the fighting of the 29th, 30th, 35th, 44th, 9th, and 1st Divisions. The fighting in July was a bitter, slow-motion struggle. There were heavy rains, creating a honeycomb of muddy fields enclosed by the hedgerows. These were created by waist-high banks of earth matted with dense roots, out of which grew weeds, bushes, and trees. The fighting was steady and bitter. Unit after unit passed us as they moved into combat. We saw many casualties who were wounded shortly after passing our hospital.

Casualties were treated at aid stations and moved to collecting companies and clearing companies for expedient care and then sent on to the nearby field hospital. The field hospital was a 150-bed unit. The most severely wounded were brought there by Jeep or ambulance. Auxiliary surgical teams often worked there. The initial plan was to move the less severely wounded further to the rear to the evacuation hospital 8M—with three hundred–bed capacity. However, the most severely wounded could not be moved easily. The result was that the field hospitals became bottlenecked in about twelve hours. Consequently, the evacuation hospital was moved near the field hospital. We would move to the battle and have a slow build-up for about ten to twelve hours, and then the casualties would pour into our unit. Depending on the intensity of the fighting, we would have our peak period over five days and then slow down. We would move to the next battle or await a resumption of the attack.

As soon as we reached our site, our tents went up like a circus. I worked opening cots. I set up our post-op center (ICU). I placed two ward tents end to end. Each ward tent held twenty cots, but I reduced this to fifteen, giving me thirty cots. I repeated this with two more ward tents (one hundred feet by sixteen feet) side by side, giving me a sixty-cot unit. I could enlarge this with a ten-bed smaller tent, which I did on two occasions.

During our rest period at Senonches, we revised our operating tents, creating a single large tent by sewing together the side flaps of our two former tents. This created a single fifty-by-forty-foot tent. We now had room for nine operating tables. Of these, one was for neurosurgery, one was for maxillofacial, three were for general surgery, one was for orthopedic surgery with an adjacent Hawley table for the spica plaster work, and two tables were for minor surgery and bums. We had two shifts of personnel working twelve hours each. We had in each shift eight to ten surgeons, five anesthetists, ten technicians, and five to seven nurses. We had four attached service departments at each corner of the tent, creating a working area shaped like a large letter H. Of these four, one was a pre-op area for eight men. Our chief of surgery usually controlled this traffic.

We had an attached area for scrubbing and writing records, and another for supplies and field sterilizer. A separate tent was available for suspected gas gangrene. Our maximum treatment in the OR was 175 in a 24-hour period. Another time we had 168. During the Normandy Campaign at La Cambe (June 14–27), La Folie (July 8–August 3), and Percy (August 6–20), France, we had 5,115 admissions and performed 3,238 operations.

Describe your involvement in the management of casualties with the Market Garden Campaign?

We left Dinant in small groups, I recall being in a Jeep. We traveled to Louvain, Belgium, and after driving in fog and rain in total blackout, we crossed the Albert Canal. During the late afternoon, gliders towed by C-47s passed over us. By night-fall of that day, September 18, all was ready. We had trouble receiving casualties at first because the Germans had closed the road. But on September 19, casualties poured into our unit. We received 512 casualties in 24 hours, the largest number we would ever receive in 24 hours. We had all kinds of wounds. I recall aspirating a chest of a young paratrooper from South Dakota. A nurse held his head in her arms like a child—and he was young. He said, "Jumping out of that plane didn't seem like such a good idea when the signal came." He had the usual high-velocity wounds with torn flesh, broken bones, and ruptured blood vessels. A medical officer had been shot through the chest going out for a casualty with a red cross flag. His buddies were irate. However, there was no love lost between the Germans and the paratroopers. At the end of September, our casualty load was decreasing. On October 8, we moved down Hell's Highway to an area between Uden and Veghel in Holland. At Bourg Leopold, Belgium, we had treated 3,432 casualties with 1,229 operations and 37 deaths—a mortality of 1.07%—a fine record.

On October 28, we moved to Nijmegen. We moved by trucks, winding up in a hilly knoll south of Nijmegen at the St. Marteen Klinik hospital. I took over the second floor wards on the east side of the hospital for the postoperative center. We then got organized and started to work. Our casualties were severe. There was a heavily wooded area south and east from the hospital called Reichswald, which was heavily fortified with Germans. Heavy artillery fire and bombing occurred in this area. Nijmegen was occupied by Canadian and British troops while the 82nd Airborne Division was clearing the area south and east of us. We had severely wounded casualties from mortar fire, which were low velocity, and one never hears them. The Germans were very accurate mortar men. We had terrible lacerating wounds of the abdomen, chest, and head. Yet the intensity of our work was not as great as the fighting around Grave. At Nijmegen, we had 1,085 admissions with 331 operations and 12 deaths.

Describe your experiences during the Ardennes Campaign.

The weather was bad—heavy snow, cold, and overcast gray skies—conditions preventing air activity. This was the beginning of a terrible forty-four days. We were supporting the fighting on the north flank of the Bulge, 1st Army territory. We received personnel from the 104th, 9th, 28th, 2nd, and 4th Divisions, as well as others. The 104th was Terry Allen's division from Ft. Lewis. Allen had previously headed the Big Red One in Africa. He was sent back to train the 104th and brought back a tough, well-trained division. I became convinced that the tougher the leader and the more demanding and thorough the training, then the better became one's chances of staying alive in combat.

My surgical wards were on the third floor with windows looking out over the open area toward headquarters and the main road that passed the area. Casualties began to pour in as soon as we moved in. The impact of the Germans was blunted by the time we started receiving casualties. Yet, we saw a mass of torn and bloody soldiers. In addition, the terrible weather made men very vulnerable. Many of our casualties were affected by hypothermia. We had twenty-nine deaths, but I felt some of the men died from exhaustion, and hypothermia added to their terrible wounds. One casualty remains in my mind. A lieutenant with the 28th, I believe, had been terribly wounded. He set out his perimeter mines and followed them the wrong way. His confusion led to his walking into his own mine. His right arm was gone, he was blinded, and only one finger remained on his left hand. As I checked the patients, he asked me to shake hands with him. I reached over and grasped his single finger. He swore at me and demanded that I shake his right hand. I had to tell this blind young man that he had no right hand. He swore mightily at his fate but did not complain. Someone said he was a piano player. He died the next day of the effects of the mine explosion. The compressed air of the explosion created such force that the covering of the intestines was ripped away from the mucosa. There was massive perforation and peritonitis in twenty-four hours.

The weather had been very overcast when we moved in, and air support had been negligible. However, on Christmas Eve the skies cleared. The night was clear, and Christmas Day was beautiful. The sky was filled with Allied bombers and fighters. The New Year began on a hopeful note. We believed the war would end in 1945. During the course of the entire ETO, the 24th Evacuation hospital had 19,213 admissions, 9,015 operations and 311 fatalities (1.61%).

What major medical advances were implemented and improved care of battlefield casualties during World War II?

The use of antibiotics (intravenous penicillin, oral sulfadiazine, topical agents like sulfanilamide) substantially reduced mortality related to infections and the concept of leaving wounds open, reduced infection rates, and enhanced wound healing. The administration of intravenous fluids such as salt solution, plasma, or blood reduced mortality related to the management of hypovolemic shock.

Elmer Potzmann

Elmer was drafted in 1943 and took his basic training at Camp Edwards, Massachusetts. He went overseas on the *Queen Mary* and landed in Gourock, Scotland, on January 1, 1944. He crossed the Channel on D-Day and landed at Omaha Beach. He served as a medic with the 110th AAA 90 mm Mobile Gun Battalion through France, Belgium, Luxembourg, and Germany. Elmer earned the Silver Star, Bronze Star, Combat Medic Badge with the Bronze Star, D-Day Medal with Bronze Arrowhead, Good Conduct Medal, World War II Victory Medal, European–African–Middle Eastern Medal, and European Theatre Service Medal with five Battle Stars (Normandy, Northern Europe, Ardennes, Rhineland, Central Europe). Elmer returned to the United States in October of 1945 and pursued a career in lithography.

Date of Birth:
May 1924

Place of Birth:
St. Louis, MO

Military Assignment:
First Army, 110th AAA 90 mm Mobile Gun Battalion

Military Duties:
Combat Medic

Highest Rank Achieved:
Technician Third Grade

Postwar Occupation:
Pressman for Lithographic Printing

Please describe your experiences on D-Day.

On D-Day, I went over on an LST and had to go into an LCI (landing craft infantry), and the waves were bouncing around about six feet high. Had to go over to that cargo net, and I'm carrying eighty pounds with my field pack and everything. That LCI looked like a bathtub down there bouncing around, and I told the sergeant, "I'm not going to make it." He said, "You better come on down, 'cause if you don't make it you're going to end up in the drink." Well, I let go and landed right in the center of that. It was lucky. But they made two mistakes. The first mistake was that they loaded us with eighty pounds and gave us these Mae West life preservers, which were good if you weren't carrying that extra weight, but when you're carrying that extra weight you're top-heavy, so the life preserver didn't do any good. Then they put flotation devices on these fifty-four-ton tanks, and they didn't allow for the weight related to the extra gasoline, the extra ammunition, and thirty infantry men who were on there. When it went off into the water, well, what happened? They all drowned; it was just like a steel coffin.

When we got onto the beach, we were up in the hedgerows, and one of my closest friends was cleaning his semiautomatic .45 hand gun. We had a couple of hours, and they told us to clean all of our shooting equipment. Well, there were about four or five rounds in that hand gun, and he didn't have the safety on. He didn't unload the chamber. I was about a hundred yards, and all of a sudden I hear this gun shot. What happened was as he was cleaning it, he was looking into the barrel, and when it went off it went right through his forehead, and it blew the back of his head off. So they hollered medic, and since I was a combat medic, I rushed over there. He was bleeding profusely. I give him a shot of morphine in each arm, and I told him, "Private Robert Potter, you're going to be okay." I then bandaged him up and put him on a stretcher with the help of some others. They were going to take him to the field hospital, and I told the captain, "He's not going to make it." Well, the aid station was five miles. He got halfway there, and the word come back that he had died.

I was a frontline combat medic. I carried two seven-pound pouches, and in there was surgical scissors, bandages, aspirin, sulfanilamide, and sulfadiazine powder, and you can't do a big job up on the front lines with all the chaos and activity. So my job was to administer first aid, which means that I could bandage wounded soldiers, or if someone had a broken arm or a broken leg I could make a temporary splint and have somebody evacuate them back to the Battalion Aid Station or the field hospital, whichever was closer. There was no back echelon for me whatsoever, so my job was just to give first aid treatment. Do what I can, tag them, and then they would be evacuated. Now, I'll back up just a little bit. When I hit the beach, I made the D-Day invasion at ten in the morning, and the captain told me, "You're going on that beach, be brave and do your best." He said, "Don't worry about too many casualties or the dead or the dying because there are going to be too many for you to administer first aid to." He said, "So once you hit the beach, no matter what you hear or what you see, take cover and find a safe place or otherwise you won't be able to help anybody. You've got to protect yourself, because if they lose you then they lose their medical part of the invasion." So I went in and did my best, and I took cover, and there was a lot of them that were hollering for first aid, but I couldn't as one individual take care of all of them, I don't want to exaggerate, but I would say that there were hundreds of guys that got wounded and you can't take care of everybody. You can take care of the ones that are the most critically wounded or the ones that you can get to. But there's no way that you're going to survive and administer medical treatment to everyone on the beach, because the Germans had every inch of it covered.

Did your training provide you with a good idea as to what to expect on the battlefield?

Well, you train and you train and you train for this, and you train for that. But some of the battlefield training that you got was not in the training program because there are the unexpected things that come up in the battle. When we went up into the Bulge, we got up there and were on what they call a rest area; we were going to rest. They told us that there was no enemy activity up there—maybe a little sporadic sniper fire up there—but we found out that that wasn't true. Now, with what we encountered in the Battle of the Bulge, we were never adequately trained for those conditions during my training period for the simple reason is that you don't know where you're going to go. You can train, but you can't train for everything, because each and every battle is different, and the weather up there was really something different. This was something we were not trained for, and we were not equipped to get into.

When you think about your military experiences, what sort of emotions do you feel?

I can't really describe them because I'm feeling them now—talking about all of this. I'm feeling them now. Whenever I talk about anything like that, it upsets me, and it's something that I can't control. And sometimes I have to get away from everything and get in up there on the riverbank or something, just sit there, and try to forget about it, and be quiet. It's tough. It's hard. I'm not the toughest one, and I'm not the weakest, but it bothers me. It continues to wake me up during the night. It bothers me today.

John Summers, M.D.

Date of Birth:
February 1923

Place of Birth:
Olney, IL

Military Assignment:
Third Army, XX Corps Artillery, 284th Field Artillery Battalion

Military Duties:
Surgical Tech, Battalion Aid Man

Highest Rank Achieved:
Technician Third Grade

Postwar Occupation:
Pediatrician

John was drafted in April of 1943 and took his basic training at Camp Grant, Illinois. He landed in Abergavenny, Wales, in July of 1944. John was transferred to the battlefield a month later and served with the 3rd Army in France and Germany. He was awarded the Purple Heart, Silver Star, Distinguished Unit Badge, three Overseas Service Bars, the American Campaign Medal, and four Battle Stars (Northern France, Ardennes, Rhineland, Central Europe). John returned to the United States in December of 1945 and pursued a career as a pediatrician.

Talk about your role as a medic and what that meant for you on a day-to-day basis.

Well, in general, we had teams that went out to see the wounded. There were, I think, three teams, I forget exactly, but we went out and took care of the wounded immediately, at the site if we could. We had modified our Jeep so that we could carry two stretchers on it, but generally we just needed the one. And we'd go out and take care of the individual who needed the attention, and then we took them back to the aid station, and there our captain, the doctor, would do what he could. If he could handle it, the person went back on duty. If he couldn't, we evacuated the person back to the clearing stations, where they took care of the more seriously wounded ones. The little stuff, we just handled ourselves. The little scrapes and bruises. We didn't get very many serious wounds, because whenever we got injuries, it was from counter-battery fire—their artillery firing at us. And that was it, it hit you, and you were killed immediately. So we had a few cuts and scrapes and bruises that we handled right there.

What's the worst set of injuries that you had to handle?

Oh, why we had eight, nine, or ten deaths. Not right in our area but with our men, and we had to handle those when they came back. Most of the injuries were related to shrapnel, and that could be serious. On one of the runs I made to A Battery, the soldier had been hit in the back of the head and was living, but we knew he wouldn't he living in an hour, and he didn't.

Was there ever enemy fire near you?

Oh, yes, every day. We would get incoming rounds, yeah. But they weren't pointed at me, it seemed, because I didn't get close to anything like that until the man I told you about when we were in a very sort of peculiar circumstance where we were actually under direct fire from mortars. And at that time, we'd picked up this man who I told you we had taken back to the aid station, and there was mortar fire dropping all around us. Every ten seconds, a round would come in, and I got hit by either a piece of wood or a rock or something and hung on and told the driver to drive faster.

What role did the weather play during the Bulge?

Don't even talk about it. It was cold. And you couldn't get comfortable. We medics, we were lucky because we had five hundred blankets around that we could wrap up with, but the others weren't that lucky. The medics, they almost always found a sheltered place to put up our aid equipment and our litters and things like that. We were almost always in a sheltered spot, so we didn't have it as bad as the poor soldiers who were up in front. But it was terribly cold. And rainy and snowy and everything.

Did you get a lot of weather-related injuries?

We got some. We didn't get nearly as many as, of course, the infantry did, because they were standing in water most of the time, but we got some foot injuries and frozen fingers, but they were generally handled by us, and we did that.

What were the greatest lessons you learned from your military experience?

Patience. CE, not TS. Yeah, and try to understand another point of view other than your own, because we were associated with all sorts of people, and the happier everyone was, the better it was for everybody. But I would say that there was another thing, that you learn not to be upset by the little things. There's always bigger things to worry about.

What advice or pearls of wisdom do you have for future generations?

Don't get into a war. I mean, there are better ways. But do what you think is best for you at the time and do it well and do it happily. I mean, anybody can scream and cry and think it's the worst thing that ever happened. But it isn't.

Les Korsmeyer

Les enlisted in the Army Air Corps in September of 1942, took his basic training at Jefferson Barracks, Missouri, and received additional training at Seymour Johnson Field, North Carolina, Fort Meyers, Florida, Amarillo, Texas, and Bury St. Edmunds, England, before flying his first mission in May of 1944. Les flew a total of twenty-six missions with the 94th Bomb Group and received the Good Conduct and World War II Victory Medals and the European–African–Middle Eastern Service Ribbon with two Battle Stars, Distinguished Unit Badge, Air Medal with three Oak Leaf Clusters, and the American Theatre Ribbon. He returned to the United States in November of 1945 and pursued a career in the retail lumber business.

Date of Birth:
November 1920

Place of Birth:
New Douglas, IL

Military Assignment:
8th Air Force, 94th Bomb Group, 332nd Squadron

Military Duties:
Waist Gunner in a B-17

Highest Rank Achieved:
Staff Sergeant

Postwar Occupation:
Owner, Retail Lumber Company

When you first joined the Army Air Corps, did you want to be a gunner, or did you think about being a pilot?

No, I just wanted to get into the Air Corps, and getting into the Air Corps was a long process. First, you would do training like mechanics school, and then you would get stepped up the line, and then finally you'd get to the process at the end where they would make up the crews. Then, the officers would assign you to a certain crew. Our crew was made up of six enlisted men and four officers, and we trained and learned together. We were like one big family.

What was your impression of England when you arrived at Bury St. Edmonds?

The type of heat you have in those huts we stayed in was from a round stove, and you would throw charcoal briquettes into it, and that's how you got your heat. The English were very accommodating. They were glad we were there, and therefore, they treated us pretty nice. We went back to school, and they would show us slides of the enemy planes, and you had to name what plane that was, so you'd be able to recognize it if you ever saw it in the air later on when you were on a mission.

So if you shot it down, you would know what kind of plane you shot down?

Yes, because you would have to report on the mission after we got back to the base. We'd have a briefing, how many were hurt, and if you saw a plane go down you always had to count the parachutes 'cause there's supposed to be ten of them. Sometimes you didn't see any, and when that plane was hit it would spin to earth just like a top, and you knew that they weren't going to get back unless they parachuted out and were able to be picked up by the underground. The underground were people over there that were helping us if we had got shot down, so we wouldn't be taken prisoner. The Germans were putting a lot of flak into the air, trying to hit our planes. Flak is a hunk of iron that would break into little bitty sharp objects, and the sharp objects would do a lot of damage; it would cut fuel lines, oxygen lines, and make a lot of holes in the side of a plane or any place it would hit. Then, when we got back at night, we'd have to patch those holes for the next day, but it is real sharp. And if it hit a person, it would tear your body up too, so some of the crew would sometimes have to get patched up as well when they got back.

Do you remember your first combat mission?

My first combat mission was in France. I can't remember right now what it involved, but it was just more or less to get us used to going on a mission, since a lot of us hadn't been on a mission yet. When you got to twenty-six missions, you got to go home. You never found out where you were going until the night before, about ten o'clock. It was generally a place where you could stop communications or transportation of some kind, like refineries, rubber plants, ball bearing factories, places like that. So you'd dash back to bed then till about three in the morning, when they'd wake us for breakfast. After breakfast, they'd come by and pick us up with a truck and haul us out to the lines. We would get into the airplane, and the pilot would start the engines up and make sure everything was working before he got out of line. Then, they would all wait for the time, and the commanding officer in charge would take off, and we'd all follow in rotation to make up the flight, trying to keep together.

Are there any particular combat missions that stand out in your mind for one reason or another?

I think the mission that really stands out in my mind was my second one on D-Day. We went out the first time in the morning and dropped smaller bombs to make foxholes on the beachhead that our guys could get into when they landed. But we found out they had concrete emplacements built there, and our bombs would just bounce off them. So they took P-38s, which were escort planes, strapped bombs underneath them, and skimmed the bombs across the water into the emplacements to tear them up. We got up at 2:30 a.m. on D-Day and then came back, loaded up for another mission, and got back that night. Each base was marked by letters on the ground that would light up so you could find your way back in the dark. Our base was Bury St. Edmonds, and we were over the base getting ready to land, and I looked out of the top window. A plane went over the top of our formation, and somebody hollered, "Bandits." Bandits meant that there were enemy planes around, and when that happened, you had to break up your formation to land and then scatter and hide out someplace if you could. But he got a few planes out of our group while they were getting ready to land, so they didn't have a chance. It was a JU-88, and they had a barrier around the whole area on the outside that should have caught that plane before it got in, but they were probably relaxed, like everybody else. We had taken off our flak suits and our heated suits, and we had unloaded our guns, since we were getting ready to land. We had to fly around a while without our heated suits on, so we learned the hard way not to be so eager to get out of them.

On missions, how often was flak fired at you, and how often would you encounter enemy aircraft?

You usually encountered both. The flak was usually over a city or over somewhere they could get the planes before the planes got to their target. And you had to go through that in order to get your targets, 'cause the target was always where that flak was coming from—like some big refinery because they had to protect that with the flak. There was a big black puff of smoke, and you knew you had to go through it. For protection, we'd turn out tinfoil or tinsel, like you have on a Christmas tree. The radio operator was in charge of the tinsel. He'd put it in the chute, and it would scatter and mess up their radar on the ground. But the more tinsel he'd throw, the more flak they'd throw up at us. You'd hope you were lucky, and they wouldn't do anything but make a hole in the airplane that we could patch up when we got back.

How many gunners were in the crew?

It was the job of the tail gunner to keep watch out the back. The engineer rode up there where the turret was, and he could watch over that, and we had two guns in the front where the bombardier and navigator were. Then, we had what we called a little belly gunner underneath which somebody rode in, and there were two guns down there. The only trouble with being down there was, if something happened to the plane, you didn't have a chance to get out of there. I was a waist gunner, on the left-hand side of the plane. We were supposed to protect the airplane using our .50 caliber machine guns, and they carried quite a wallop. When you saw enemy planes approaching, you had to be careful so you didn't hit one of your own planes when you shot through there. And we never shot at anything on the ground, because we were too far away.

How much information were you given during the preflight orientations?

Well, they might say we have to eliminate this target because they're doing too much damage out of there. Maybe a base was doing a lot of transportation in and out, or they were getting a lot of stuff in there that they shouldn't get in there, and so that had to be eliminated. We had to try to destroy all that stuff so it wasn't used against us, like a refinery, ball bearing, rubber plant, or anything that could keep them going. If you would hit a refinery today, you'd go back over that area tomorrow with another mission again. If it was still burning, you knew you were doing some good. I think our biggest mission was when we went to Munich, Germany, for three straight days, and it was ten hours each to go over and come back. But we had our C-ration candy, which kept us going until we got back to the base.

Clarence Pratt

Clarence was drafted in 1943 and took his basic training at St. Petersburg, Florida. After receiving additional training at Salinas Air Base, California, he went overseas and landed in Framingham, England, on November 11, 1943. He served with the 9th Air Force and was attached to the 365th Hell Hawk Fighter-Bomber Group in France, Belgium, and Germany, participating in the Normandy, Northern France, Rhineland, and Central Europe campaigns. He earned the Good Conduct Medal, European–African–Middle Eastern Theatre Ribbon, World War II Victory Medal, Merit Plaque, and European Theatre Service Medal with four Battle Stars. Clarence returned to the United States in December of 1945 and pursued a career at Edison Brothers Shoe Company.

Date of Birth:
June 1923

Place of Birth:
Cadet, MO

Military Assignment:
9th Air Force, 1221st Quartermaster, 84th Service Team

Military Duties:
Quartermaster

Highest Rank Achieved:
Private First Class

Postwar Occupation:
Edison Brothers Shoe Company

As a quartermaster, what kind of things would you do on an average day?

I was assistant in the orderly room to the company clerk, you might say, but there was a lot of extra jobs, such as filing. I was a principally a Jeep driver, but I also handled mail and the morning reports at headquarters. And a lot of times when they were shorthanded on some of the work, I'd fill in. Every morning, the boys would have to go out and get the rations for the whole base. Then, they'd bring them into a big warehouse tent, and they'd have to be broken down for every outfit on the base. I don't know who did it, but it was a big job. He had to divide those rations according to how many personnel were in each outfit. Others were involved with the clothing warehouse, going to the dump, getting clothing, keeping them supplied, and especially the pilots. They had to have the best food. And then the gasoline. You had to go to the dumps and pick up cans of gasoline for the motor pool. So different guys would get different supplies. But then in a service group you would have also a signal corps, who were near us. They had a truck with all their stuff in it. They had their living tents around it, but they were our next-door neighbors. And there were other headquarters groups, and I can't think of them all, but the service group kept the air base going.

When we were in Metz, we stood guard duty together. We had German barracks, but they had no water, no electric, and no lights, no heat. And those German planes would come, these barracks were like two stories, and they'd come around the barracks real low so the antiaircraft couldn't hit them, and then they'd circle back and hit the field. I stood in the window up there and watched them as they come down, and then they'd go round and hit the field. But they'd stay low so the antiaircraft couldn't shoot at them at times. And I guess I was there until the Bulge ended.

Describe your experience during Operation Boddenplatte.

New Year's morning, they hit our base. I got pictures of that. I got a book of the 365th Fighter Group, and I cut out a lot of the pages and printed them. They knocked out about twenty planes of ours on New Year's morning of 1945. These were German planes coming over and making their last stand. Hitler was going to try to pull our troops over there, and he had the signals of his own all silent. Some of their people shot down several of their own planes that night. They hit a lot of English bases. They hit a number of our bases that night. I think they destroyed something like one thousand planes, but they also lost one thousand that night.

Robert Dains

As a young man, Robert was always interested in flying, so he thought he'd like to be an aeronautical engineer, and that's when the war caught up with him. He went through navigation school and graduated as a second lieutenant navigator in July of 1943. Eventually, he went overseas, arriving in England in April of 1944 just in time to train for the Normandy Invasion, and he dropped paratroopers at two in the morning into Normandy to start the invasion. Later, he got the opportunity to volunteer to serve on a B-26, flying in over thirty missions before the war was over. He participated in the Normandy, Northern France, Ardennes, Rhineland, and Central Europe Campaigns, earning five Battle Stars, the Air Medal, American Theatre, ETO, and World War II Victory Medals.

Date of Birth:
October 1921

Place of Birth:
Millersville, IL

Military Assignment:
439th Troop Carrier Group, 94th Squadron

Military Duties:
Navigator in a B-17

Highest Rank Achieved:
First Sergeant

Postwar Occupations:
Cartographer

When the Bulge started, were you in the air during that period?

I'd been in the infirmary for a few days, and when I got out it was on December 23. On Christmas Day, I flew a mission in support of the Battle of the Bulge. It was a beautiful day; the air was clear, and the sky was bright. Fresh snow was falling on the ground, and our target for that day was the town of Bitburg. Now, they had antiaircraft at Bitburg, and we'd flown in that area before, but we never went to that target because the Germans were pretty good, and they would shoot at you and put shells out at very extreme ranges of their guns. So we always made sure we stayed out beyond their range. But on Christmas Day, Bitburg was the target, and they said the Germans were bringing up supplies over the road through the town. We were supposed to go out there and destroy the town and throw as much debris and rubble around as we could, create as many bomb craters as we could to interrupt the flow of supplies. So we went out on the mission, and we got to the initial point, but when we tried to open our bomb bay doors, they were frozen shut, and we had to make a second run. By the time we went around again and got our bomb bay doors open, the rest of the formation had already dropped their bombs. I've never seen such accurate and concentrated bombardment in my life as I saw there. They deliberately destroyed that town. I could see the bombs breaking over the town, and then we dropped our bombs. One of our men got a piece of flak in his engine, and he had to pull out. On the way in during the second run, a piece of flak came up through the nose. That day I was up in the nose with the bombardier, and I don't know how I ever escaped. I had a flak suit on and shards of Plexiglas got stuck in my flak suit, but I didn't get a scratch on my face. The bombardier had a garrison cap on. He didn't have a flak helmet on because he thought it got in the way of his using the bombsight. So he had a hat on, and he had his head down, and he ended up with all kinds of shards sticking in the top of his hat. But neither one of us got a scratch, and we just brushed the shards away onto the floor and went ahead.

Was that the time you were most afraid during service?

No. Things like that happened too fast. You don't have time to be afraid until afterwards, when you have time to think about it. Probably one of the times I was most afraid was when I was going in on D-Day, because I never had experienced combat before. You didn't know what you were going to get into, whether you were going to live till the next day. There were a number of times when things would happen—near misses, midair collisions. One time, we were on a bombing mission, and one of the planes got out of formation and created a prop wash, which is a big swirling mass of air. We were flying in formation, straight and level. The next instance, we were standing on our wing. The whole formation was thrown into that. How we ever avoided a midair collision in those airplanes, I don't know. But after it was all over and you got things straightened out and back into formation, then you got scared. Of course, you were always scared. No question about it.

What would you say your most important contribution was, you personally?

Well, I guess taking part in the Normandy Invasion was perhaps the highlight. We left England and went across the Channel down close to the water, and we came in from the backside of the Normandy Peninsula. During the invasion, they landed on the eastern beaches, but we came in from the western side, and if you can imagine planning an air operation without any regard to the possibility of clouds over the target, well, we did. I can't believe to this day that our military experts did that. When we got to France, there was a layer of clouds at about twelve hundred feet, and this was a common occurrence, I understand, historically, over the Cherbourg Peninsula. But they hadn't planned on it. So when we got there, and we'd been told to go in low until we got to the coast of the Cherbourg Peninsula and then climb to fifteen hundred feet. Well, when we hit the clouds at twelve hundred feet and no one had been briefed on what to do and since we were all green troops, it was like a covey of quail that got flushed. We all went different directions; some went up on top of the clouds, but we stayed below and had a discussion in the cockpit. "What should we do?" And I said, "We should stay below the clouds so we can see where we're going." The copilot said, "Yeah, but we're going to get shot at." I said, "Well, we can't worry about that. We got to get the troops on the target."

So the pilot agreed with me, and we stayed below the clouds and went along there a little bit. All at once, there were paratroopers coming down through the clouds all around us. Somebody had gone up above the clouds and dropped their troopers, so we flew right through a string of those guys. We never physically contacted any of them with the airplane, but perhaps our prop wash spilled their chutes. We'll never know. But we went along a little farther, and fortunately we had put the radio operator looking out the top of the aircraft through the astrodome, because all of a sudden here's a plane letting down through the clouds right on top of us. We dove down a couple hundred feet and leveled out, and this guy got his orientation and went drifting off into the night. We went along a little farther, and there's a German machine gun position dead ahead on the course, and he starts shooting at the flight ahead of us. Well, he hit the lead plane on that flight and shot him out of the sky. He fell off, hit the ground, and exploded into a ball of fire. Nobody got out of that plane. All I could see was the wing tips and the tail sticking out. And so we're coming up to the same place where this fellow got shot down, and this German started shooting at us. Well, they had a lot of tracers in their gun that night, and so there was a stream of green fire coming up towards the plane. It started getting so close that the copilot threw up his arms to protect his face because he thought the bullets were coming right in the plane. I dropped my maps and grabbed hold of the armrests of the pilot and copilot's seats. I had my flak suit on and my flak helmet on, and I looked down at the floor of the plane because I thought that would be the best way to protect my face from anything that came in. Well, believe it or not, those shells got up so close outside of the plane that I could see everything inside of the plane from the glow of the tracer bullets. And then they stopped.

If that German had held his trigger finger down one more second, I wouldn't be here today. But we went on past there, and I guess he started shooting at somebody behind us, because that was the end of the fireworks as far as I was concerned. When we got to the drop zone, the pilot cut back on the throttle, nosed the plane up a little bit, and when the airspeed hit 120 miles an hour, we gave them the go signal, and out they went. When the engineer in the back said they were all out, we were down to 105 miles an hour. So I knew we got our troopers out all right, 'cause that was the proper airspeed for a drop. More recently, I've had an opportunity to study the records, and over 60 percent of our troopers were right in the drop zone, so I guess we did a pretty good job. I was always confident we had done what we were supposed to.

Wilbur "Speed" Barton

Speed was drafted in June of 1942 and went to Camp Walters, Texas, for basic training and later to Camp Bowie, Texas, for additional training. He went overseas on Easter Sunday of 1944, landing in Glasgow, Scotland, and traveling to Southampton. He crossed the Channel on June 12, landing on Omaha Beach. Speed served with his quartermaster unit in France, Belgium, Germany, and Czechoslovakia, receiving the Good Conduct Medal, World War II Victory Medal, Army of Occupation Medal, and the European–African–Middle Eastern Service Medal, with five Battle Stars (Normandy, Northern France, Ardennes, Rhineland, Central Europe). He left the service in September of 1945 and pursued careers in trucking and as an operating engineer.

Date of Birth:
May 1921

Place of Birth:
Collinsville, IL

Military Assignment:
1st Army, 501st Railhead Quartermaster

Military Duties:
Quartermaster Supply, Railhead

Highest Rank Achieved:
Private First Class

Postwar Occupation:
Trucking

Did the training give you a reasonable perspective of what to anticipate in regards to your military duties?

We came back from maneuvers with a car company, and we spent eight months on maneuvers learning to be a car company. But about two weeks after we got back, they told us we weren't a car company anymore. We were a railhead, and everybody in the company said, "What is a railhead?" Do you know when we finally found out what a railhead was? In France. None of us knew what a railhead was. As far as training with a railhead, we never had any training, but it didn't take us long to figure it out.

What did you do on Christmas Eve or Christmas Day of 1944?

I was walking guard duty, and they came out and asked me if I had any Christmas cards, and I told them where they were. After I got off guard duty and was walking around, it was snowing and everything else. I walked two more blocks to see a Christmas tree. It had a little light above it, and that was the prettiest Christmas tree I ever saw. But I don't remember a special meal on Christmas Day.

Anything else you would like to discuss?

Well, I would like to tell the time that a one-star general served me hotcakes. I had a staff car, which was a sedan, and I had it parked out where a sedan had no business to go. A Jeep was supposed to be out there, but I took a major and this general up to get breakfast. We drove right into the field kitchen, right up to the table almost. By the way, we had left at four o'clock in the morning. None of us had had any coffee or nothing, and I heard this general ask the major I was driving if I had breakfast. The major said that I could eat after I finished, and that general chewed his . . . out. He said, "Enlisted men eat first, and you know that as well as anybody else does." He said to me, "Driver, do you want a cup of coffee?" And I said, "Yeah, but I didn't have my canteen with me." He said, "Come with us and we'll get something to eat." We're drinking out of china. Now, that's when Melmac first came in, and I walked over to the stove, and the sergeant who was the cook took and poured me a cup of coffee. And I was going to stand up and drink it. and the general says, "Sit down over there." I said, "No, sir, I can stand here and drink this." He said, "When a general tells you to sit down, you sit down," and I did. And I'm sitting there at that table by myself, nobody around me. They were all standing around, and that general went over there and got some hotcakes from the stove and brought them over there. He said, "Get yourself around these." The general told me to do it, so I had to do it. He said, "Now you can go. When you get home, you can tell your grandkids that you had a one-star general served you hotcakes." I went back to my company and told them that, and they all told me I was a . . . , but I wasn't. True story.

Marvin Cox, Sr.

Marvin was drafted in March of 1943 and took his basic training at Camp Polk, Louisiana. The 8th Armored Division was a training division before going overseas, and Marvin spent about nineteen months with them training the cadres that formed several other Armored Divisions. His role in ordnance was keeping the vehicles running—the tanks, half-tracks, 6 x 6s. Marvin was awarded the Victory Ribbon, the American Theatre Ribbon, and the European–African–Middle Eastern Theatre Ribbon with three Battle Stars, as well as the Good Conduct Medal and two overseas ribbons. After he was discharged from service in March of 1946, Marvin began a long career as a tool and die maker at Anheuser-Busch.

Date of Birth:
October 1922

Place of Birth:
St. Louis, MO

Military Assignment:
8th Armored Division, 130th Ordnance Company

Military Duties:
Ordnance Vehicle Repair

Highest Rank Achieved:
Technician Third Grade

Postwar Occupation:
Tool and Die Maker

What do you think was the most important contribution your unit made?

I'd say the real heroes were the infantrymen and the tank men, who really had to go up and fight. I don't figure myself as a hero. Maybe in civilians' eyes we were, 'cause somebody had to keep the vehicles going, or the troops couldn't have done anything—if they didn't have vehicles that could operate. The ordnance kept the weapons going too, so if a gun got broken or a part got worn, we'd overhaul it. Sometimes we'd have to go to a line company and work on a vehicle over there, because they couldn't get it back to our area. Sometimes we had to go where their staging area was, up at the front line, but I was up there only one time. There were two tanks knocked out in a field, and the first lieutenant who was in charge of our platoon wanted us to go out. We had a tank retriever up there, and he wanted us to go out to work on the tanks or grab them with a tank retriever and pull them back and work on them. One had a track blown off, and I don't know what was wrong with the other tank, but our company commander, who was a captain, went along with us that time. And they were arguing about it. My company commander wouldn't let us go out. We were lying underneath the tank retriever to protect ourselves from the shrapnel, 'cause the Germans were shelling us with their mortars. These shells were popping out in the fields all around there, and we laid in that snow while they were arguing. And the company commander told him, "Those tanks can rot out there. My men mean more to me than those tanks do. We can always get another tank, but you can't get another man." So we didn't go after the tanks until it was safe to go.

Where were you when you heard that Germany had surrendered?

After Germany surrendered, we were down in Czechoslovakia. We were there a couple months. Before that, we went into a factory in Braunsweig, Germany, and I confiscated a whole set of tool and die maker's tools—really expensive, but they were all in metric. There were micrometers from approximately a half a foot up to about a foot. I carried them in my duffle bag and wanted to send them home, but the officers would not sign off on them. So we were billeted with a family in Czechoslovakia, and the father was a tool and die maker, and when the Germans took over Czechoslovakia and the Sudetenland, they confiscated his tools. He was in the Czech army when we got there, and we were billeted in his house. When he came home on the weekend one time, I gave him all those tools, 'cause I couldn't send them home. What good was I carrying them around then? So I gave him those tools, and that man cried like a baby, he was so happy. And it made me happy too, that I gave them to somebody who could really use them and who really appreciated them.

Vincent Kemper

Vince enlisted in November of 1942 and took his basic training at Camp Santa Anita, California. He crossed the Channel in July 1944 and landed at Monfreville, France. Vince served with the 544th Ordnance Maintenance Field Army Company through France, Belgium, Holland, and Germany. His unit was responsible for receiving new tanks from the States and making them ready for the front line. The 544th readied over 2,600 vehicles, artillery pieces, and trucks. Vince earned the Good Conduct Medal, American Campaign and World War II Victory Medals, and the European–African–Middle Eastern Service Medal with five Battle Stars (Normandy, Northern France, Ardennes, Rhineland, Central Europe). Vince returned to the United States in December of 1945.

Date of Birth:
June 1922

Place of Birth:
St. Peters, MO

Military Assignment:
1st & 2nd Army, 544th Ordnance Maintenance Field Army Company

Military Duties:
Mechanic

Highest Rank Achieved:
Technician Third Grade

Postwar Occupations:
Automotive Parts, Aircraft Manufacturing

What was the International Harvester Battalion?

I went into active service February of 1943 and signed with the International Harvester Battalion. It was a group the company devised. We all had something to do with mechanics, trucks, and vehicles. Some worked on tanks, guns, anything that needed work. And we were adaptable.

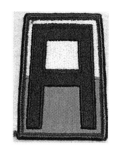

Did the weather cause any problems with the equipment?

It was hard to get things warm enough to clean them. We did it, but it took longer. We worked outside in big areas usually without a cover. Sometimes we were stationed in old quarries, but we usually had indoor quarters. When we were in Belgium, we worked indoors, so we didn't have to worry about the weather as much.

How did the vehicles get to where they were needed?

The ones ready for the frontline troops were picked up by those troops. The guys were transported to our area to pick up the vehicles, and then they would drive them into combat. We filled them with gasoline, rations, and ammunition.

Compare American equipment to German equipment.

When the war started, German equipment was superior. Later, American equipment became equivalent to the Germans', especially the guns. The Germans had their 88s, which could knock out a tank in one hit. We didn't have anything like that. Eventually, the Americans fitted the 90 mm guns on their tanks, which made the tanks heavier and made a huge difference.

What was the best lesson you learned from your military service?

Do your job well, because otherwise somebody could get hurt. And if you had trouble with your task, ask someone for help so that you could complete the work.

We couldn't have won the war without you.

There wasn't a thing that our company couldn't work on. We got tanks from the States, and you could drive them on the road; that's it. They were no good for anything else. All of the parts were generally in two big boxes tied to the back end. When we got them, we had to take them apart. The machine guns were in there. And the big gun on the front of the tank was full of Cosmoline, a heavy preservative that we had to clean off. The equipment was new, but we had to service it and make sure it was in fighting condition. Sometimes some of the vehicles didn't have the extra pieces they were supposed to have, but we had to send them on. When the 544th Ordnance Heavy Maintenance was disbanded, a number of the men came home six months before I did. But I stayed over just to help out; a few more months wouldn't make any difference to me. That's how I looked at it. Some of us started an Ordnance Training School.

Anyone you'd like to mention?

A local boy used to help us out. Some of the fellows went over there recently and talked to him, and he's now a mechanic. He said that he got his training from watching and helping out. He had an old American Jeep he put together.

Joseph Keough

Joe was drafted from the enlisted reserves in August of 1942 and took his basic training at Ft. McClellan, Alabama. He served with the 36th Machine Records Unit through France, Belgium, and Germany. During the Battle of the Bulge, he was pressed into service as a machine gunner. Joe earned the Combat Infantry Badge and was awarded the American Campaign, Army of Occupation, and World War II Victory Medals and the European Theatre Service Medal with five Battle Stars (Normandy, Northern France, Ardennes, Rhineland, Central Europe). Joe returned to the United States in November of 1945 and pursued a career in medicine.

Date of Birth:
August 1920

Place of Birth:
New York, NY

Military Assignment:
1st Army, 36th Machine Records Unit (Mobile)

Military Duties:
Machine Gun Emplacement During Bulge

Highest Rank Achieved:
Technician Fourth Grade

Postwar Occupation:
Chiropractor

You initially started with machine records and then you were transferred?

I was in the Advanced Section of Communications where we kept records of all the men, the number of people killed, wounded, missing, AWOL. Every day, we would collect the morning reports from the companies and sort, tabulate, and forward this information to the generals, so they would know exactly how many men they had in each unit, on any date, at any time. There were so many men lost in the first week of the Bulge; the 106th Division was so decimated, they were no longer a division. So we were assigned as replacements to take up the slack.

On December 16, we were bombed out of a barracks in Namur, Belgium. Then, our colonel called for all the people with infantry basic training. About ten of us were infantry-trained, and he said we were needed at the front. So we packed our stuff and got on a truck.

The Battle of the Bulge was the extent of my combat. I and six other guys were machine gunner emplacements, and we took turns. Two of us maintained the emplacement, while the other guys tried to sleep or get warm. We'd be at a roadblock, bridge, on a roof, or in a burned-out building. We moved around for six weeks doing that. After the Battle of the Bulge, I returned to my original outfit.

During battle, did you learn how to do things better?

Yeah, how to stay warm and alive. I wore everything I had under my overcoat and still cold. Snow, below-freezing temperatures, no place to get warm. We took turns, and when it was your turn on the gun, you were there. We wondered if the machine gun would fire; it was so cold. Then it would be someone else's turn, and we'd try to find a place to warm up, have a little fire, K-rations.

What are your impressions of communications during the Battle of the Bulge?

Very confused. The company commanders didn't know how many men they had, but they were supposed to report the number in their morning reports. So the platoon sergeant would bring you some K-rations or ammunition while checking how many men were there. Then, he'd fill out his form, and they'd run tabulations on that.

The unit I was in would run locator files. We could run names through the machine and find out who was in a unit and where that unit was. Then, the generals would know how many units they had and how strong each unit was. We'd run them on a daily basis.

What was your most important contribution during a battle or just helping a fellow soldier?

I didn't do anything heroic; I was just a cog in the wheel. I was a sergeant, and I tried to be a good soldier and follow the rules.

In my noncombat job, I was in charge of monitoring all the officers in the 1st Army, and I would run reports every day on the officers' status: wounded, killed, missing, whatever. The reports would go on up the line. That was my job; someone had to keep track of casualties.

James Kyle

Jim was drafted in 1943, took his basic training at Camp Adair, Oregon, and went overseas on the SS *West Point* with his division, arriving at Marseilles in mid-December of 1944. He served with the 70th Infantry Division through France and Germany, earning the Combat Infantry Badge and two Battle Stars. Jim returned to the United States in May 1945 and worked as an auto mechanic.

Date of Birth:
August 1921

Place of Birth:
Fenton, MO

Military Assignment:
70th Infantry Division, 275th Infantry Regiment

Military Duties:
Mechanic in Service Company

Highest Rank Achieved:
Technician Fourth Grade

Postwar Occupation:
Auto Mechanic

What were your career plans before you entered the service?

I was a mechanic when I was drafted. I could have been deferred because we did defense work, but I wouldn't have felt right. So I went to Camp Adair. They told me I was too young to be in ordnance, which I wanted, and put me in infantry maintenance, as a mechanic. We serviced all the vehicles. We were only supposed to do second maintenance, carburetors, etc., but we did everything. We had all the infantry training, including bayonet drill. I had an M1 rifle and a toolbox.

Did you know what to expect about the weather and battlefield conditions?

We were there for the coldest winter in fifty

years. We landed in Marseille, France, to plug a leak in the Bulge. By the third day we were up on the front—all the trucks and equipment lying in the snow. And we stuck out like a sore thumb, 'cause we didn't have any camouflaged equipment. It was so cold, if you held a piece of steel too long, your hand would stick to it, and we couldn't work in heavy gloves.

We were always in front of artillery and behind the front lines. They'd shoot the artillery shells over our heads, and your helmet would lift up when the gun went off.

Day before Christmas of 1944, they towed in a two-and-a-half-ton truck hit by a German 88. The projectile hit the right rear, traveled diagonally through the truck, took off the top of the transmission and the driver's foot, broke open the engine block (you could see the pistons), and went out the headlight, never changing course. It made you a believer.

The scariest thing was repairing vehicles hit by a mine. A vehicle like that would be in a field not far from the road, and the Germans would tie a potato masher grenade to any fencing by the vehicle. So you'd be dropped off with your toolbox, M1 rifle—any parts you might need—and you had to walk in the track of the truck so you wouldn't step on a mine. Then you'd poke around where you were going to work with your screwdriver 'cause the vehicle might also be booby-trapped. And if you got that vehicle running, you'd hustle out because if there was a sniper, he'd fire at you.

Your greatest hardship?

The cold was our greatest enemy, and we worked 24/7. Once in a while, we'd have a shed to work in, and then we could use lights. We washed parts in gasoline, and during the day we could burn a bucket of dirty gas and warm our hands.

One time, we couldn't get spark plugs, but we found this factory where they had boxes of 14 mm sparkplugs. So we used them, even though ours used 18 mms. The 14 mm didn't last very long, especially if you revved the engine too fast. So we put extra gaskets on the plugs, and they worked fine. We learned to make do.

How was communication during the Battle of the Bulge?

No communication; no supervisors. We didn't even know what town we were in.

Do you have any advice for future generations?

So many people say the Holocaust never existed, but I saw where they lined up Jews, shot them, and buried them. How can people not believe it?!

Stewart Piper

Stu was drafted in January of 1943 and took his basic training at Camp Sibert, Alabama. He went overseas on the *Saturnia* and landed in Cherbourg, France, on September 7, 1944. He served with the 26th Infantry Division through France, Germany, Czechoslovakia, and Austria and participated in the Normandy, Northern France, Ardennes, and Central Europe campaigns. He earned the Combat Infantry Badge and was awarded the Bronze Star, Good Conduct Medal, Expert Marksman, Army of Occupation Service Medal, and four Battle Stars. Stu returned to the United States in January of 1946 and pursued a career in sales.

Date of Birth:
August 1923

Place of Birth:
Greene County, IL

Military Assignment:
26th Infantry Division, 101st Infantry Regiment

Military Duties:
Information and Education Unit

Highest Rank Achieved:
Sergeant

Postwar Occupation:
Salesman of Paper Products

Tell me about your job putting out the news bulletin.

Our job was to print a one-page headline news bulletin every day. We got our information from a shortwave radio we had. We'd mainly listen to BBC Europe, but we also picked up Axis Sally or German stations and particularly Goebbels, their propaganda minister. I listened to him for weeks, telling us how badly we were

losing the war, to surrender, to give up, and all that. And we knew damn well he wasn't telling the truth to his people. But they did have intelligence information and would say things like, "To the 26th Yankee Division just new in action. How about your wives, how about your family?" They would talk like that, but the average GI couldn't hear it because he didn't have access to radios like we did. And the Germans also printed up leaflets and stuff and dropped them on our troops. Of course, we did the same thing to try to get them to surrender. Our bulletin was made from one sheet of eight-and-a-half–by–eleven paper, and we cut it in half to make four sides. We used a typewriter and a mimeograph machine and then cut it and stapled it. But that was only part of our job. Basically, we were in supply, and so we also had to load the trucks to get the ammunition and gasoline and all the other stuff to the troops. The bulletin was just a sideline, but each regiment had to have one so they could keep the guys informed daily about what was going on.

So after you prepared these bulletins, what happened to them next?

From the little farmhouse or barn or wherever we happened to be, we had to get these bulletins to the battalions or to Regimental Headquarters. The battalions were supposed to get them to the companies and then down to the foot soldier. The idea was to get the news to the troops, who would pass them on to one another, but that didn't happen very easily. And it was strictly headline news, just what was going on. There was no editorial stuff or anything; it would just say that we're not losing the war. We'd mention what was happening on the different fronts in Europe and the Pacific, but we couldn't say anything that would unnecessarily encourage or give false hope to our troops. Nothing like the war would soon be over, even though in September and October rumors were flying because we had cleared the Germans out of France into Belgium, and there was talk that the war might be over by Christmas. Well, that didn't happen, because we know what happened on December 16.

Do you remember where you were when you heard that Germany had surrendered?

We were in Czechoslovakia, and the day the war ended, we lost eighteen men in our unit who were unloading German ammunition that blew up. I was sitting just like this in a chair, this little hamlet, and all of a sudden I find myself sitting on the floor with plaster and glass all over the place. I was probably a couple of hundred yards away from where they were unloading the ammunition inside a building, and several of my buddies were killed. This was on the last day of the war.

Frank Camm

Lieutenant General Frank A. Camm served in three wars before retiring from military service in 1977. As a young officer with the 303rd Engineer Combat Battalion in World War II, he supported the 311th Infantry Regiment in successfully frustrating the German attack through the Ardennes Forest towards Liege, Belgium; his engineers inspected the strategically important Roer River dams for explosive charges so that the 78th Infantry Division could continue into the Rhine River Valley. Reaching the Ludendorf Bridge at Remagen, his was the first complete Allied company to cross the Rhine with all its equipment. He commanded the 303rd Engineer Battalion in Berlin from September 1945 to June 1946. In the Korean War, he commanded the 2nd Engineer Combat Battalion and received another Bronze Star. In 1967–68 in Vietnam, he was assigned as project manager of the highly sophisticated, electronic sensor-driven "McNamara Line." Upon retirement in 1977, he was appointed to head the collection of national human, signals, and photo intelligence for the Central Intelligence Agency until 1979, when President Carter appointed him to direct Civil Defense, Continuity of Government, Mobilization of Civilian Sector, the National Stockpile, and planning for natural disasters in the Federal Emergency Management Agency. His decorations include four Bronze Stars, including one for valor in World War II and Korean War, three Legion of Merit Medals (Vietnam, Pentagon, South Pacific Division of Engineers), the Meritorious Service Medal (Pentagon), and the Distinguished Service Medal.

Date of Birth:
March 1922

Place of Birth:
Fort Knox, Kentucky

Military Assignment:
78th Infantry Division, 303rd Engineer Battalion

Military Duties:
Combat Engineer Company Commander

Highest Rank Achieved:
Lieutenant General

Postwar Occupations:
U.S. Army until 1977; Corps of Engineers Troop and Civil Works Commander; Nuclear Weapons Assembly & Strategy

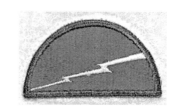

Please describe your training prior to being sent overseas.

After six weeks at the Basic Engineer Officer Course, I led a platoon at the Engineer Replacement Center at Fort Belvoir for six weeks before reporting in April of 1943 to B Company, 303 Engineer C Battalion, 78th Infantry Division at Camp Butner, North Carolina. There I trained an engineer platoon in basic, individual, and combined arms training for eight months and went to Tennessee winter maneuvers in January of 1944. There I commanded C Company during maneuvers and river crossings against two other divisions. In April, we moved to Camp Pickett, Virginia, and continued training of our men and seven infantry Ammunition & Pioneer and Anti-tank platoons in combat obstacles and assaulting fortified positions. We also trained the 311th Infantry Regiment in river crossings.

What were the more memorable battlefield engagements of your outfit?

I was a captain at the time, and company commander of C Company. Our combat role was almost exclusively in support of the 311th Infantry Regiment Timberwolves (78th Infantry Division). Our combat began in early December 1944 in the Hurtgen Forest where Lieutenant Siegele's platoon was involved in maintaining the regiment's main supply route (MSR), a mile stretch of hub-deep mud. Several of his engineer demolition teams spent a day assaulting enemy pillboxes with the 3rd Battalion, when they found themselves cut off behind enemy lines until nightfall when they could sneak back to friendly forces.

Meanwhile, the rest of C Company supported the 309th Infantry in its initial drive into the Siegfried Line at Simmerath and then moved back to Rotgen to protect Division Headquarters against German paratroopers spearheading the Wehrmacht's winter offensive into the Ardennes. From December 26 to January 29, C Company bolstered Timberwolf defenses against the Germans' northernmost penetrations in the Battle of the Bulge by ringing the defenses with 10,000 yards of triple concertina barbed wire, 7,545 antitank mines, 205 antipersonnel mines and 47 trip flares, and preparing 21 craters and three bridges for demolition. They did most of this work at night in no-man's land and blew up eleven pillboxes. In one of these attacks, one of my medics, Private John Coyle, won the division's first award of the Distinguished Service Cross for heroic action in treating men under heavy fire until he himself was seriously wounded. Meantime, C Company trained the Timberwolves to use demolitions and flame throwers in assaulting pillboxes and busily cleaned snow off roads at the front with their bulldozers, causing the Germans to mistake them for the noise of 7th Armored Division tanks moving up for the "big push."

The big push began with Lieutenant Monroe's platoon struggling through six feet of snow to clear the 1st Battalion's road into Huppenbroich and Lieutenant Timm's platoon breaching eight minefields in support of the 2nd Battalion's struggle for Kesternich.

When we reached Schwammanauel Dam, several of our men braved sniper fire to search through its bowels for explosive charges that could detonate at any time to blow them to eternity. Their search netted four prisoners and knowledge that the dam's penstock was damaged, causing the Roer River to flood for several more days.

During a subsequent rest period, C Company maintained the Division MSR from Witzerath to Schmidt, buried dead horses and cows, trained the Timberwolves in river crossing, demolitions, and booby traps, and developed three innovations conceived in the recent fighting. These involved: (1) installing A-frame hoists over winches on the platoon supply trucks; (2) devising simple H-frame footbridge spans for each squad to use in hasty stream crossings; and (3) using machine guns to detonate visible mines protected by enemy fire. These innovations proved useful in subsequent combat engagements.

On March 8, C Company crossed the Remagen Bridge with the 311th Combat Team, becoming the first complete Allied company to cross the Rhine. They opened the first water point on the far shore, but German artillery soon destroyed it with a direct hit. Until American vehicles could drive back across the Rhine, Lieutenant Monroe's men operated captured German boats to ferry some five hundred wounded back and laid artillery communication lines across that helped blunt the first German counterattacks.

On March 13, the Germans honored Captain Camm's birthday by losing a German Panther Tank in a minefield at Honnef. This was the first and only enemy tank destroyed by 78th Division mines. Supporting the Timberwolves' expansion of the Remagen bridgehead, C Company breached five abatis (felled trees blocking a road), four minefields, and two steel roadblocks.

After the division closed on the Sieg River, Lieutenant Timm's platoon built a twenty-eight-foot timber bridge one night only eight hundred yards from enemy outposts and C Company bolstered defenses along the Sieg with seventeen minefield road blocks and one abatis.

To mislead the Germans, C Company feinted at crossing the Sieg River by hauling bridge-crossing pontoons in sight of German observers and building an A-frame footbridge halfway across the river. On April 6, C Company placed three footbridges over the raging Sieg River for attacking doughboys of the 309th and 310th Infantry Regiments and then crossed to build three bridges along the Division MSR to Morsbach and breach two abatis and an S-mine antipersonnel minefield.

On April 9, C Company hastily installed an antitank barrier against a possible tank attack and then swept forward with the Timberwolves, breaching two blown overpasses, one crater, and twenty-six log roadblocks and building another bridge and two culverts. In the race to collapse the Ruhr Pocket, Sergeant Steffen and his Jeep driver were captured and had to accompany Volkssturm troops for nine days scrambling madly to the rear. In the meantime, a German tank column captured Lieutenant Siegele and his driver and placed them atop a German tank that advancing Timberwolves recaptured just two hours later. The Timberwolves went on to seize Wuppertal, ending C Company's participation in active combat in World War II.

Did you gain insights with respect to how to conduct yourself on the battlefield?

Yes. We learned we could greatly bolster soldier's confidence in attacking pillboxes. We did this by placing infantry platoons in a captured pillbox to experience interior reverberations of bullets fired against the pillbox embrasures. We also had them place sheep in the pillbox and had them rush in to recover the sheep after tossing a satchel into the back entry and exploding it. After finding the sheep dead with blood gushing out, they realized the strain that firing on embrasures and exploding charges would place on Germans inside pillboxes. After this training, they successfully attacked dozens of pillboxes, as we attacked through two successive lines of fortifications in the Siegfried Line.

Describe the role that the weather played during the Bulge?

It was extremely cold, covering enemy mines and booby traps in deep snow and quickly freezing our mines at roadblocks, requiring us to replace them daily. In one instance, one of our men was blown up when he struck an antitank mine while trying to remove it. Heavily overcast skies prevented air support for a couple of weeks. We had many severe cases of trench foot. Lacking adequate warm clothing and boots, we struggled to put on layers of clothing and tried to keep our socks dry. But we couldn't make fires, because they'd attract enemy fire. Some men managed to find warm spots inside nearby German homes and barns. When there was time, some dug deep holes, covered them with logs and branches, and built small fires inside. We also provided plenty of hot meals and coffee.

Are there any individuals you would like to mention regarding their impact on your company?

I want to pay tribute to Lieutenant Maurice Phelan, Private Pearl Albaugh, Private Harold Fisher, Private Kenneth Hart, and Private Kurt Storkel, who dashed through heavy fire into a German dam, captured six German machine gunmen and riflemen, and searched the dam until they determined that it was not packed with explosives. We were afraid that the Germans would blow the dam and flood thousands of Allied soldiers crossing their final major obstacle on the way to the Rhine River. I would mention our mess sergeant, Staff Sergeant Pearson, whose kitchen truck served the first hot meal to Allied soldiers east of the Rhine. I would also cite Lieutenant Bill Monroe's men, who commandeered two forty-foot German riverboats to evacuate casualties across the Rhine River and installed our division's first communications cable across the Rhine, enabling our artillery to frustrate the first German counterattack, undoubtedly saving many lives.

What did you do on Christmas Eve or Christmas Day of 1944?

I drove a few miles back to my father's 78th Division Artillery headquarters and dined with my father in a basement. After we toasted our family back home and my twin brother flying in India, my father told me we'd received orders to fight the attacking Germans without retreating and advised me that my engineer company was being thrown into the front line to fight as infantry, blocking a road entering our right flank. This led me to hasten back to my company and deploy it behind so many mines and booby traps that the German couldn't get through.

What was the saddest moment or moments during this battle or during your time in military service?

These were the occasions when I lost each man killed or wounded. My company lost seven killed in action, seventeen wounded in action, and thirteen non-battle casualties.

Were there any moments of comfort or happiness during your tour of duty?

Yes, when I unexpectedly encountered my father at the front. While I was studying an enemy minefield to decide how to breach it, a series of enemy mortar shells began exploding closer and closer to me. Expecting the next one to arrive too close, I jumped into a ditch and landed on top of an unseen person. He turned out to be my father. When the smoke cleared, I asked what he was doing so far forward and he replied he was checking on the quality of his artillery fire. When newsmen later asked him how he felt about firing artillery over his son, he replied, "Like I do firing it over everybody else's fine son."

What was the most important contribution made by your squad, platoon, company, or battalion during this battle?

My company enabled the three thousand-man 311th Infantry Regiment that we supported to pass over every physical barrier encountered and continually allowed them to evacuate the wounded and bring forward ammunition, food, and reinforcements.

How did you cope with your battlefield experiences?

Well, having trained my platoon, then company, in the 303rd Engineer Combat Battalion in the 78th Infantry Division for one and one-half years before entering combat in Germany in December 1945, I enjoyed good relations with my men. We suffered seven killed and thirty injured, but this was less than our other engineer companies suffered. My father in the same division was a Regular Army Artillery colonel, whom I managed to dine with almost weekly after fighting ended. He served as an excellent mentor.

Socrates Dendrinelis

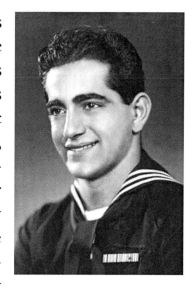

Soc enlisted in June of 1944 and took his basic training at Great Lakes Naval Base near Chicago, Illinois. After basic, he was transferred to Camp Shumaker and was subsequently assigned to the Asiatic-Pacific fleet aboard the Liberty Ship *Corina*. He, along with other seamen aboard the *Corina*, were dispatched to Teleliu at the latter phase of that invasion and subsequently participated in the Okinawa invasion. He was then later transferred to the Destroyer *Mervine* as a radio striker, seaman 1st class. He was awarded the Victory Medal for the Okinawa invasion and Asiatic-Pacific Medal (one star). Soc returned to the United States in July of 1946 and pursued a career with *TV Guide* magazine.

Date of Birth:
March 1926

Place of Birth:
St. Louis, MO

Military Assignment:
USS Corina, USS Mervine

Military Duties:
Seaman, Radio Striker

Highest Rank:
Seaman 1st Class

Postwar Occupation:
Worked as a Circulation/Field Representative for TV Guide Magazine

What were you doing before America became involved in World War II, and what were your future plans?

Very simply, I graduated from Ben Blewett High School on January 26, 1944, when I was seventeen years old. I turned eighteen a few months later, March 11. The war was already in full swing. I didn't want to be drafted to go to the Army, so I chose the Navy, and I enlisted in June of 1944.

What did your training consist of?

Well, one thing that I specifically remember at Great Lakes was that we'd go into a visual class and they would flash silhouettes of Japanese airplanes and German planes and ships on a screen. They were very, very small, and they would only flash them for a split second, and we were expected to identify them in that short time. At the beginning, I couldn't, but after a while you were able to identify them real quick. You were on watch constantly, and you were expected to identify any kind of craft, airplanes, or ships that were at sea while you were at watch. So this was good training. That's something I never did forget. Never did forget that part of it.

Describe your first ship?

My first ship was a Liberty Ship that probably needs to be defined because a lot of the younger people wouldn't know what a Liberty Ship was. It was just a cargo ship that had five holds that were loaded with pontoons. There were sixty Seabees aboard, and we were assigned to join a big convoy to go in on the invasion of Okinawa, and our job would be to build these pontoon barges during the invasion.

What were the pontoon barges to have been used for?

The Seabees had built a platform on the starboard side in the back and on the port side up front. They'd lay a big long angle iron about sixty feet long and bring these big pontoons out, put them in a string, and then get two more angle irons on top and make a string of these and dump them in the water. They'd get about four strings of these and then they would attach a big motor unit to the back of this barge. Unfortunately, we were hit by Kamikaze before we were able to start this operation. But even after we were hit, we stayed there and completed our job of building these pontoon barges, even though we were under fire constantly with Kamikaze planes.

So you would help the construction battalions build these since there were no dock facilities?

Correct. We did this in the middle of Buckner Bay, right there in Okinawa. There were ships all around us. I never saw so many ships in all my life. When we left Ulithi atoll, there was every kind of ship imaginable, including battleships. As I recall, the first day we got to Buckner Bay, an ammunition ship had gotten in our berth by mistake and the Kamikaze hit it and blew the ship up. There were sailors all over the water. A lot of people were killed there. We were so close to each other that when the Japanese planes would come over we'd be shooting at each other. When you missed the Japanese planes, sometimes you hit one of your own ships. So when they saw what was happening, they ordered us to stop shooting when the planes came over. Our planes would come over and lay a smoke screen over the entire bay and would counteract them as best they could, but the Japanese would still come over and drop bombs hoping they'd hit one of us because there were so many ships moored in Buckner Bay, and sometimes they'd succeed.

And this was where you were serving when your ship came under attack for the first time?

Yes, we were in Buckner Bay, and I'll never forget the night we got hit. Kamikazes could be either small boats or airplanes. Most people think that they're just airplanes. This Kamikaze boat came off of the island of Okinawa. We had spotlights from our ship on it as far out as probably three hundred yards from the ship, and unfortunately, the officer of the deck that night had given an order that if we saw anything suspicious to report it and request for permission to shoot, which was probably one of the dumbest orders I ever heard because we had a spotlight on it all the way. We didn't get one shot fired at this Kamikaze, which we could have probably blown out of the water if we were allowed to. It succeeded in hitting our ship below the waterline and cracking it in half. We immediately were taking on water. Fortunately, the buoyancy from these hundreds of pontoons that were on our ship in all five holds kept the ship from really sinking and I would also credit the motor mechanics as well. They immediately starting pumping out the water, and they somehow managed to right the ship. After that, the Seabees brought the angle irons out and literally welded the ship back together. You could literally see where the deck was completely split. I mean about an inch and a half to two inches of steel, and they welded these big angle irons to hold the ship together. Having done that, then we proceeded doing what we were supposed to do: building these pontoon barges, even though we were constantly under Kamikaze attacks and under general quarters.

Were there other boat or aircraft attacks that were aimed specifically at your ship?

No. No, that was the only one that hit us. But, another time after I had graduated to the radio shack, it was broad daylight and the guns were going off like crazy. After I ran outside to see what was happening, from the captain's deck I looked up and saw this Japanese plane coming in right at us. There was no question that he was coming at us. Then the gunners mate, Wyatt Berg—will never forget his name till the day I die—waited until it got within range. I don't think he missed a single round, and he shot that Japanese Kamikaze plane down and it blew up. Parts of it landed on our deck, and I have pictures of a wing that stuck in a raft that we had on our ship, and the gas tank flew across the deck and hit a buddy of mine in the head. Luckily, he had his helmet on.

I felt even more sorry for the Army and Marines who were fighting on the shores, because when they hit there, it was a big surprise. The battleships had been pounding Okinawa for weeks before that, and they thought that a lot of damage had been done, we'd just walk in there. But that wasn't the case. They were there waiting for us; they were in caves. It was quite an experience. I consider myself very lucky to have survived it.

Then, after the Seabees examined our ship and indicated that our ship was not seaworthy, they would not give us permission to leave. But after about a week or so of constant Kamikaze attacks, Captain Ben Kerner, an old Merchant Marine captain, requested permission to leave, which they granted. We made it all the way back from there to Pearl Harbor and then San Francisco. At night, a lot of people slept on the deck in life rafts. Some days we were lucky and the ocean was rather calm, but other times it wasn't and it would creak like a haunted house. You never knew if that ship was going to break up right in the middle of the ocean. But when we got back, the engineers came aboard and couldn't believe it. They immediately condemned it, and we were all reassigned to other assignments.

On another note, I've always been a very positive and optimistic person all my life, and it paid off because more than once I could have gotten killed easily, even on the *Corina*. While I was still on the Deck Force one day, my job was to be on top of these pontoons to position the big angle irons in such a way so the Seabees could rivet them and connect them together.

When I was on top of the pontoon, I just stepped under and on the other side of this angle iron as one of the hooks gave away and fell into the water, and if I hadn't stepped on the other side when I did, it would have taken me right with it, and I would have been gone. So I have a good guardian angel. I never for one minute ever questioned that there were several other times in my Navy experience where I could have been killed. One time, when I got assigned to the other ship, I could have been washed off the ship right in the middle of the ocean. Again I wasn't, but that's another story.

Eve Dayhuff

Do you remember your parents or older people discussing the Nazis before they came to power?

They didn't like them. They knew the Nazis were coming along with a war, and that's all I ever heard. The people in my family and the people I knew were all against Hitler because they knew there was going to be war, and the Austrians really didn't care that much for the Germans.

I understand that Hitler once came very near to you and your family.

Well, Hitler came from Linz, and we lived on the Linzer Street and they had to march through the big street. Crowds of people formed to see the Germans marching in, and all I saw was Hitler's hand and his wrist, and that's about it. But I saw the German soldiers, and they were scary to me because I was only ten or eleven years old at the time. It was close to Hitler's birthday, which was April 10 and then that's all they celebrated, the Germans.

When Germany got involved in the war, how did your life change?

Well, it changed completely because my real father was drafted and assigned to an Intelligence unit. My stepfather was also drafted and fought with Rommel in Africa. But my real father, we really didn't know what he was doing; only we knew he was an officer. I never saw him in uniform, even when he came home, he was always in civilian clothes, which we thought was kind of odd. And he had a stepsister who was living

Date of Birth:
December 1927

Place of Birth:
Vienna, Austria

Wartime Activities:
Student in Austria During the War; Worked in a U.S. Army Air Base in Langenlaben, Austria, Shortly After the War

Postwar Occupations:
Famous-Barr, Bookkeeper, Homemaker

in Yugoslavia. A few days before the war was over, he visited her and she wanted to hide him and he said no, I have nothing to be afraid of. He said all I did was I did my job. Three days later somebody called her and said he's captured and needs some food. So she brought him food and when she got there, there were Russians, or whatever they were, with the machine guns. She went in the room, and he had a typewriter and he was typing lots of papers. So next day, she came again, and he had a brand new uniform on, and he said they're shipping me away. And that's the last we ever heard. He had a secretary, and nobody knew she was Jewish. Her father later went to Yugoslavia in 1948 and found out that they both got shot. He was not a Nazi, and that's all we ever knew.

Did you have enough to eat and clothes to wear during the war?

Well, we didn't have too many clothes, not like kids have here, but we had enough to eat and everything. But naturally when the war came we had to go on rations. And then it was bad, because you got maybe a stick of butter for a family a week, and that was for cooking. You maybe got for the whole family one and a half pounds of meat, and you saved that for Sunday dinner. And after the war ended, it was pretty bad, but I could not complain because we used to have lot of linen that we traded for food like sheep and cows and stuff like that with the farmers.

Was there evidence of the Nazis in Austria through this war?

Oh yeah, there were Hitler youth, the boys and the girls who wore uniforms. Since I was young, I wanted to be one too, but my family wouldn't let me. They didn't want anything to do with it. There were the Jewish people that wore the yellow star on their clothes. At the beginning I went to grade school, and girls would disappear. We would ask the teacher where they went, and they said that they're on vacation or that they moved. And then later on we found out they were Jewish and they had disappeared.

You mentioned American bombing raids.

Yeah, we got bombed. The war was over officially I think on May 8, 1945, but in Vienna it was practically over at the end of April because the Russians took over. After I graduated from boarding school, I wanted to stay three weeks longer, and they wouldn't let me 'cause there were girls from out of town, and they needed to stay there. And three weeks later their building got bombed, and they all got killed. The bombing was directed not on the school, but behind the school where soldiers were living in barracks. They tried to bomb that. The school looked like a castle, so the Americans could not have known that it was a school.

What are your feelings, looking back on that time?

It seems like a bad dream. After all these years have passed, it seems like it wasn't so. I never talk about it because the young people really are not interested. You have to live it to know how it was. But we lost a lot of people; I lost my grandmother, who was a very strong Catholic, went to church every day. When the Russians came in and bombed our town, and she got killed and they never found her. Lots of people died a month before the war was over.

What was your worst experience during the occupation, by the Russians or the Americans?

Well, naturally during the war it was when we got bombed. Because we lost everything.

Do you consider yourself lucky for having survived?

I consider myself very blessed. Not lucky. I would say blessed. I guess God has something else in store for me. But sometimes it just goes that way. However, some of my family died; all my friends, boys I grew up with—most of them got killed in the war. And then after the Russians left, we didn't have enough food. Of course, the Americans helped a lot then.

Do you think that the experiences that you had in Austria, as bad as they were, did they help you later in life?

I'm sure it made me a stronger person because I went through hell, and I'm not just talking about myself, but the elderly people, there was a lot of sadness, a lot of regrets. But I definitely say you are a stronger person if you experience that and survive.

Allyne "Bobbie" Ganz

Date of Birth:
October 1927

Place of Birth:
Owatonna, MN

Wartime Activities:
Jostens Factory Stamping Out Aviator Wings

Postwar Occupations:
Jostens (Ten Years)

At school, were there any organizations you could join or ways you could contribute to the war?

Oh, yes. By that time my brother was in the service, I'd write to him all the time and send him cookies and different things. At first, he'd write back and say the cookies were broken, and I had heard someplace if you popped popcorn and packed it around the cookies, it would help. And he said that it did help, so that's something we always did. So they had a little popcorn to go with their cookies.

What sort of items did you miss from the shelves as the war got going?

Well, the rationing was on, and gasoline, tires, coffee, and sugar were hard to get. My mother used syrup instead of sugar for baking and cooking. And for coffee, I think they used chicory instead of coffee, and that became popular, but I don't remember my folks using it. Oh, and shoes were scarce.

I think it was harder for the head of the household; I just don't remember a lot of it. But we lived on a small farm, so my father would butcher, and we had a garden, so food wasn't a problem to my family. We never sold any of the food, no. Probably gave extras to relatives and neighbors.

Did you have an opportunity to help with the war effort?

As soon as I was old enough, I did get a wartime job at Jostens Manufacturing. You've probably heard of Jostens class rings and announcements. Well, they were in Owatonna, Minnesota, my hometown. A portion of the jewelry plant they turned into military where they made airplane parts and pins and medals for the service. I stamped out aviator wings; that was my job. I had relatives who worked there, and they told me about the job, so I applied and got it. This security pin is what I had to wear when we'd come in the door. I mean, it was pretty well guarded. I worked from seven in the morning I think until six at night. And sometimes overtime too—Saturdays were very busy.

The rationing probably prevented you from spending too much money.

That's true. With ladies' nylons, they used the nylon to make parachutes, so ladies' nylons were out for a while. So a lot of us would take a black marker or pen and mark the back of our legs. That was the style at that time. That line was on the nylons before, so it made it kind of look like you still had them on. We couldn't buy new shoes, 'cause they were rationed and probably, there were not as many clothes either. I was at that age when I really wanted to buy clothes for myself, you know, when you first start working, but a lot of them weren't available like they normally would be.

What was the greatest effect the war had on your life, and how did that impact you?

Well, it brought closeness to families, and we learned to appreciate peace. And I sure thank all the soldiers for what they did too; because of them we have a free country.

If you could give some advice to the youth of America today, based on your experiences during World War II, what would that be?

Appreciate your country, the freedom you have, and be thankful for our military because they saved our country. I go with my husband to classroms and see little children and older ones too at different schools. And I think the littler, younger ones are more appreciative of what our guys did. But it's interesting, and we're happy to be able to do this, to let the younger generation know what their forefathers went through.

Vyrlene Gibson

Date of Birth:
June 1927

Place of Birth:
Browns Valley, MN

Wartime Activities:
Telephone Operator at Ft. Lewis, WA, Service Club

Postwar Occupations:
Telephone Operator; Bookkeeper

What were you doing before America became involved in World War II?

Well, I lived in South Dakota. My parents were farmers, and I was going to high school when it started.

Do you recall when you first heard that America had been attacked at Pearl Harbor?

We heard it on the radio, because that's the only thing you had in those days. My parents didn't like the radio much but you had to take it in stride.

When the United States declared war, what changes did you notice around you?

Well, the only thing I noticed was that some of the young men in high school were drafted and went off to war.

How long did you remain in South Dakota then?

I lived in South Dakota until June 1944. During a tornado, I lost my mother, dad, and brother, and our farm was flattened. I was in the hospital too. I then went to live with a lady in Wilmot, South Dakota. My dad was an Oddfellow, and they took care of widows and orphans, but I didn't realize it at the time 'cause I was too young. So I stayed with a lady who took care of me for that next year and saw that I finished high school. My aunt in Tacoma, Washington, asked me to come out and stay with her for the summer. So I did. I also thought I needed to do some work, since I didn't have a whole lot of money. So I got a job with the telephone company as an operator, and they asked for volunteers to go to Ft. Lewis, Washington, to work in the service club. I volunteered, and that's where I met my husband.

And you worked on a military base?

Yeah, at the service club. I had to take a bus from Tacoma to Ft. Lewis, Washington, every day to work at the service club. There were two or three other gals working with me at the telephone, 'cause those soldiers were always making phone calls or getting phone calls from their family.

As a civilian during the war, how did you receive most of your war news?

From the paper and on the radio. When I was up in South Dakota, I can remember having gas rationing. We didn't have gasoline machinery for our work in the fields, but we did have an old Ford to take us back and forth to town for our supplies. It was very primitive in those days.

Were there patriotic organizations you were invited to or expected to join?

No, this was a little town of about five hundred. And there weren't organizations like that. I did write letters to different boys I knew in the service.

Were you growing most of your own food at this time?

Oh, yes. When I lived on a farm, my mother always had a big garden, and she canned food every year, and that's what we lived on.

Glenda Goelz

Date of Birth:
October 1923

Place of Birth:
Ellsinore, MO

Wartime Activities:
*Office Worker in a Defense Plant;
USO*

Postwar Occupations:
Secretarial Work

Pearl Harbor happened several months after you graduated. What were your plans at that time?

My parents wanted me to start college, and I wanted to come to St. Louis because war plants were opening. But being seventeen or eighteen, I kind of had other things on my mind. Not the war so much, but then, we realized that those war plants were going into high gear. So I got a job in personnel at Emerson Electric. We did the hiring, and they made turrets for tanks and planes. I worked there throughout the war.

What other ways could women contribute to the war effort?

Many of them joined the service. Very good friends of mine went into the Marines, the WACs and the WAVEs, which were newly created branches for women. During the war, I joined the USO. It was in Kiel Auditorium at that time in downtown St. Louis. I played the piano for the servicemen, so the soldiers, sailors, Marines, and Air Force men all wanted to sing their song. You can only play one song at a time, but it didn't make any difference to them: The sailors sang "Anchors Aweigh," the soldiers sang the caissons, and the airmen were singing "Off we go into . . . ," so it was very funny.

Did the war affect the availability of goods or services that you were used to?

Oh, yes, eventually. The ones that unmarried girls my age would have paid more attention to would have been nylons and sometimes makeup. There were certain things in lipstick that had to be used for the war effort. And we could no longer get nylons, so we painted our legs—leg makeup. That was a hoot 'cause it rubbed off on your clothes, but it did the job. Cigarettes were rationed, and there were a lot of things rationed later, but since I wasn't running a household I didn't miss them much, like coffee and sugar—automobiles. And then later on we didn't get much meat. People with automobiles were probably the most affected. Most young people didn't have automobiles then. We used public transportation, but people with automobiles had rationed gasoline, and then they couldn't get tires.

At your war-factory job was security great?

Oh, yes. We wore badges and had to go through a guard headquarters to get to your office or place in the factory. I know girls in the factory that had to dress certain ways—they had to wear hairnets—but we didn't in the office.

There was an act of sabotage at Emerson during the time I was there. There was a lockdown in the factory. It was two German brothers (don't ask me how they came to be working there), and from what I heard, they threw tools in some of the machinery on the assembly lines, which damaged a lot of equipment and shut down some assembly. Emerson was, I think, under the control of the Army-Navy. I know the big brass came, and there was a lockdown, and the brothers were taken away. I don't know what happened to them after that. I'm sure more of that happened in places like the small arms ammunition plant and other places that I was not aware of. There were a lot of things kept under wraps; it was necessary.

Did you or your household contribute in other ways to the war effort?

Yes. My first year in St. Louis I lived with an aunt who gave pots and pans, and I believe that they contributed grease, too. Cans of grease were used for some sort of thing. And we had blackout drills once a month. You had to have blackout curtains, and they'd practice blackouts because we really thought that we might be attacked, particularly on the coasts. So we just stayed in and made sure the windows were blacked out.

Do you recall where you were and what you were doing when you heard the war was over?

On VE-Day, I was at work, and everybody just went berserk. I believe I was working overtime, but my apartment-mate and I and everybody that could went downtown. We got on the trolley and got about as far as 20th or 18th Street and could go no further because of the people. They just couldn't move. And all the church bells were ringing, so it was very exciting. I don't remember how we got back, but we must have walked a lot of the way in the wee hours of the morning.

Dorothy Haberl

What was your situation before America became involved in the war?

I was in high school. And after high school I wanted to make a living because everything was converting to war work. So I went to the Chevrolet Fisher Body Plant on Kingshighway and Union Avenue and applied. They converted to making wings for the Navy dive bombers. Never held an electric tool in my life, but we had a week's training. The job training was excellent. If you drilled a countersunk hole and made a dimple, that was a no-no, because that plane, when it was under pressure, the air could rip the wing off. The same way with the riveting: If you made a dimple while you were riveting, somebody's behind you bucking, so okay, that was the training. Passed it. First day on the job, walked in and there was a sea of big airplane wings. It took your breath away! So I climbed up on the scaffolding, and the left wing section that sits next to the fuselage on the Navy dive bomber was the part we worked on. I enjoyed it; I really did. And I worked with mostly young girls my age because all the guys were in the service. So we felt we were contributing.

Did your mother or people of the older generation object to women wearing pants or working?

Not at all, because my dad had been in World War I. No, in fact I think they kind of liked the idea because it was one of the better-paying jobs back then.

And the clothes we wore were another good

Date of Birth:
December 1924

Place of Birth:
Baden, MO

Wartime Activities:
Riveter on the Left Wing Section of Navy Dive Bombers at the Chevrolet Fisher Body Plant

Postwar Occupations:
Manager of the Fine Jewelry Department at Famous-Barr (Crestwood Plaza) (Twenty-Three Years)

thing. We had to wear slacks and long-sleeved shirts. Nothing billowy. And your hair had to be either tied up in a bandana or in a hairnet. And you had to wear safety shoes. I remember I had a ration coupon, and I wanted to go to Baker Shoes and get a cute pair of pumps. But I had to spend my coupon for those safety shoes! I had to walk two blocks to catch a bus, transfer to another bus, and then walk to my job. The first week in those shoes was horrible.

How many days a week did you work and what were the hours?

Five. And it was an all-day shift. I'm sure there was a night shift, but I lucked out with day shift—seven in the morning till four or five in the afternoon.

So you worked in the aircraft industry after Pearl Harbor was attacked?

Yes, because it took a while before all industry in St. Louis converted. You could make clothing for the soldiers or ammunition at a company on Broadway or at the big ammunition plant on Goodfellow. Everything changed. I wasn't necessarily thinking about working on aircraft. There was an opportunity, and I was hired, gave it a chance, and I loved it. I felt, I'm doing something productive.

Were you rewarded for meeting production goals?

We were, yeah, I have some at home. I have shown the different things I was given at DAR. If you had so many hours to complete a job and the job was done well, you got a little E for Effort pin. And that was a big thing to us.

With most American industry transferred to wartime production, what sort of deprivations did you experience?

Everything was rationed: coffee, meat, women's things, leather, cosmetics, tax on jewelry, but who needed it? We had a bigger thing to solve. No one was deprived. You had enough ration tickets to survive. No one was hurting.

Where were you when you heard that Germany had surrendered?

Yeah. Downtown, and Washington Avenue went bananas. Everybody was out in the street, confetti was pouring out the windows. It was a wonderful thing. And thank God part of it was done. We felt the same way when they dropped the bomb on Hiroshima and Nagasaki; no one felt that was too much. We were glad; it saved our men and women.

Helen Keilholz

Do you recall where you were and what you were doing when you heard that Pearl Harbor was attacked?

I remember very much when it happened, but I don't remember where I was. It was terrible. You know, everybody was shocked.

Did people realize that America was going to become involved in this war?

I don't think they realized that it was going to be as bad as it was.

Well, of course only men were allowed to serve in combat. What ways could a woman contribute to the war effort?

Well, my parents and I planted Victory Gardens, and we had food stamps. Everything was rationed, like the gas. Of course, we didn't have a car, but we had to eat things that weren't rationed. And we could plant vegetables and things on empty lots, that we would use for our family and that would be ours, you know. So we could plant whatever we wanted to grow. You could plant whatever you wanted, your vegetables and whatever, and they were yours.

So you mentioned rationing.

Sugar and meats. I know we ate a lot of brains. My mom fixed them 'cause we didn't have to have a food stamp for that, and there wer things that we had to be careful and not use too many of them. Make them last.

Date of Birth:
January 1928

Place of Birth:
Loose Creek, MO

Wartime Activities:
Sold War Bonds, Saved Scrap Metal, Wrote Letters to Servicemen

Postwar Occupations:
Notre Dame High School

Were you involved in any of these activities tied to the war effort?

I was very much involved with the bonds. I went from door to door asking people to sign up to buy war bonds, and my dad and I saved my money. My dad matched everything that I made. The bond was $18.75, and it would become a $25 bond. So I would save half of the $18.75, and he would pay the rest. And at Notre Dame, the girls who would sell the most war bonds in their class would be allowed to be on the stage with their father on Father's Day—a dad and daughter day—and I was up there with my dad, so I was really proud.

Apart from food and the rationing, what sort of deprivations did you experience? Clothes, anything like that?

Oh, yeah. Shoes, I know. And stockings, nylons. We couldn't get nylons at that time, so we would paint our legs and draw a line with our eyebrow pencil up, to make it look like we had stockings on.

How about when Japan surrendered and the war was over? How did your hometown and your family celebrate?

Well, I guess that's when we went downtown. We took a bus downtown, my girlfriend and I and everybody was happy. Yes. I was with my girlfriend, and we went downtown and all the servicemen were there. We got kissed by the servicemen.

Did you have any close male friends who served in the war?

I wrote to servicemen, you know. We were supposed to write to servicemen and keep them happy and all this. Just letters to servicemen that you didn't know? Yeah, that I met like through my sister's friends that she knew. And so there was one boy that I wrote, a sailor that I wrote to more, and there were soldiers. But I was more for sailors at the time.

Do you feel that Americans today are informed about the Second World War or do you think there's lessons that we've learned once but since have forgotten?

I believe they have forgotten, the younger generation. I don't think they have any idea what the men went through for World War II. And with making this quilt, I feel honored to have been allowed to have made this quilt. Of course, I can't take full credit, cause Rudy Reitz was the one that got all the patches for me and told me where he wanted them. So I just designed it the way he said he wanted it.

Millie Knize

Where were you and what were you doing when the war started?

I was just nineteen years old. We knew something was going on, but we didn't have televisions and very few had radios, so we weren't paying attention to the rantings of that German guy. So I didn't pay enough attention. Now, my family did, and I noticed a difference in them. They became very subdued and would listen to every news broadcast. Guess I wasn't that interested then.

Since you were in charge of your own household, did you contribute to the war in any way?

We had to give up our pots and pans that we didn't use. They would be piled on the street corners. Rubber tires were collected and then melted down. Even the children got involved. They took their wagons and collected tires and pots and brought them to collection areas. We were supplying not only our Armed Services but also all of our Allies who had been devastated for years. So there was a shortage of everything, and for everybody to get their equal share, the president issued ration books with stamps. Even if you had money, which people were making more money now than during the Depression, often you'd go to the store and there'd be nothing on the shelves. Many times I'd go to the butcher shop, and there'd be nothing. I'd have to have eggs or vegetables for supper, which is why we planted Victory Gardens to supplement the food shortage.

Date of Birth:
June 1919

Place of Birth:
St. Louis, MO

Wartime Activities:
Waitress; Mother

Postwar Occupations:
Dining Room Manager, Musial and Biggies (Four Years); Goaltenders Club (St. Louis Blues, Ten Years); Century 21 (Five Years)

What items would have been rationed?

Flour, sugar, butter, milk, everything that we took for granted, even hair-pins. You couldn't buy a washing machine or an electric icebox. Children's shoes were rationed. We were allowed two pairs a year, so if the shoes got too short we cut the toes out. Everybody was in the same boat, it was the way it was then; there was no complaining or griping. We had a slogan: "Use it up, wear it out, make it do, or do without." So you just did the best you could.

Describe your reunion with your husband after the war.

My husband left from and returned to Jefferson Barracks. The whole family went to meet him. Our little boy was about two and a half years old and had just seen pictures of his father in a uniform. So my husband walked up and we embraced and our little boy looked up at this soldier, and he said, "My daddy's a soldier too." And my husband said, "I'm your daddy, son" and picked him up and hugged him. That was a joyful day.

The Second World War demanded and changed the lives of women more than any time before.

Women's lives changed drastically during World War II. Before 1939, America was recovering from a ten-year depression where men sold pencils and apples on street corners just to feed their families. They would hop freight trains from city to city, looking for jobs. If you lived near railroad tracks like we did, you were visited by hobos four to five times a week. They would knock on your door and ask for jobs and something to eat. And my mother would always feed them. If the person fed them, they'd mark an X with chalk on the sidewalk so the next hobo would know that the people would feed them. But we got wise to that and would wash the Xs off of the sidewalk.

It was a man's world, and men ruled the country. They literally wore the pants. A woman could never be seen wearing trousers. We wore a dress or a blouse and skirt. We even wore little white gloves! Women were pampered and raised and educated to become wives and mothers. Boys were educated to become fathers and take care of their families. Very few girls even went on to high school; many graduated from grade school and went right to work. When I was fifteen years old, I got a job; there were no child labor laws then.

And then Hitler invaded Poland, so the president said we should prepare ourselves. So we opened new airplane factories, shipyards, and ammunition places; started production of tanks and trucks and things for defense; and everybody started to work. But like I said before, you had money but you couldn't buy anything. So people bought and saved war bonds to finance the war effort. Almost everybody had a bond taken out of each paycheck. Some had enough for a down payment on a home after the bonds matured ten years later. And children would bring change to school to buy stamps to fill a book from which they'd buy a bond.

Then in 1941, the Japanese bombed Pearl Harbor and all the young men were drafted and even some older men volunteered. Soon, factories, shipyards, etc., needed workers. So the call went out to the women, those pampered women who couldn't do that. But the country recruited us with the slogan "We Can Do It" with the image of Rosie the Riveter, and we were told if you can use a mixer in the kitchen, you can use a drill. And by God, Rosie the Riveter was born. So we climbed scaffolds, went under trucks and tanks and learned to weld. We exchanged our dresses for dungarees and overalls. (The girls nowadays can thank their grandmothers for wearing jeans today.) We even ran the railroads and steam locomotives and flew transport planes across the Atlantic Ocean. And after the war when the men came back, and the women lost their jobs, it was pretty rough. We couldn't go back to the way we were before. And I think that was the beginning of the feminist movement.

Pat Mohrmann

Date of Birth:
July 1934

Place of Birth:
St. Louis, MO

Wartime Activities:
Student

Postwar Occupations:
*St. Louis Suburban Journals
(Twenty-Four Years)*

Do you recall the time before America became involved in the war?

I was in grade school and unaware of what was going on, except when my parents would talk about it. They were very concerned because my father was eligible to be drafted even though he had three children who needed his support. Those kinds of things I remember, but the war itself didn't really affect me until it actually happened.

Where were you when you heard the Japanese had attacked Pearl Harbor?

My father was working, but my mother heard it and was very upset and telephoned everyone she knew. I heard her discuss it, which was the only reason I was aware. My father was very quiet, but he was worried he would have to go; he was still a young man.

As America became embroiled in the war, how did your life change?

My father became an air raid warden. We had special drapes to keep out the light, and we had to keep the lights off. We all had cellars with outdoor entrances that became our bomb shelters where we kept water and food. And as school children, we had bomb drills. We'd kneel down on the floor and cover our head like that was going to help.

My family life changed a lot because when the war broke out my father was finally making more money than he had made in a long time. He was a cooper and made barrels so we could buy shoes and other things. Shoes were rationed, but friends would give us their ration coupons that they didn't need so that I could have more shoes, since I kept growing out of them.

What other kinds of items were rationed?

Food, sugar, coffee—my parents suffered for the coffee. I remember going to the store with the coupon books for vegetables and meat. But since everybody had to ration it didn't really affect me that much.

Did you gather scrap metal or save fat like some children did?

I didn't, but I remember a park on the way to my grandmother's house that had a beautiful wrought-iron fence. They took it down during the war for scrap, and they never put it back.

How did you hear news about the war?

My parents listened to the radio, and when they were upset, we wanted to know why they were upset, so that's how we heard news about the war. And we did see newsreels on a regular basis at the movies.

Is there anything that I haven't asked you about that you'd like to mention?

My life has been affected because of other people who were involved in World War II. And it indirectly affected me when I found out about the atrocities that happened. I don't believe that the men and women who went through that could come back the same people they were before. It's impossible. My husband didn't like the war. He couldn't kill a fly, so he certainly didn't want to kill people, and it was very difficult for him. He was only eighteen years old when he went—just a kid.

Do you recall the victory celebrations and how your life changed when the war ended?

When it was announced on the radio that the war was over, people drove around in their cars honking the horns and hanging out of car windows. We lived across the street from a big church, and people went in the church and rang the bell for hours. It was a big celebration, and I remember thinking it might have been a bit soon to be celebrating, but we were so happy.

Dorothy Pendleton

Date of Birth:
November 1926

Place of Birth:
St. Louis County

Wartime Activities:
Issued Ration Books

Postwar Occupations:
Shoe Factory, Parkmoor Office, School Secretary (Thirty Years)

In what ways did you contribute to the war effort?

That was limited because of where and how we lived, but we recycled. Clothing and shoes were handed down, or mended. We raised all of our own vegetables and canned everything for wintertime food. And we had chickens and pigs too, so we even had meat. Cooking fats and oils were saved for making ammunition. "Save" and "Make Do" were our mottos.

Were there scrap metal drives?

Oh, yes, even the children were involved. My youngest brother who was six had a pedal fire engine he decided to give to the scrap drive. And we gave old cooking pots and anything made of metal.

How did rationing work?

It came about because the best of everything went to the servicemen. And that was as it should be. So people raised their own as best they could. But it became difficult to buy canned foods, meat, butter, and later, gasoline and shoes. And rationing became necessary because some would buy large amounts and store them. So the government came up with a fair distribution plan—rationing. Each family received ration books according to their size.

I helped distribute the ration books at the community school. People signed up for books of stamps. Each item that was rationed would have a corresponding book. And you couldn't buy those rationed items without the stamp. Large families fared better because they got more stamps. People would trade stamps all the time. I had friends who lived in the city, and it was more difficult for them. Where it was hard for us to ration was transportation, because we had no public transportation where I lived. So we depended on our old rickety car. Our key phrase was, "Is this trip necessary?" So we had to think and plan ahead. But we did sometimes have to go to the doctor. After rationing started, tires, gasoline, and car parts were scarce. So we could run out of gas, have a flat tire, or a breakdown at any time.

Did you join any organizations that supported the troops?

I was part of the Gold Star Mothers organization. We made flags for our loved ones in the service. You've seen them in windows. It's a horizontal flag with a red border, a white field, and a blue star for every living person and a gold star for every person who died in the military.

How often did you receive letters from your fiancé?

When he was in England en route to battle, he wrote frequently, but letters were censored—any places or dates were cut out. The first lieutenant had to censor the outgoing letters. He didn't write much after he got into the Battle of the Bulge. He said it was difficult for him because he knew that somebody besides me was reading his letters, and he couldn't describe what was going on. So he would write generalities. I'd go two weeks without hearing from him.

World War II altered the role of women in American society.

I wasn't the typical World War II woman because I was only fifteen when the war started. But women had to do jobs the men had done, because most of the men were gone. So women operated trains, worked in the mines and on farms, and especially ran the factories that made the war equipment. They literally put on the pants and removed the housedresses and aprons. There were also women pilots who ferried planes to Europe. We were not allowed in combat, but we did everything else.

Are there any lessons you learned from your experiences?

Patriotism, working hard, and sticking together to get a job done; tenacity and how to get by; how to make do. I'm glad I lived in that time, not glad that we had the war, but my experiences are a part of who I am.

Jodie Saul

Date of Birth:
February 1925

Place of Birth:
Cora, IL

Wartime Activities:
Worked for the Navy in Bremerton, WA

Postwar Occupations:
USO; Worked in Hospital With Veterans

What were you doing during the war?

I came to St. Louis from Illinois in 1943, and I was hired by McDonnell. I worked in the office at first. But I heard if you trained you could be a riveter and make more money. So I did. I worked as a riveter for about six months on the C-47s. We repaired damaged cargo planes. My shift was seven o'clock in the morning until 3:30. One day, we were working on a C-47 wing, and a piece of the steel flew back and hit my left eye. I still do not have full sight in that eye. After my recovery, McDonnell took me back and gave me an office job. I worked there for a year.

Where were you when Pearl Harbor was attacked?

I was home. We heard it on the radio, and we were shocked.

How did you hear about McDonnell hiring?

I moved in with my aunt and uncle in St. Louis, and he worked for McDonnell, but later he joined the Navy and was shipped to Washington.

Did you have all the food, clothes, and extras you wanted?

We had to go without hose because you couldn't purchase or afford them. We still went to the movies and there were streetcars and busses for transportation. I couldn't afford a car. I had plenty to eat, just maybe not always the things that I wanted.

How did you hear news about the war?

We listened to the radio. I was also dating a soldier, and he wrote me. And we read newspapers.Also when we went to the movies we saw the latest news and pictures from overseas.

Did you work for McDonnell for the entire war?

My aunt and I left McDonnell when she wanted to see her husband in Washington. So we drove to Bremerton, Washington. I never dreamed I would do that. Washington was wonderful.

What did you do in Washington?

At first I worked in a store; then I got a job with the Navy. I worked in the office pool, but then I was promoted and worked for an officer for six months. Then I worked for a jeweler. That was my last job before I came home.

How did the end of the war impact you?

I came home in 1945, and my boyfriend was discharged from the Army. He was in Normandy, but he was okay. He came home and soon after we were married.

Were you engaged before he left?

No. My father told me, it was best that we remained friends, and if we still loved each other, we could get married when he came home.

Did women work after the war industries closed?

Sure, because they had to start over, but I didn't go back to work. My husband got a job with the Corps of Engineers, and I went with him. About two years later, we had a child.

Do you have any war memories you would like to share?

I'll always remember visiting the big damaged ships in the harbor in Bremerton. Going onboard and seeing how they lived, their quarters, was an experience and education because it was not pretty. And all the sailors and officers at sea did not get paid until the ships came in. So we had to check their fingerprints so they could get paid. It was fun.

Is there anything you'd like to add?

I just wish more people realized what the military went through then because we didn't have the weapons we have today. The war was devastating. My husband had a difficult time adjusting because of all he went through.

Kathryn Vinke

Date of Birth:
January 1924

Place of Birth:
Woodstock, MN

Wartime Activities:
Office Worker at Buda Co.
(Diesel Engine Manufacturer)

Postwar Occupations:
Homemaker

When did you realize America was in this war and that this total war effort would really involve a change in lifestyle in the United States?

Well, probably soon after Pearl Harbor, because as soon as rationing came in, we could just have so much sugar, so much meat, and canned goods I don't think that was really rationed. But sugar and meat and I think that was probably all that was rationed at that time. And we got stamps. You would go to the butcher, give him so many stamps, and you could get so much meat. So depending on how many children were in the family, that would determine how many coupons that you received for the food. I had to go to work after high school to help support the family because my parents had six children, and there were four younger than I. I gave my parents half of everything I earned, and I started out at sixty dollars a month, so they got thirty and I got thirty.

Where did you work?

I worked at the Buda Company, which made diesel engines. This company was in Harvey, Illinois, and my father and my aunt worked there. So my aunt got me this job where I worked in the accounting department and I stamped invoice numbers on the invoices. I worked from eight in the morning until five in the afternoon, and we worked on Saturdays till noon.

The rationing system expanded as the war continued. What did you find to be the most difficult or disagreeable part of rationing? Was there a particular commodity that was exceptionally missed?

Now, my mother canned everything, and my grandparents were from Minnesota, and they would come out and visit my mother and dad. They would bring canned meat, so we always had canned meat. We had canned vegetables and canned fruit, and we could buy potatoes by the sack, so we really were not suffering that much by rationing. We had most everything that mom wanted to cook.

With rationing being as intense as it was, what could you do with the thirty dollars of your part of your paycheck?

I probably bought clothes and saved my money to buy war bonds. That's what we did through our payroll at Buda. They took a certain percentage out, and they would buy war bonds for you. They would take a certain percentage out, and they'd accumulate it until they had enough to buy a $25.00 war bond for $18.75.

With rationing and with so many of the American boys being overseas, what could you do for fun on the weekend?

My goodness, I don't know. We just really didn't do much. I mean, we would go take the bus and go to Roseland, which was a shopping area, and just maybe look in the stores and then take the bus back home. So we really did not do much.

When rationing was dropped or slowly phased out, what commodities did you find especially valuable that you could store up and buy a lot of?

Well, nylon hose were one of the things. And I don't know really that there was that much more. We had a good life during the war; it wasn't as if we had suffering from the rationing. Maybe my mother and dad thought they did but as I was growing up I didn't feel like I was deprived.

If nylons were rationed or unavailable during the war, what did you wear instead?

They were unavailable. There were rayon stockings, but they didn't look as nice as the nylon ones did.

What was the lesson learned?

I think that you learn that you had to accept things as they came and just work around them.

Glossary

ASTP – the Army Specialized Training Program was established in December 1942 to identify, train, and educate academically talented enlisted men. Due to the impending invasion of Normandy, the program was ended in early 1944.

B-17 – the Boeing B-17 Flying Fortress; an American four-engine heavy bomber, primarily involved in the daylight precision strategic bombing missions.

B-26 – the B-26 Martin Marauder; an American twin-engine medium bomber.

Bailey Bridge – a portable pre-fabricated truss bridge, designed for use by military engineering units to bridge gaps up to 200 feet in length.

BAR – Browning Automatic Rifle; a family of automatic rifles. The rate of fire was adjustable, with a choice between "fast-auto" (500–650 round/min) and "slow-auto" (300–450 round/min).

Bazooka – a portable antitank rocket launcher, named from a slight resemblance to the musical instrument of the same name.

Bofors Gun – a 40 mm antiaircraft auto-cannon designed by the Swedish firm of Bofors.

Bouncing Betty – an antipersonnel landmine developed by Nazi Germany in the 1930s and used extensively in open areas to attack unshielded infantry.

Cat Eyes – blackout marker lights.

C-46 – the Curtiss-Wright C-46 Commando; a transport aircraft used by the United States Army Air Forces.

C-47 – the Douglas C-47 Skytrain or Dakota; a military transport aircraft used to transport troops, cargo, and wounded.

Caliber – the length of a weapon's barrel divided by the diameter of the bore.

Camp Lucky Strike – One of the Cigarette Camps; hastily-erected collections of tents and wooden huts set up in the forests and fields to the east and southeast of Le Havre. The camps included Camp Herbert Tareyton, Camp Wings, Camp Home Run, Camp Philip Morris, Camp Pall Mall, Camp Old Gold, and Camp Twenty Grand.

Cosmoline – a yellowish, light-amber, or greenish colored ointment-like substance, having a slight fluorescence, petroleum-like odor and taste, used in the storage and preservation of firearms.

Dachau – the first Nazi concentration camp opened in Germany, located on the grounds of an abandoned munitions factory near the medieval town of Dachau, about ten miles northwest of Munich.

Dragon's teeth – square-pyramidal fortifications of reinforced concrete used on the Siegfried Line to impede the movement of tanks.

DUKW – a six-wheel-drive amphibious truck that was originally designed by General Motors Corporation during WWII for transporting goods and troops over land and water and for use approaching and crossing beaches in amphibious attacks.

Flak – the FlaK 30 (Fliegerabwehrkanone 30) and improved FlaK 38 were 20 mm antiaircraft guns widely used by various German forces throughout WWII.

Focke-Wulf – the Focke-Wulf Fw 190 "Würger" (Butcher-bird); a single-seat, single-engine fighter aircraft of Germany's Luftwaffe; over 20,000 were manufactured during WWII, including around 6,000 fighter-bomber models.

Forty and Eights – French four-wheeled boxcars used as military transport cars (the term itself refers to the cars' carrying capacity, said to be forty men or eight horses).

Half Track – a vehicle with regular wheels on the front for steering, and caterpillar tracks on the back to propel the vehicle and carry most of the load. In WWII, they were used primarily as armored personnel carriers, but also saw duty as mortar carriers, self-propelled antiaircraft guns, self-propelled antitank guns, artillery haulers, and armored fighting vehicles.

Howitzer – a type of field artillery. Classic howitzers are distinguished from other types of cannon artillery by their trajectory in that they tend to fire at high angles and deliver plunging fire.

International Harvester Battalion – the 544th Ordnance Maintenance Field Army Company. Composed of experienced mechanics, the men had been recruited or drafted into the Army from the International Harvester Co.

JU-88 – the Junkers Ju 88; a Luftwaffe twin-engine multi-role aircraft, used as a bomber, close-support aircraft, nightfighter, torpedo bomber and reconnaissance aircraft.

Junkers – The Junkers Ju 87 or Stuka was the best-known German dive-bomber in WWII.

LCI – Landing Craft, Infantry; an amphibious assault ship for landing large numbers of infantry directly onto beaches. Around 1,100 LCIs were built in American yards and provided under lend-lease to the Allies.

LCT – Landing Craft, Tank; an amphibious assault ship for landing tanks on beachheads.

Liberty Ships – cargo ships built in the United States; eighteen American shipyards built 2,751 Liberty ships between 1941 and 1945.

LST – Landing Ship, Tank; designed to support amphibious operations by carrying significant quantities of vehicles, cargo, and landing troops directly onto an unimproved shore.

M1 Rifle – the M1 Garand (aka the United States Rifle, Caliber .30, M1); the first semi-automatic rifle in the world to be generally issued to infantry, officially replacing the Springfield M1903 rifle as the standard service rifle of the United States military in 1936.

M1 Carbine – the M1 Carbine (aka the United States Carbine, Caliber .30, M1); a lightweight semi-automatic carbine.

M3 – "Grease Gun" (aka United States Submachine Gun, Cal. .45, M3/M3A1); a submachine gun developed by the United States during WWII as a cheap substitute for the Thompson submachine gun.

M3 tank – the Light Tank M3; an American light tank, used by British and Commonwealth forces prior to the entry of the USA into the European theatre.

M4 tank – the Medium Tank M4 was the primary tank produced by the United States for its own use and the use of its Allies during World War II. Production of the M4 Medium tank exceeded 50,000 units, and its chassis served as the basis for thousands of other armored vehicles such as tank destroyers, tank retrievers, and self-propelled artillery.

M-51 – M-51 Quad .50-caliber Machine Gun on Trailer Mount; "Quad Fifty"; truck-drawn, trailer-mounted guns which were capable of pouring a deadly hail of lead at low-flying aircraft. They were also devastating against ground targets, although as an automatic weapon over 11 mm in caliber, by the international conventions then in force, this weapon was only to be so employed in self defense.

Malmedy Massacre – refers to a war crime (assassination of disarmed American prisoners of war) perpetrated on December 17, 1944, by Kampfgruppe Peiper (part of the 1st SS Panzer Division).

Marching fire – a fairly dense skirmish line of infantry, with armored vehicles following closely behind them. The men and vehicles marched forward toward the assumed enemy defenses as artillery fired in support.

Mauthausen – a large group of Nazi concentration camps that were built around the villages of Mauthausen and Gusen in Upper Austria, roughly twenty kilometers east of the city of Linz.

Messerschmitt – Me 262 Schwalbe (German "Swallow") was the world's first operational jet-powered fighter. It was mass-produced in World War II and saw action from late summer of 1944 in bomber/reconnaissance and fighter/interceptor roles.

Nissen hut – a prefabricated shelter that consists of a sheet of corrugated steel bent into half a cylinder and planted in the ground.

Nordhausen – a city at the southern edge of the Harz mountains, in the state of Thuringia, Germany. It is the capital of the district of Nordhausen. Sometimes used to refer to the WWII concentration camp of Mittelbau-Dora in which approximately 20,000 prisoners lost their lives in an eighteen-month period.

ODs – Olive Drab; the color of the standard fighting uniform for U.S. GIs and tanks during WWII.

P38 pistol – the Walther P38; a 9 mm pistol that was developed by Walther as the service pistol of the Wehrmacht at the beginning of WWII.

P-38 – the Lockheed P-38 Lightning; a WWII American fighter aircraft that had twin booms with the engines mounted forward and a single, central nacelle containing the pilot and armament.

P-47 – the American Republic P-47 Thunderbolt; the largest single-engine fighter of its day and was effective in air combat but proved especially adept in the ground attack role.

P-51 – the North American P-51 Mustang; an American long-range single-seat fighter aircraft that entered service with Allied air forces in the middle years of WWII and became one of the most successful and recognizable aircraft.

"Repple Depple" – Repple Depple stood for Replacement Depots and was the most reviled system of the Army. The replacements were treated like cattle, with a number but not a name.

Rolling Barrage – a military tactic in which massed artillery support an infantry advance by firing continuously at positions just in front of the advancing troops.

Saint-Lô – Due to the city being a strategic crossroad in France, Saint-Lô was almost totally destroyed (95 perccent according to many estimates) during the Battle of Normandy.

Sainte-Mère-Église – a small town and commune of the Manche département, in the Cotentin Peninsula near the coast of Normandy.

Saint Vith – an important road and railway junction and was fought over in the 1944 Battle of the Bulge during WWII. The town was largely destroyed during the ground battle and subsequent U.S. air attack.

Screaming Mimis – rockets fired from a nebelwerfer, a six-barreled rocket launcher whose bombs wailed as they flew through the air. The nebelwerfer was a German towed rocket artillery piece, which had six 150 mm barrels, from which it fired rockets; a full salvo spread over a period of ten seconds.

Shelter Half – also known as a "pup-tent"; a simple kind of tent designed to provide temporary shelter and/or concealment. Two sheets of canvas or a similar material (the halves) are fastened together with snaps or straps to form a larger surface. The shelter-half is then erected using poles, ropes, pegs, and whatever tools are on hand, forming an inverted V structure.

SS Waffen – the Waffen-SS ("Armed SS") was the combat arm of the Schutzstaffel. Headed by Reichsführer-SS Heinrich Himmler, the Waffen-SS saw action throughout WWII.

Stalag IV-B – one of the largest prisoner of war camps in Germany during WWII. The main camp was located 8km NE of the town Mühlberg in Saxony, just east of the Elbe river and about 30 miles (50 km) north of Dresden.

Stalag VII – a German POW camp located just north of the town of Moosburg in southern Bavaria, Germany. The camp covered an area of 85 acres. At the time of its liberation on April 29, 1945, there were 130,000 prisoners from at least 26 nations on the camp roster.

Tank Destroyer – a self-propelled antitank gun, used primarily to provide antitank support in combat operations but do not fit all the criteria of a tank. They may mount a high-velocity antitank gun but have an open turret, no turret at all or run on wheels instead of tracks.

Teller Mine – a German-made explosive common in WWII. Equipped with a built-in carrying handle, the mine was a plate-shaped (Teller is the German word for plate) device used for antitank warfare.

Thompson submachine gun – the M1A1 (aka the United States Submachine Gun, Cal. .45, M1A1).

Tiger tank – the Panzerkampfwagen VI Ausf. E Tiger I; a heavy tank developed by Germany. The Tiger I was in use from late 1942 until the German surrender in 1945. The design served as the basis for other armored vehicles, including the Tiger II, or King Tiger tank, and the Sturmtiger self-propelled gun.

V-1 – the Vergeltungswaffe-1, V-1, also known as the Flying bomb, Buzz bomb or Doodlebug; the first guided missile used in war and the forerunner of today's cruise missile. The name Vergeltungswaffe, meaning "reprisal weapon," was coined by German propaganda minister Goebbels.

V-2 – the Vergeltungswaffe 2 ("Reprisal weapon 2"), was the first ballistic missile used by the German Army primarily against Belgian and British targets towards the end of WWII.

Victory Ship – a type of cargo ship produced in large numbers by North American shipyards during WWII to replace shipping losses caused by German submarines.

Water-cooled machine gun – the Browning Model 1917 Machine Gun; a heavy machine gun used by the U.S. armed forces in WWI, WWII, Korea, and to a limited amount in Vietnam. It was a belt-fed water-cooled machine gun that served alongside the much lighter air-cooled Browning M1919.

Wehrmacht – the unified armed forces of Germany from 1935 to 1945, consisting of the Wehrmacht Heer (army), the Kriegsmarine (navy) and the Luftwaffe (air force).